Easy Crafts for Hard Emotions

100 Ways to Say I Love You
OR HATE

DEVYN WENSLEY
Creator behind StainedHands

Copyright © 2024 Devyn Wensley

First published in 2024 by
Page Street Publishing Co.
27 Congress Street, Suite 1511
Salem, MA 01970
www.pagestreetpublishing.com

All rights reserved. No part of this book may be reproduced or used, in any form or by any means, electronic or mechanical, without prior permission in writing from the publisher.

Distributed by Macmillan, sales in Canada by The Canadian Manda Group.

28 27 26 25 24   1 2 3 4 5

ISBN-13: 979-8-89003-973-6

Library of Congress Control Number: 2023945224

Edited by Marissa Giambelluca
Cover and book design by Elena Van Horn for Page Street Publishing Co.
Photography by Katelyn Prisco

Printed and bound in the United States

Page Street Publishing protects our planet by donating to nonprofits like The Trustees, which focuses on local land conservation.

DEDICATION

This book is dedicated to the most wonderful lady I know, my mother, who has sacrificed everything for me to follow my (wildly out-there) dreams without doubting me a single step of the way.

Contents

Introduction | 7
Craft Basics | 8

A LITTLE REMINDER THAT I LOVE YOU — 11

Tiny Love Letters — 12
A Cutie for My Cutie — 14
We Are a Perfect Match — 16
A Little Stamp of Love — 17
You Rock (Literally) — 18
A Doodly Gesture — 19
Piece of Candy — 20
Pocket Kisses — 21
Rip-Up Card — 22
What Makes Up My Heart? — 24
The Way to My Heart — 25
Old Timey Scroll — 26
Stickers of My Affection — 28
An X-Small Delivery — 30
Shrink Plastic to Grow Love — 32
You Blow My Mind — 34
Scratch-Off Love Letter — 36
Cuddles from Afar — 37
Message in a Bottle — 38
Fiery Feels — 40

ROMANCE OR REVENGE? — 43

The Never-Ending Card — 44
DIY "Operation" Game — 46
Loopy for You — 48
Baby, You're a Firework — 50
Instagram IRL — 52
Machine Claw Game — 54

Puzzle to My Heart — 57
A Cozy Cup of Love — 58
Love: Delivered to Your Door — 60
You Make My Heart Bounce — 63
My Favorite Sweet Treat — 64
You Rock My World — 66
You Are a Snack! — 68
I'm So Glad You Popped into My Life! — 70
Tootsie Rolls® for My Tootsie — 72
Map of Our Love — 74
Matchbox TV — 76
iLove Your iMessages — 79
Listen When You Miss Me — 82
Mine to Be Mine — 84
Instant Love (Ramen Noodles) — 86
Ticket to My Heart — 88
Antique Love Letter — 90
Passport to My Heart — 92
You Are My Favorite Song — 96

CONFESSING YOUR LOVE — 99

2000s Flip Phone — 100
Lemon Juice Secret Letter — 102
You're My Muse — 104
Decipher Your Love — 107
You Give Me Butterflies — 110
Secret Bookmark — 112
I Love Learning about You — 114
Read between the Lines — 116
Will You Wear Your Bow Tie (Pasta)? — 118
The Love Equation — 121
Mirror Writing — 122
Conceal to Reveal — 124

FAMILY IS FOREVER (?) 127

Home Is Wherever My Family Is	128
Thank You for Helping Me Grow	131
My Family's Cookbook	133
Everlasting Flowers	136
My Mother's Purse	138
Opening Doors	140
Family Flowers	142
You Were My Cocoon	144
My Father's Wallet	146
Dollar Bill	148
Surprise Party in a Box	150
It's Been a Bumpy Road	152

FOR YOUR BFFS OR YOUR FRENEMIES 155

For the Record, You're My Best Friend	156
Paper Dolls	158
Pops of Affirmation	160
I'm Always Watching You (Eye Ring)	162
You're a Work of Art	164
Friendship Bracelets	167
Faux Photobooth Pictures	168
Faux Photobooth	170
Lil' Heart Book	173
You're My Rock	175
Friend-Chips	176
Friends Are like Stars	178
Color Our Friendship	180
Capture Our Memories	182

NEVER MIND. YOU SUCK. 185

You're Such a Tool	186
You're Not a Treat	188
Sad Meal	190
Sad Fries	191
Sad Nuggets	192
You're an A-Hole	194
Hangman	195
A Taste of Their Own Medicine	196
Baby, You Got Baggage	198
You're Dead to Me . . . Literally	200
Bloody Knife	203
Pack o' Smokes	206
I Can't Stand You	208
You're So Sour	210
Bandage for My Boo-Boo	212
Douchebag Day	214
You're a Sour Grape	216

Templates	218
Acknowledgments	250
About the Author	251
Index	252

Introduction

I can envision lots of different people picking up this book: a grandmother buying a copy for her grandchildren, someone getting this for their partner right before Valentine's Day, a future professional crafter developing their skills, a follower of my social media accounts and so many more from all walks of life. Whoever you are, given that you have decided to read this book, we can all agree that we want to express ourselves just a touch more than words usually allow.

As lovers, we understand that relationships are not effortless. Far from it. Relationships with our loved ones may actually be the most challenging ones we have. We show people we love them in a million different ways, from doing a household chore, cooking dinner, being there when they need us and much, much more. Love takes effort, and I would argue that love itself is effort.

I realized how much we crave these different forms of love when I started posting a series on TikTok called "Cute Ways to Say I Love You" (@stainedhands—if you're curious [*wink, wink*]). This series accumulated 150 million views on TikTok alone and even more on Instagram and YouTube. We as a society want to show love and we want to be loved in ways that transcend words. So let this book be a stepping stone to being more proactive and creative with your feelings.

And if anyone questions the reason for saying "I love you" in a more artistic way, remind yourself that we are working to tell the people in our lives that we love them in a way that won't fall on deaf ears. And the best part? Love isn't about how artistically inclined you are; just the mere fact that you are putting in the effort is love in and of itself!

I can already hear some skeptics saying, "Then why the 'Never Mind. You Suck.: Crafts for Exes and Enemies' (page 185)? Doesn't this negate the whole point?" Well, it would be silly if I thought all relationships ended in "Happily Ever After," which is why I started a separate series on TikTok called "Cute Ways to Break Their Hearts" that forms the basis for this chapter.

While this second series of videos polarized some of my fans, I still love it because it shows that art is a form of healing and processing emotions, whether it's a joyful feeling or not. And if you are not a fan of this pivot, then I do hope you are able to see these crafts for what they are: a lighthearted way to grieve unfortunate relationships and not as a way to spread hate or negativity. In fact, while writing this book, I kept imagining you, my reader, showing up at your best friend's house after going through a breakup and making tons of "I hate you" crafts together while you laugh, cry and vent about it all. (In fact, if you end up having a craft party to commemorate a betrayal or heartbreak, SEND ME PICS!)

Overall, I want this book to serve you through your love and through any hurt you may experience. The point of this book is to connect, whether that be with other people or yourself. And I hope more than anything that you are able to find your perfect way of expressing yourself with the help of these pages.

Devyn Wensley

Craft Basics

I so appreciate the beauty of inexpensive materials. I firmly believe that crafting shouldn't break the bank, yet you'll walk into an art supply store and mysteriously come out with your bank account totally empty. It is simply not fair. So, my aim for this book is to guide you through projects using items you might already have lying around. I love creating without the need for a last-minute run to the store, because truly, there is nothing worse than not having what you need right in the middle of a craft. So, dig through your trash and let's start crafting!

TOILET PAPER ROLLS

We use toilet paper rolls a lot around here. In fact, my mother collected these for me so I now have a stash of fifty at my disposal at all times. We'll use these for any round tube shape. I also use them all the time to make mini containers with lids on either side.

TOILET PAPER CONTAINERS

Let me run through how to make these little containers. Cut your toilet paper roll into two same-length tube pieces. Cut one of these toilet roll halves directly through the center of the tube. With your hot-glue gun, assemble the tube back together overlapping the tubes slightly (¼ inch [6 mm]). You will notice that this toilet paper roll half is just small enough to fit easily within the other half.

Now to transform the tubes into a container, trace the top of each of the tubes on a piece of heavyweight paper and cut out the circles. On the rim of each toilet paper roll half, apply hot glue and attach the circles to each of the tubes. Slide the smaller tube into the bigger one and you have a small container!

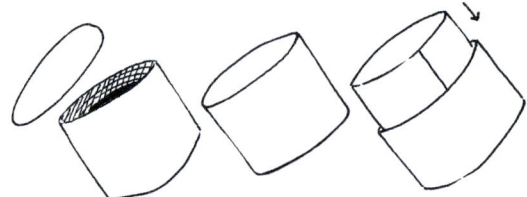

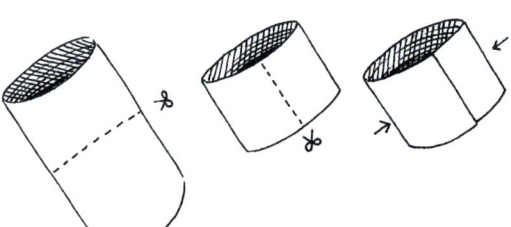

CUTTING CARDBOARD

I'm such a professional crafter that I forget how hard it is to cut cardboard. It really gets your fingers hurting after a minute. (Mine are simply the equivalent of a WWE fighter's . . . but for thumb wars.) But there are a few rules when cutting cardboard to both make your life (and your crafts) better.

Cardboard has two internal orientations that you may not be able to see from the outside. The internal texture appears as rows that go along the inside. When cutting cardboard, you can cut along these rows to get a cleaner cut or fold along one of these rows to get a nicer fold rather than going against the grain.

A Sticky Suggestion: Working with Glues

If there's one craft supply to invest in, it's the hot-glue gun. I have a love-hate relationship with it—using it so often that I forget to turn it off, occasionally leading me to get an unexpected third-degree burn. Like, seriously!? Regardless of the annoying burns, a hot-glue gun is a very effective tool for almost all of the crafts in this book. I have to recommend it because it is so quick and easy to use, but if you absolutely cannot get a hot-glue gun on your hands whether it's because you're clumsy (which, girl, I totally get—CLEARLY) or you're young and/or broke and don't want to spend the $30 on it, then I totally get it. For most of the crafts in this book, if you do not have a glue gun, using other types of glues and tapes will work for the most part. (Cardboard will probably be the trickiest of these without hot glue, so steer clear of the cardboard crafts if you do not have a hot-glue gun.)

Here's a brief guide to glues I recommend, depending on the materials:

- Paper on paper: Multi-purpose glue (I use Elmer's®) or a glue stick
- Cardboard on cardboard: Hot-glue gun and hot-glue sticks
- Hydrophobic materials (e.g., plastic): Hot-glue gun and hot-glue sticks
- Fabric: Hot-glue gun or sewing materials (not covered extensively in this book)

Folding

Achieving a perfect fold can be elusive, especially with thicker paper. When working with materials like cardstock or watercolor paper, I've come up with an ingenious way of doing this. (Okay, I'm sure someone more professional than me has done it first, but I am going to take credit for it anyways.)

Measure the exact fold points on the top and bottom of the paper. Line up the markings with a ruler, and gently etch the surface with a craft knife (I use X-Acto®) or blade. Fold the paper along this etched line, and stand in awe of how perfect your fold is.

Chrome Marker Magic

The mirror chrome marker is my favorite tool that turns anything it touches into a reflective surface. It comes in chrome, gold and copper. It can be a little annoying getting started with it, so keep these tips in mind:

- Always prep absorbent surfaces (like paper or cardboard) with acrylic paint, gesso or water-based glue (I use Mod Podge®) before using the chrome marker.
- A single layer ensures a shiny and metallic finish.
- Allow sufficient drying time (a few hours) for the metallic effect to set, or heat-set it with a blow-dryer to prevent smudges.

Now craft your little heart out knowing these tips will probably save your butt while you're working.

NOTE: When crafting a project where a template is needed, find the template(s) from the back of the book (pages 218 to 249) and trace them onto heavyweight paper for best results. Use a light box or a window to help trace each of the indicated fold lines.

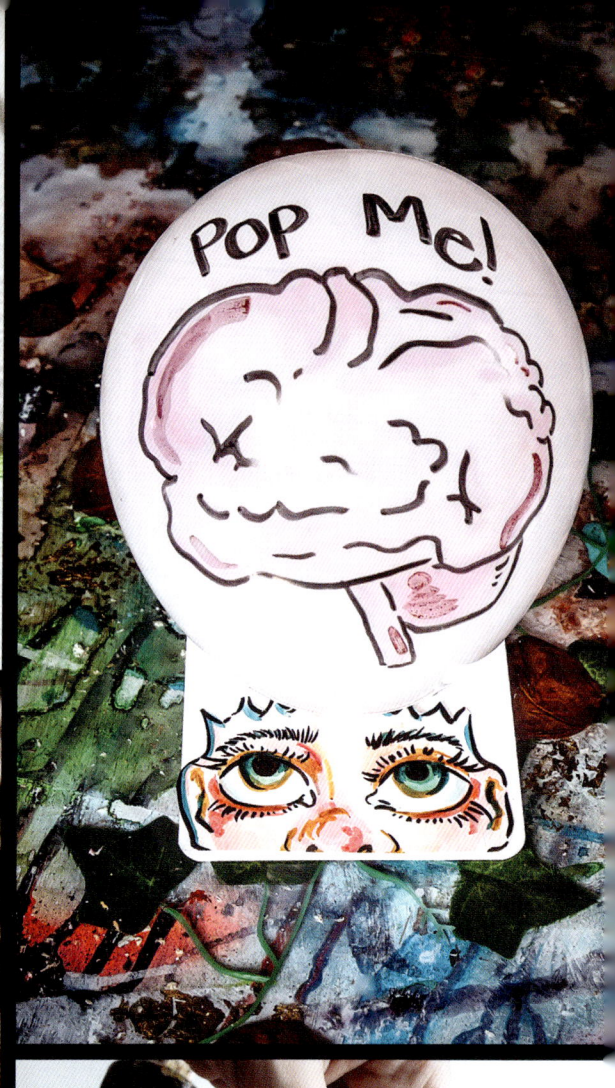

A Little Reminder That I *Love* You

CRAFTS YOU CAN DO IN UNDER 10 MINUTES

I think we've all seen at least one video of a YouTube or Instagram craft channel discussing these "super-easy and not-at-all stupid craft ideas in 5 minutes." Meanwhile, they are making prescription glasses out of hot glue or stuffing their pillows full of marshmallows to make it fluffier. While I'm sure the title of this chapter is bringing back those utterly awful flashbacks, I assure you these crafts really ARE 10 minutes or less. I would know, as I timed and vetted each one myself!

But don't hate on the quickies either! Short little crafts are my bread and butter! They don't take a significant amount of time or artistic skill (in most cases), but they still have the ability to give your partner a big smile and an acknowledgment that they are loved and appreciated.

Tiny Love Letters

When I discovered how to make tiny love letters, I was instantly hooked. I've made hundreds of them and don't plan on stopping. They're not just easy to make—you can create 10 or 20 in just 30 minutes—but also perfectly sized to hide under pillows or in your partner's wallet. Imagine the delight in finding a tiny love letter tucked away in your shoe!

MATERIALS

Printer paper

Glue

TOOLS

Ruler

Scissors

Black pen

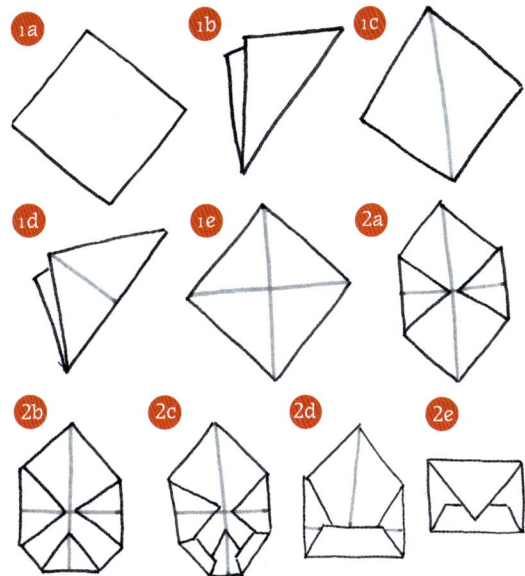

STEP 1

Let's begin crafting our teeny tiny love letter. Start by cutting a 2 x 2-inch (5 x 5-cm) square from a sheet of printer paper. Turn this square so it looks like a diamond, with a pointed corner facing you. Take the bottom point and fold it upwards to meet the top point, creating a crease down the center. Unfold it, and then rotate the paper so a side point is facing you, and repeat the fold, creating another crease. These creases will guide the rest of your folds.

STEP 2

Keeping the paper in its diamond shape, fold the left and right points to meet in the center at the crease line, being careful not to exceed past this crease. Now, take the bottom point and fold it slightly below the center crease, creating two new bottom corners. Fold these new corners inwards slightly towards the middle. Then, visually divide the bottom half of the envelope and fold the bottom half upwards, again, not exceeding the middle crease. Secure it with a small amount of glue to create a little pocket. Finally, fold the upper point down so that its tip meets the center crease.

Now you have a miniature envelope! To add an aesthetic touch, use a black pen to accentuate the folds and the exterior of the letter. You can also attach a tiny heart to the center of the envelope. To insert a note, cut a piece of paper, write your heartfelt message and slip it inside the envelope. These aren't just adorable by themselves; they're also the perfect addition to An X-Small Delivery (page 30) and the Machine Claw Game (page 54).

A Little Reminder That I Love You

A Cutie for My Cutie

♥💔♥💔♥💔♥💔♥💔♥💔♥💔♥💔♥💔♥💔♥💔♥💔♥💔

You know Cuties® tangerines? (Or any brand of tangerine or clementine?) Well, they actually make for a perfect loving subject matter. We're going to make a little "peel to reveal" illustration inspired by the way you unravel the actual fruit.

MATERIALS

Printer paper

Heavyweight paper

Sticker from a piece of fruit

TOOLS

Ruler

Scissors

Coloring utensils

Color printer (optional)

Multi-purpose glue (I use Elmer's)

Acrylic marker

White gel pen

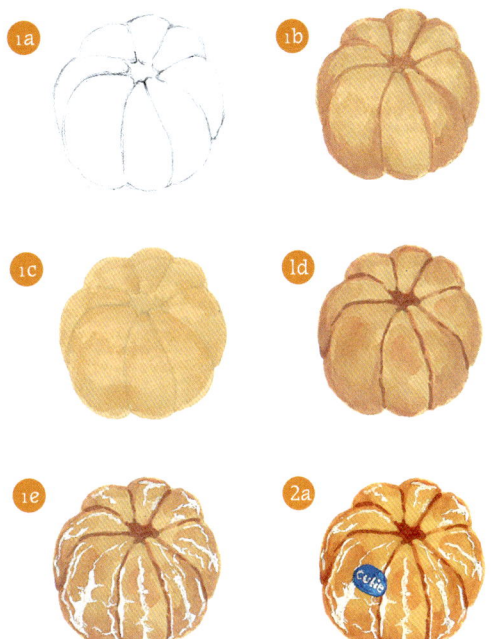

STEP 1

For full transparency, this craft does require a certain level of artistic skill, but if you are not comfortable with that, you can certainly cheat and print out the pictures instead. (I promise I won't tell anyone.)

Start by drawing (or printing) your unpeeled Cutie on a piece of printer paper measuring no more than 2¾ x 2¾ inches (7 x 7 cm). If you're going the hand-drawn route, alcohol markers are great for this, but really, any coloring tool will do. If you decide to draw your Cutie, make sure you do it on some heavyweight paper, and if you decide to print it out, add some glue to the back of your printed-out Cutie and apply it to a piece of heavyweight paper and cut off any paper that goes past your picture.

TIP: Don't skip those shiny white highlights—they're what give your fruit that juicy, can't-wait-to-eat-it look!

STEP 2

Once you are happy with how your Cutie looks, grab an acrylic marker and overlay the Cutie with a secret message. We are going to write, "You Are a Cutie," but it's up to you if you want to write directly on top of your drawing, or you can get extra sneaky with it by incorporating a fruit sticker with your hidden sentiments.

STEP 3

Next, cut out your Cutie, careful to leave no white edges. Trace this shape onto another sheet of paper, and cut that out too. This will be your "peel." Give the peel an authentic Cutie look with shades of orange and a touch of darker orange for shadow. Use a white gel pen to add tiny highlights, mimicking the texture of a Cutie's skin.

Here's where the magic happens. Make a small cut in the center of the peel. Place a fruit sticker over the incision—it's the key to your "peel to reveal." When they remove the sticker and start peeling, they'll uncover your sweet message hidden inside.

A Little Reminder That I Love You

We Are a Perfect Match

♥💔♥💔♥💔♥💔♥💔♥💔♥💔♥💔♥💔

This one is very easy and requires no skill, so if you're looking through this book and having a panic attack because you're running out of time to make a Valentine's Day card, don't worry. (This is speaking from the personal experiences of all those poor souls who sent me Instagram DMs, wanting to show their love but not being able to draw a stick figure to save their lives!) So, to quickly add a spark to your relationship without too much fuss, listen up and get your matchboxes out because we are going to set this last-minute card ablaze!

MATERIALS

Heavyweight paper, such as bristol or watercolor paper

1 match

1 matchbox

TOOLS

Ruler

Scissors

Writing utensil

Tape

STEP 1

Firstly, get your piece of paper and cut it into a small rectangle. I cut mine to measure 2¼ x 4½ inches (5.5 x 11.5 cm), but it doesn't really matter for this craft. Holding the paper vertically, at the top, write, "We Are a Perfect . . ."

STEP 2

Then in the center of your card, tape a match onto the paper. Bonus points if you add a drawn flame, little hearts or even a ribbon to secure the match to the card, but ultimately, just a match and the text suffice.

When they receive the gift, they will read it as though it says, "We Are a Perfect Match," which is just the right amount of cute and cheesy, if I do say so myself. Stuff this bad boy right into the matchbook that you stole the match from, and leave it there until your partner oh, so conveniently needs a match. Once opened, they'll be hit with a simple-yet-adorable token of your adoration (along with access to that match they needed). This little box of (unsuspecting) love is the perfect thing to stuff in your partner's camping bag or to set beside your partner's favorite candles for maximum discoverability.

A Little Stamp of Love

♥💔♥💔♥💔♥💔♥💔♥💔♥💔♥💔♥💔♥💔♥💔♥💔♥

Not everyone is into the whole romantic-note-under-the-pillow thing. If that's you, how about a stamp? Yes, a stamp. It's a fun, slightly quirky way to remind your partner of your love, and it's perfect for leaving little surprises on the most unexpected things. Plus, the materials might just be sitting in your trash can right now.

MATERIALS
Thin Styrofoam™ takeout container

Printer paper

TOOLS
Scissors

Marker

Pencil

Ink pad

STEP 1
First we need a Styrofoam to-go container. We need the thin comp foam type, which can be found in disposable dishware like foam cups, plates and bowls. My pro tip? Choose a container with flat sides for the best results.

Start by cutting out the flat parts of the container. Then, on a piece of paper, brainstorm your stamp design. It could be something sweet like a heart, a classic "I love you" or a little inside joke that'll bring a smile to your partner's face.

STEP 2
Next, trace your design onto the foam with a marker. Be gentle. We don't want to indent the foam just yet. Once you are happy with your design, take a dull pencil and press down along the negative space of your design. Remember, whatever is not indented will show up when you stamp.

STEP 3
Now, grab that ink pad and start stamping! Get creative with where you leave your marks. Stamp on a disposable dinner napkin, the end of a paper towel roll or even a sheet of toilet paper. Do be careful not to get the ink anywhere that will come into contact with food. And hopefully with this craft, you'll be able to find ways to subtly remind your special person that you love them.

You Rock (Literally)

This is another super-duper easy craft that you can whip up in just a few minutes, as long as you have the great outdoors at your fingertips (or even some gravel that has fallen loose from your street or pavement). Create this craft for anyone who rocks your world.

MATERIALS
1 small rock

Heavyweight paper, such as bristol or watercolor paper

TOOLS
Measuring tape

Scissors

Marker or pen

Hot-glue gun and hot-glue sticks

STEP 1
Measure your rock and cut your paper to be five times the size of your rock. Write on the paper, "You R   C K." Make sure you leave enough space for the rock to fit in the middle of the "R" and the "C" so it can take the place of the "O" in "rock." Extra points if you stylize the words. For example, I am making the text around the rock very bold along with little lines to emphasize the actual rock.

STEP 2
Hot glue your rock into place. Now that your little note is ready to be unveiled, stuff it in your friend's or lover's shoes to really catch their attention, or let it sit in a houseplant, ready to be discovered. This is the perfect way to let them know how awesome they are in the least expected of ways.

A Doodly Gesture

In the digital age, it's a rarity to actually touch a physical picture and hold it in your hands, but there is something undeniably special about possessing one. Clearly that's why Polaroid® cameras and photo booths made such a boom of a comeback in the past few years. To give your photos an extra dash of sentimentality, here's a nifty trick to enhance those already treasured snapshots.

MATERIALS
Printed pictures

TOOLS
Acrylic markers or paint

STEP 1
This craft is about giving a personal touch to those already cherished photos. Print out some favorite snaps of you and your partner on good quality paper. If you've got Polaroids, even better—they're perfect for this.

STEP 2
Grab an acrylic marker and let your creativity flow around the borders of the images. Keep it simple with classic hearts and "I love you" messages, or personalize it with doodles linked to the memories captured in the photo. Add mouse ears for that Disney trip or a speech bubble with a memorable joke your partner cracked. These doodles transform a static image into a dynamic memory capsule, a reminder of the little moments that a photo alone can't capture.

> **TIP:** If you have pictures with your ex, do the same thing! Except instead of adding hearts, quotes and doodles, draw them out of the picture entirely! You have a prom picture that you thought you looked really cute in but your monster of an ex is ruining it? Turn them into a ghost or a tombstone (because they're dead to you [wink, wink]).

Piece of Candy

For this craft, we're showing your partner just how "sweet" you think they are. It's like Valentine's Day, but without the commercialized pressure and overpriced chocolates. These little candies are perfect to store anywhere to surprise your partner on Easter or as a go-to stocking stuffer.

MATERIALS
Printer paper

Tissue paper

TOOLS
Ruler

Scissors

Pen or marker

STEP 1
Let's get cracking. Cut a piece of printer paper that's 5 x 5 inches (13 x 13 cm). Precision isn't the name of the game here. In fact, I just ripped mine out of my sketchbook. The key is to make sure this piece of paper can transform into a scrunchable ball. That's your only mission.

STEP 2
Once you've scrunched it into a little ball, smooth it out and write a sweet message for your better half. Extra points for staying on theme—anything with "sweet" or "candy" will hit the mark. Use a pen or marker instead of a pencil. We don't want the note smudging in the scrunching process.

STEP 3
When the ink is dry, and your message is set, scrunch that paper back into a ball. Next up, the tissue paper. I used a 5 x 5–inch (13 x 13–cm) square. Place your scrunched-up message in the middle and twist the tissue paper around it to secure the ball in place. If the tissue paper's looking a bit too long on the sides, trim the excess to your desired length. You can jazz up the outside of your candy if you prefer, but I opted to keep it simple. And voilà, you've got yourself a DIY paper candy. Hand this over to your loved one or hide it in their candy cabinet, stocking, Easter basket or anywhere this little candy love note will blend in. How sweet!

Pocket Kisses

Sometimes a little kiss can bridge even the widest distance. Whether you're continents apart or just in different zip codes, you can still send a smooch their way. Luckily, there is a way to give them a little piece of your luscious lips without having to travel the distance every time! And hey, even if you see each other every day, who wouldn't love a pocketful of kisses?

MATERIALS
Paper (any kind)

TOOLS
Multiple shades of lipstick

Scissors

Pen or marker

Perfume (optional)

STEP 1

I'm starting with a plain piece of printer paper just because that is what I have on hand, and it will be the easiest to cut once we get to that step. Get out some lipsticks. Unfortunately lip gloss, lip oils or lip stains will not work. In fact, the more pigmented, the better—this is not the time to go natural.

Now for the fun part: Pucker up and plant those kisses all over the paper. Don't hold back. Really press in to capture every crease and line of your lips. You're essentially turning your mouth into a stamp, so you're going to find that you will get very nice and cozy with the sheet of paper. Feel free to switch up the colors and fill the page with an array of different colored kisses.

STEP 2

Once you have deemed the number of kisses to be an appropriate amount, cut out each one. If you really want go ham on the smooches, prepare for your hand to get sore.

Sure, a bunch of paper kisses is sweet on its own, but why stop there? Flip each cutout over and pen down your thoughts. Jot down cherished memories, little things you love about your partner, future plans or maybe a cheeky bucket list of places for future smooches.

Now, you've got a collection of kisses ready to be stashed in a wallet, slipped under a pillow or sent a million miles away. While it's a simple gesture, it carries the warmth and intimacy of your presence, even when you're miles apart.

A Little Reminder That I Love You

Rip-Up Card

Let's be real. I can totally see this craft begging to be used by a partner who totally forgot it was their anniversary and had to come up with some sort of card idea last minute. Hey, just because this card only takes 10 minutes doesn't mean it isn't adorable. In fact, it may even get more appreciation than a store-bought card!

MATERIALS

Heavyweight paper, such as cardstock or watercolor paper

Lightweight paper, such as printer paper or construction paper

Cardboard

TOOLS

Ruler

Scissors

Pen or marker

Pencil

Craft knife (I use X-Acto)

Glue stick

Coloring utensils (optional)

STEP 1

Kick things off by cutting both the heavyweight and lightweight papers to the same size, measuring 4 x 5½ inches (10 x 14 cm). On the heavyweight paper, write your heartfelt note with a pen. Keep it classic with a simple "I love you," or tailor it to the occasion. Just remember to center it, and leave a ½-inch (1.3-cm) margin on each side.

> **TIP:** If you want this DIY card to be a little cuter, feel free to color and decorate both pieces of paper.

STEP 2

Set aside your heavyweight paper for now. On the lightweight paper, lightly sketch a long, rounded rectangle with your pencil. This shape should cover your entire written message when placed over the heavyweight paper. Now, place a piece of cardboard underneath the lightweight paper. Grab your craft knife and gently press small divots along the sketched rectangle, spacing them no more than ¼ inch (6 mm) apart. These divots will guide the eventual ripping. Write, "OPEN" inside the rectangle and carefully erase any remaining pencil marks.

STEP 3

Flip the lightweight paper over, apply glue around the outside of the rectangle and align it over your heavyweight paper with the message. Voilà! You've just created a rip-up card that's ready to surprise. The divots make it easy to tear open and unveil the heartfelt message hidden beneath.

A Little Reminder That I Love You

What Makes Up My Heart?

If you could list everything that you love, what would be on it? Obviously (or I guess, hopefully) you have a lot of love for your partner, or why else would you be reading this chapter? But what else do you love? Chocolate? A favorite movie? Your favorite food? If you would trade all of that for the love you have with your partner, then this craft is for you.

MATERIALS
Heavyweight paper, such as watercolor paper

TOOLS
Ruler

Scissors

Pencil

Markers

Glue stick

Pen

STEP 1
Start by cutting a heart out of your paper that's 4 inches (10 cm) at its largest point on the sides and 3½ inches (9 cm) from the tip of the heart to the largest part of its rounded edge. Once you have your heart, use a pencil to lightly draw a line dividing it in half vertically. Then, divide this line in half again, creating four equal quadrants. Carefully cut out one of these quadrants and set it aside. Take the remaining three-quarters of the heart and color it a vibrant red. Glue this piece onto a 5 x 6-inch (13 x 15-cm) piece of heavyweight paper.

STEP 2
Now, let's focus on the piece you set aside. Cut it in half, and then divide one of those halves into one-third and two-thirds. You'll end up with three separate pieces for just that one quadrant, all of which are slightly different sizes. Color each heart sliver a different color of your choosing, and glue them into the section of the heart that was previously cut out.

STEP 3
Above your newly glued-down heart, title the sheet of paper to either say, "My Heart" or "What Makes Up My Heart." Around the edges of the paper, draw arrows pointing to each section of the heart. Beside each arrow, write something you love (excluding the largest piece). For the biggest section, write, "YOU!" in bold, capital letters, signifying that the largest part of your love is reserved for your partner.

24 - 100 Ways to Say I Love (or Hate) You

The Way to My Heart

This craft is a quick and cute card you can give to your partner any time—for an occasion or lack of occasion, because spreading love is never a *bad* idea.

MATERIALS
Heavyweight paper

TOOLS
Ruler

Scissors

Black and red markers

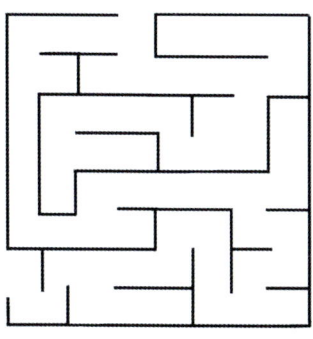

STEP 1
Cut a 4 x 5-inch (10 x 13-cm) rectangle out of the paper. In the middle of the page, draw a maze with the black marker (or print one out). Feel free to use mine as a reference.

STEP 2
At one end of the maze write, "You," and on the other end, draw a heart and write, "My Heart." Complete the maze with the red marker. On the outskirts of the maze, write, "You Found the Way to My Heart."

Give this gift to your partner as a small reminder that you're all theirs. If you'd prefer to make this craft a tad more interactive, change the wording to "Can You Find the Way to My Heart?" and let them complete the maze!

A Little Reminder That I Love You - 25

Old Timey Scroll

♡💔♡💔♡💔♡💔♡💔♡💔♡💔♡💔♡💔♡💔♡💔♡💔

Let's face it, you might not be the next Shakespeare, and your calligraphy skills could pass for chicken scratch, but your heart is bursting with love, and you're eager to express it in a unique way. Allow me to guide you in crafting a DIY scroll that will serve as the perfect canvas to declare your love to your special someone.

MATERIALS
2 toilet paper rolls

Printer paper

TOOLS
Paint (optional)

Paintbrushes (optional)

Ruler

Scissors

Coffee, black tea or watercolors

Lighter (optional)

Hot-glue gun and hot-glue sticks

Pen or marker

STEP 1
To begin, ensure your toilet paper rolls are free of any remaining paper. These will serve as the foundation for our scroll. You have the option to paint them, but I preferred to keep their natural cardboard color, adding only a touch of watercolor paint to give the tips a weathered appearance.

STEP 2
Once you're satisfied with the toilet paper rolls, it's time to work on the paper. Cut a piece of paper measuring 4½ x 8 inches (11.5 x 20 cm), and for that aged look, soak the paper in black coffee, black tea or watercolor. Allow it to air dry or speed up the process with a blow-dryer. You can even lightly scorch the edges of the paper with a lighter to enhance its aged look.

STEP 3
When the paper is completely dry, attach each end to the length of the toilet paper roll with a little hot glue. Ensure that the paper's edges run parallel to the roll's length to avoid any distortion when you unravel the scroll.

STEP 4
Now that the foundation of your scroll is prepared, it's time to pour your heart out in the form of a poem to your beloved. Given the dramatic nature of this gesture, feel free to embrace old-timey words like "thy," "alas," "thee" and such. Because these poems are supposed to be terribly melodramatic, I asked the most dramatic person I know (my boyfriend) to write me up something good. Here's what he came up with:

> What is thy desire with me?
> To turn my heart into ribbons?
> Thou shan't do any of the sort.
> I feel thy love; I feel thy smile warm my back.
> I feel thy warmth from across the world.
> While I abide for your return to bring
> the greatest prize of all,
> My warmest of loves.

When you finish composing your poem, be sure to write it in your most elegant cursive, and don't forget to embellish the first word to be godishly ornate and extravagant—seriously, why did they do that? Now, when it's time to reveal your affection, clear your throat as obnoxiously as possible, climb onto a table and declare your love with passion. (Bonus points if you throw in an old English accent!)

A Little Reminder That I Love You

Stickers of My Affection

Who knew that a simple sticker could be a vessel for affection? Just like A Little Stamp of Love (page 17), stickers are a fun way to leave little love reminders anywhere and everywhere.

MATERIALS
Printer paper

Wax or parchment paper

TOOLS
Coloring utensils

Scissors

Packing tape

Perfume (optional)

STEP 1
First, let your creativity flow and create some charming illustrations. For this project, I'm crafting little affirmations for my partner. Think cute and thoughtful, like a candle with "You Light Up My Life" or a heart saying "You Have My Heart." If you're the artsy type, go wild with your designs. If not, no pressure—you can always print out your desired images. Just remember to keep them small enough to fit the width of standard packing tape.

STEP 2
Once your artwork is ready, cut around it, leaving no white edges. Now, grab your parchment paper and lay down a strip of tape, sticky side down. Carefully place your drawing facing up on the tape. Then, seal the deal with another strip of tape on top, making sure the drawing is snugly sandwiched in between. Trim the tape around the drawing, leaving a small margin to ensure the tape fully encapsulates your art.

STEP 3
When it's time to surprise your partner, just peel off the parchment paper and stick your homemade love token wherever it'll catch their eye. Bathroom mirror? Check. The cover of their favorite book? Perfect. Their wallet? Absolutely. It's all about finding those everyday spots to sneak in a little reminder of your affection. Get ready to sticker bomb your partner's day with little bursts of love and creativity. Who knew packing tape and parchment paper could be so romantic?

A Little Reminder That I Love You - 29

An X-Small Delivery

There's an undeniable thrill in receiving packages delivered to your doorstep—a feeling that captures the essence of Christmas morning. It doesn't even matter whether or not you've bought it yourself; it still arrives like a surprise gift! And when that package is a present from a friend or loved one, the anticipation of what's inside adds an extra layer of excitement. Well, this gift idea is a small package brimming with love, perfectly complementing our Tiny Love Letters we created (page 12).

MATERIALS

Tiny Love Letters (page 12)

Template (page 231)

Heavyweight paper

Kraft paper or an old grocery bag

Twine

TOOLS

Ruler

Scissors

Hot-glue gun and hot-glue sticks

Tape

STEP 1

Let's start by crafting 15 to 20 tiny envelopes and love letters from page 12 and setting them aside for the moment. Using heavyweight paper, follow the template provided on page 231, folding along the gray lines and gluing the tabs to create your little box. Fill the box with the tiny love letters, and once filled they should all fit snugly within the box.

STEP 2

It's time to give the package its final touch. We'll wrap the box with kraft paper. If you do not have kraft paper on hand, you can easily deconstruct a paper bag from your local grocery store. To wrap your little box, begin by cutting a sheet of kraft paper measuring 6½ x 4 inches (16 x 10 cm). Place the box in the center of the kraft paper sheet, making sure the paper extends beyond the box on each side by at least half of the box's width. Now, place the box face down on the cut piece of paper. Bring one long side of the paper up to the middle of the box's back and secure it with a small piece of tape. Then, fold the remaining long side over so that it overlaps the first side, taping it down to create a neatly covered surface.

STEP 3

Now to finish off the ends of the box, gently push the sides of the paper inward, forming two flaps against the box. You will now have two triangular shapes at the sides. Flatten these triangular flaps against the box. Then, methodically fold the top flap down against the box and secure it with tape. Repeat the same steps for the bottom flap, folding it upwards and taping it securely. After finishing one end, replicate these steps on the other end of the box to finish it off.

STEP 4

Once the package is wrapped in kraft paper, add a finishing touch by tying a small piece of twine into a little bow at the top. Now you have a delightful little package ready to be delivered to your lover's doorstep. Let's just hope they don't accidentally step on it before unveiling the heartfelt surprises inside!

Shrink Plastic to Grow Love

♥ 💔 ♥ 💔 ♥ 💔 ♥ 💔 ♥ 💔 ♥ 💔 ♥ 💔 ♥ 💔 ♥ 💔 ♥ 💔 ♥ 💔 ♥ 💔 ♥ 💔 ♥ 💔

Many of us have fond memories of playing with Shrinky Dinks®, those magical sheets of plastic that shrink and harden when heated. They're perfect for crafting keychains, jewelry charms and other tiny treasures. But did you know that you likely have this shrinkable plastic in your home already, possibly in your recycling bin?

This type of plastic often houses our favorite takeout and restaurant meals. However, it's crucial to know that not all plastics are created equal, as there is only one type that will shrink, harden and flatten the way we need it to. This type of plastic is labeled #6 on the recycling code, so before you heat up plastic (and deal with the corresponding fumes), check to make sure it says #6. Once you've sourced the right type of plastic, focus on sections that are completely flat. When creating your design, remember that it will shrink to about one-third of its original size, so start big!

This is an easy idea to start with, but once you get the gist, there are so many fun and unique ways to use this overlooked art material!

MATERIALS
Piece of #6 plastic

2 jump rings

TOOLS
Sandpaper

Red acrylic marker

Scissors

Hole punch

Baking sheet

STEP 1
Preheat the oven to 310°F (155°C).

Start by drawing a large heart on the plastic. Sand your plastic and color it in with a red acrylic marker. Cut out the heart, and then cut it in half in a chevron pattern. Using a hole punch, punch holes at the top of either side of the broken heart.

STEP 2
Place the pieces on a baking sheet, and heat it in your oven for 10 minutes, or until you notice the plastic has shriveled and flattened. Use the holes we punched earlier to attach jump rings and add them to a bracelet, necklace or keychain.

While this makes for a perfect gift for you and your special person, there are countless other things you can make out of this magic plastic, whether it's to show your love or just to have for yourself.

A Little Reminder That I Love You

You Blow My Mind

"You blow my mind" . . . I know, kind of a juvenile saying, but don't hate. Even if it is juvenile, no one *doesn't* want to hear it. So here's a way to make this saying into such a strong visual that every time your giftee hears it, they will immediately think of you.

MATERIALS

Printer paper

Cardstock

Pink balloon

Glitter or money (optional)

TOOLS

Markers

Scissors

Tape

White glue

STEP 1

First up, channel your inner artist and draw a face on the printer paper from the nose up to the forehead. Hold off on drawing the hair, though. Instead, imagine the top of the head has "exploded" (in a totally non-gory, fun way, I promise). Here's a basic sketch to guide you, but feel free to tweak the facial features to suit your style.

Once your masterpiece is complete, cut it out and set it aside.

STEP 2

Next, write a small note on a strip of printer paper that reads, "You blow my mind." Blow up the pink balloon and stuff your note inside the balloon before you tie it off.

If you're feeling extra creative, grab your markers and doodle a brain on the balloon. Just remember to let the ink dry completely before handling it—no smudgy brains here!

STEP 3

Tape down the knot of the balloon to the middle section of the cardstock paper. Take your drawing and place it on the cardstock paper. The knot of the balloon should lay a little under the forehead. Once the placement looks right, glue the bottom and sides of the drawing and write, "Pop Me!" on the balloon. Your person will pop the balloon "brain" to reveal the note exclaiming that they blow your mind. It is such a unique way to let someone know that they are absolutely awesome.

TIP: If you're creating this for a birthday or other special occasion, feel free to add glitter, money and other goodies directly inside the balloon for them to find once it is popped!

Scratch-Off Love Letter

This craft combines the best part of a scratch-off lottery ticket (not the money, but the satisfying scratch-off) with the sentimentality of a love letter. You only need a few materials and some extra minutes to make a card that will make your lover's heart skip a beat.

MATERIALS
Template (page 227)

1 coin

Heart sticker or cutout

TOOLS
Scissors

Black pen or marker

Clear packing tape

Acrylic paint

Paintbrushes

Pen

STEP 1
We will begin by cutting out the deconstructed letter. Go to page 227 and cut out the template. Etch and fold all of the lines so they go inward. When folded inward, you may notice the shape changes to look like a simple rectangle. To give the rectangle a cute "love letter" appearance, use a black pen or marker to outline each of the fold lines.

STEP 2
Now open the rectangle back up and write a little love note inside.

STEP 3
Once you have finished writing your heart out, cover the note with the packing tape. Make sure the tape covers the entire note, but cut off any excess if it exceeds past the edges of the paper. Over the tape, add a layer of paint to sneakily conceal the note below; I chose white paint to make it really blend in and make for a more surprising reveal. Wait for the paint to dry completely and add a dime or other small coin inside and fold on the fold lines of the template.

STEP 4
To make sure the envelope stays closed, either add a heart sticker to the middle of the letter or you can even make one (see Stickers of My Affection on page 28) and secure your sticker heart to the middle of your letter, or simply cut out a little heart and glue it down to the center, ensuring each of the sides stay closed. On the reverse side of your envelope write, "Scratch me." When they open the envelope, they can use the coin to scratch off the hidden little love note inside.

Cuddles from Afar

Being in a long-distance relationship for the past three years has made me appreciate the simple joy of a little cuddle. Whether your partner is just five minutes down the road or a thousand miles away, here's a thoughtful craft that brings the warmth of a cuddle wherever they are.

MATERIALS

Heavyweight paper

Cotton balls

Paper towels or fabric

TOOLS

Hot-glue gun and hot-glue sticks

Coloring utensils

Pen or marker

STEP 1

Start with a rectangular piece of heavyweight paper, and draw two horizontal rectangles at the top of the page to serve as the basis for pillows. Add a bit of cotton to the center of these rectangles, then hot glue matching rectangle pieces of paper towel (or fabric), securing all edges onto the drawn rectangles. These little things will serve as our three-dimensional pillows.

STEP 2

On the rest of your heavyweight paper, feel free to go ahead and color your "bed" any color, acting as your "bedsheet." You can do this directly on top of the paper towel pillows as well, but I decided to leave mine white.

STEP 3

Directly below the pillows, cut a piece of paper towel (or fabric) to fit seamlessly over the rest of the heavyweight paper. Crease down the very top of your paper towel to resemble the look of a cleanly made bed. Feel free to color this paper towel to serve as your blanket. Then glue the left side as well as the bottom onto your piece of paper. Since the right side isn't glued down, you can fold it over and write something to be discreetly hidden underneath the sheet when folded back over. Feel free to write, "Wish you were here," "I miss our cuddles" or maybe even something spicier if you like.

STEP 4

Fold the sheet back and put it in the mail on its way to your partner. The little message is cutely concealed, but once the sheet is pulled back, the message is sure to transcend the physical distance.

A Little Reminder That I Love You

You have one new MESSAGE

Message in a Bottle

♥💔♥💔♥💔♥💔♥💔♥💔♥💔♥💔♥💔♥💔♥💔♥💔♥💔

Messages in a bottle have been around for as long as there have been bottles and seas to cast them in. They have appeared in so many TV shows and movies that I couldn't name them all even if I wanted to. While you're free to look for love by doing this traditionally, here is a quick craft that references this age-old way of communication without the potential littering.

MATERIALS

Heavyweight paper, such as bristol paper, watercolor paper or thick cardstock

Sand (optional)

Twine

TOOLS

Ruler

Scissors

Coloring utensils

White glue (optional)

Pen or marker

Double-sided tape

STEP 1

To kickstart this crafting journey, cut out a 6 x 4½-inch (15 x 11.5-cm) piece of the heavyweight paper. It's time to let your artistic flair take the lead. Whether your drawing skills are novice or advanced, I've got you covered with a range of designs, from simple to sophisticated. So, get out your coloring supplies and recreate one of these drawings on your paper. Feel free to color them however you prefer.

But if you're feeling a bit extra and want to elevate your craft, here's a little twist: Add some sand for a truly beachy vibe. After coloring in your sandy base, apply a smidge of white glue to the areas where you'd like some texture, and then sprinkle on the sand. This just adds that extra oomph that your craft may be begging for.

STEP 2

Now for the heart of this craft: the message. Jot down a heartfelt note, a quirky message or even a cheeky comment on a small piece of paper. Once your ink is dry, roll it up and tie it with a piece of twine. Add a tiny bit of double-sided tape to your message, just enough to stick it onto the bottle without causing any paper casualties.

STEP 3

To cap it off, I scribbled, "You have one new message," at the top of the paper, and voilà, your craft is ready to be gifted. Whether it's for a loved one, a sibling, a crush, a romantic partner or even a teacher, this craft's charm lies in its versatility. The message you tuck inside is what truly personalizes it, making it a fitting gift for just about anyone in your life.

A Little Reminder That I Love You

Fiery Feels

If you have some fiery feelings, then you may be struggling to find the perfect card for your crush or partner. Luckily, I got you covered with this sizzling craft. Beware, as it involves controlled burning, so make sure to follow safety guidelines.

MATERIALS
Paper (any kind)

TOOLS
Drawing and coloring utensils
Water
Matches

STEP 1
Safety first: Perform this craft in a well-ventilated and fire-safe area. Keep the burning controlled, and be ready to extinguish it promptly. Always have a cup of water or a fire extinguisher nearby. (Seriously, I'd really rather not wake up to find out someone set themselves on fire because of one of my craft ideas.)

STEP 2
Once you have everything you need, let's ignite the passion. Begin by drawing a flame on a piece of paper. Feel free to choose what type of paper you want for this craft; as long as it lights, you're good to go! You can go simple or take advantage of the chance to unleash your inner artist.

STEP 3
Light one corner of the paper on fire with a match, ensuring it doesn't spread too far or disrupt the drawing. Keep a close eye on it, and either blow out the fire or dunk it into the water. As always, exercise caution when using fire.

STEP 4
Since embers may continue to affect the paper, use water to spray or dunk the burnt corner. This helps contain the burnt area and prevents it from spreading beyond our designated corner. In any empty space of the paper, write the message, "You're so hot." The end result is a visually captivating and symbolic piece of art that conveys your hot feelings. This craft is a unique way to infuse passion into a simple message.

A Little Reminder That I Love You

YOU ROCK!

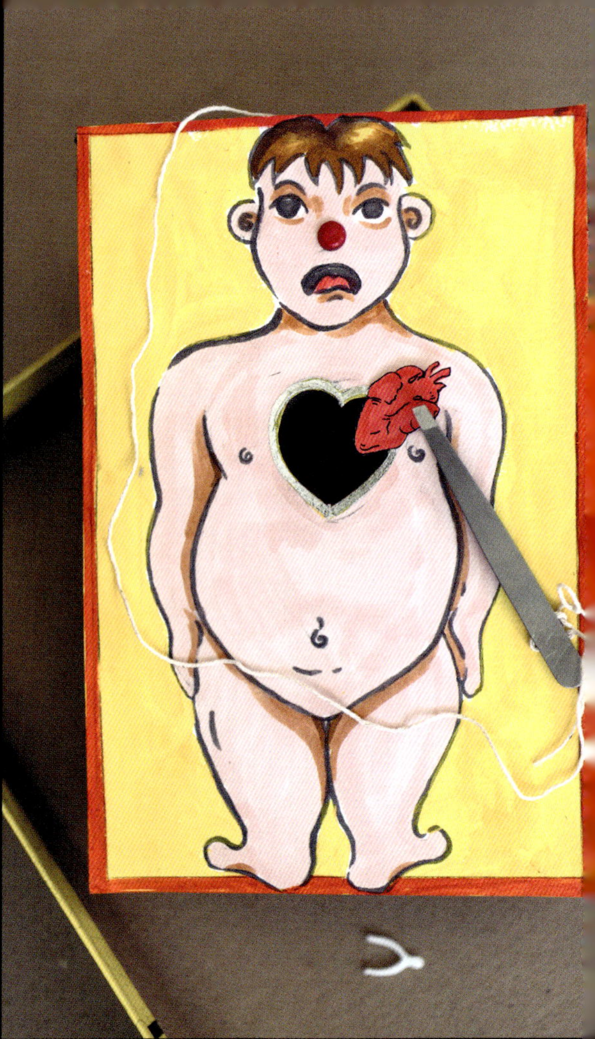

COUPLEGOALS
COUPLEGOALS and the cutest couple is .... Devyn and Isaac! # couplegoals
View all 100 comments
Harrystyles they really are the cutest couple I've ever seen

BABY, YOU'RE A FIREWORK!

Romance or Revenge?

GIFTS FOR YOUR CURRENT OR FORMER PARTNER

Of course, there are many different types of love, and throughout this book we are going to spread our appreciation (and discontentment) to the various relationships in our lives. But there is something about romantic feelings that needs its own spotlight, whether that be a heart full of ooey gooeys or a shattered chest that just feels like an ouchy.

And you know what? Sometimes just saying "I love you" or "I hate you" simply isn't enough. So here are a whole bunch of different crafts to let your current or former romantic partners know just how you feel about them through something a little more tangible than words.

The Never-Ending Card

♥💔♥💔♥💔♥💔♥💔♥💔♥💔♥💔♥💔♥💔♥💔♥

Have you ever felt so overwhelmed with love for your partner that you feel like it could literally burst from your chest? There is so much that you could say to them: what you adore about them, the future you want with them, what made you fall in love with them, etc. Sometimes it feels like there aren't enough words or there isn't enough space on a piece of paper for you to write it all out on. If you have ever felt like this for a partner (or an ex, for that matter), then you need this craft.

We're going to make a card that will look and seem normal enough at first until you open it to reveal an endless stream of thoughts and feelings folding out. Caution: If you are not in a committed relationship with this person, it may be a little off-putting for them to get this without warning. I know, sometimes we have the most to say about people we aren't yet in a relationship with, but proceed with caution because I don't want any of y'all to receive a restraining order. (And if you do, I will not be held legally liable.)

MATERIALS

Heavyweight paper

Cardstock

Paper (any kind)

TOOLS

Ruler

Scissors

Decorative tools

Tape

Glue

Pen

A TON OF FEELINGS

STEP 1

We are going to start off cutting out a 9 x 5-inch (23 x 13-cm) piece of heavyweight paper. Place your sheet horizontally and create a crease that goes down the page at 4½ inches (11.5 cm) and fold. Now that it's all nice and folded, you should have a typical-looking card. Feel free to decorate the front cover however you choose. I chose to decorate my cover using graphic cardstock and a little gold trim that I found at the bottom of my craft closet. (You never know what you'll find there!) And I used cardstock scraps to decorate the inner left side and the outer edges on the right. We don't need to totally cover the right side because we'll be covering most of it with our note.

STEP 2

Now let's create the pages for our never-ending note. Cut out multiple 5 x 3¼-inch (13 x 8-cm) pieces of paper. I recommend cutting out at least five, but the more you have to say to this special person, the more pages you will need! Tape the pages together at the top and bottom and fold them at the tape crease. Now that you have a stack of paper all connected together, take the first piece of your stack and glue it directly to the card, in between the cardstock scraps or to the left page of your card. Unfold all of the pages so it appears to be one very long piece of paper and begin writing your love note.

I definitely do not recommend this craft if you're trying to do it the day before an anniversary or a Valentine's Day dinner. This type of thing can't be rushed, or your partner will feel it. Obviously, life gets in the way, and we're not always thinking about how much we love the people we love (even though it's not a bad habit to start!). But when it's really late at night, and your sleeping partner is cuddled up in your arms, and you feel an immense amount of gratitude for having them in your life, write down how you feel.

Here are some prompts to get your gears turning:

- ❤ How grateful you are for them
- ❤ What they've done to improve your life
- ❤ What they've taught you
- ❤ How you've grown together
- ❤ How you both have overcome challenges
- ❤ How you see your future together

This is the time to be vulnerable and to truly speak from your heart. (I know it's cheesy, but it's true!)

DIY "Operation" Game

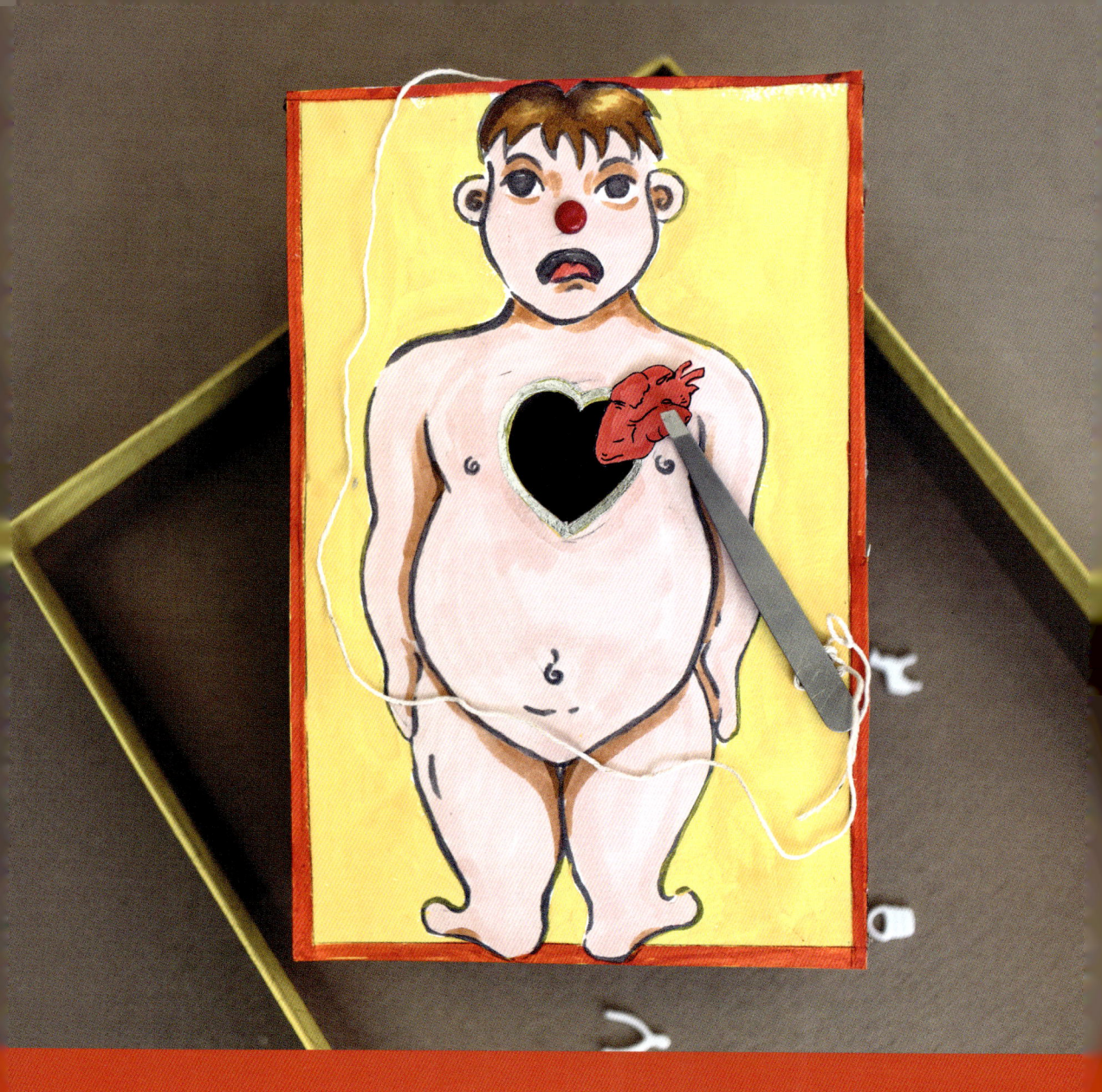

♥💔♥💔♥💔♥💔♥💔♥💔♥💔♥💔♥💔♥💔♥💔♥💔♥💔

Remember the childhood game Operation® where you had to carefully extract objects from a man's body without setting off the buzzer? Let's bring back some nostalgia and show our love with a homemade version. While it won't be as high-tech as the board game, it's a creative way to express your affection, nonetheless.

MATERIALS

Heavyweight paper, such as bristol or watercolor paper

Cardboard

1 toilet paper roll

String

Tweezers

TOOLS

Ruler

Scissors

Coloring utensils

Craft knife (I use X-Acto)

Hot-glue gun and hot-glue sticks

Silver chrome marker (optional)

Pen or marker

STEP 1

Cut out a 6 x 9-inch (15 x 23-cm) piece of heavyweight paper. Let's start with creating an illustration of a person, inspired by the game. Feel free to reference my illustration or try your hand at making one yourself. Color and outline the person and all their features. Carefully cut out the area where the man's heart is located with your craft knife, add a touch of hot glue to his nose and once dry, color it red to mimic the game. Color the area outside of the person yellow except for a thin red border along the perimeter of the paper. For extra detail I also added some silver chrome marker around the cutout to look like metal from the OG game.

STEP 2

Now, cut out a 6 x 9-inch (15 x 23-cm) piece of cardboard. We want to create a box with this piece of cardboard as the base, so cut out two 9 x 1½-inch (23 x 4-cm) pieces of cardboard and two 6 x ½-inch (15 x 1.3-cm) pieces and glue them to the sides of the large cardboard base using hot glue. In the center of this box, place a 1-inch (2.5-cm) piece of the toilet paper roll, ensuring that the cutout in the chest area aligns with the toilet paper roll. Apply hot glue to each side and the rim of the toilet paper roll, and then align your paper with the man and press it down so the hot glue sticks to the paper.

STEP 3

Draw a heart on a small piece of heavyweight paper. You can choose to make it look like a realistic organ or a simple heart, depending on your preference, but be sure to color it so it looks like a real piece you would find in the original game. Cut out the heart and write on the back, "My heart is all yours." Attach the piece of string to a pair of tweezers and glue the other end of the string to the box. This is to ensure that tweezers don't get lost and you can properly play it like you would play a real game of Operation.

You are now free to give this craft to someone you love. Ask them if they want to play a game of Operation, or simply give it to them. This craft is versatile and suitable for expressing your feelings to a best friend you've fallen in love with, to someone you've been dating but haven't made it official with yet or even an ex! Just replace "My heart is all yours" with "You ripped my heart out!"

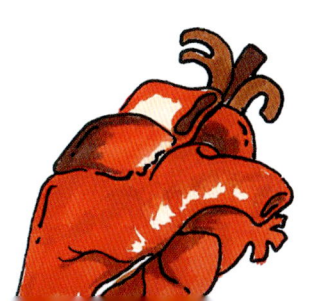

Romance or Revenge?

Loopy for You

♥💔♥💔♥💔♥💔♥💔♥💔♥💔♥💔♥💔♥💔♥💔♥💔♥💔♥💔♥💔

Have you ever stayed at a hotel with free breakfast and been greeted by those totally adorable single-serving cereal boxes? There's something oddly satisfying about them—maybe it's their tininess that speaks to my soul, or maybe it's the joy of having a whole cereal box to myself. Maybe it's a bit of both, and I will be using both of these endearing characteristics to create this next craft. In this chapter, I'll show you how to create a mini cereal box with a twist. It's a special way to let someone know they have your heart, all while channeling the essence of your favorite cereal.

MATERIALS

Template (page 219)

Parchment paper

TOOLS

Scissors

Markers or colored pencils

Ruler

Hot-glue gun and hot-glue sticks

Pastel paint (light red, blue, green and orange)

Paintbrushes

STEP 1

Begin by cutting out the template on page 219 for your mini cereal box. Now that we have our box, let's decorate. Begin by either printing a picture of the Froot Loops® mascot or, if you're up for an artistic challenge, coming up with your own original cereal box design. Then write, "Loopy for You" in big white letters.

> **TIP:** You can also emulate the early 2000s with a prize hidden inside the cereal box as an opportunity to give your partner a little gift, such as jewelry or tickets to their favorite sports game.

STEP 2

Once your cereal box is completely colored, we can add a creative opportunity to write a love note. Instead of the usual nutrition facts, write, "Little Love Facts" on the back of the box in bold letters and begin writing attributes about your partner that you find endearing. I chose to write, "love, sassiness, charm, friendliness and sweetness," but feel free to expand on this based on your partner's attributes. At the end of each line, I wrote a percentage, imitating the daily intake percentage that you would find on typical nutrition facts. Now that the box is complete, we can go ahead and create the cereal. Go to page 118 (Will You Wear Your Bowtie) for a visual guide.

STEP 3

To create the heart-shaped "cereal," add short lines (no longer than ¾ inch [2 cm] long) or dabs of hot glue all around the parchment paper. Precision is not crucial here, but leave 1 inch (2.5 cm) of space between each dab. When the glue dabs have had a few seconds to cool but are not yet completely solid, add another dab to each original dab, connecting the tails at the bottom. This will allow the hot glue pieces to form a heart shape.

STEP 4

While they are still attached to the parchment paper, paint each heart-shaped piece with colors that match the ones you'd normally see in fruit cereal: light red, blue, green and orange. Keep the colors pastel to maintain that cereal-box charm. Once the cereal pieces are painted and dry, place them inside your "Loopy for You" container. Close up the box and give it to your loved one as a delightful and heartwarming surprise.

Romance or Revenge?

Baby, You're a Firework

"Baby, you're a firework" is an iconic line from the 2010s that still plays in my head rent free. Let's use this cheesy line to create a gift we can give to our partner. (Earn extra points if you gift this around the Fourth of July or New Year's Eve.) While some people may light actual fireworks to tell their partner they love them, that costs money and could potentially blow a body part off, so let's use our craft skills instead.

MATERIALS

Toilet paper roll

Printer paper

Pipe cleaners

Curl ribbon (optional)

Skewer

TOOLS

Paint, including silver

Paintbrushes

Markers and other coloring utensils

Protractor

Scissors

Hot-glue gun and hot-glue sticks

STEP 1

Paint the TP roll with a fun design, because fireworks tend to be colorful and lively. You can choose from various styles like polka dots, pinstripes, thick stripes, swirls and more. To make it easier, paint the roll white first, and then use markers to add your design.

STEP 2

Once your toilet paper roll is beautifully colored, let's add the cone head. Create the cone using a protractor to draw a 2-inch (5-cm) circle from a piece of paper. Cut the circle into a Pac-Man shape from the center point. Twist the Pac-Man shape to connect the corners and form a cone, gluing to hold it in place. Color the cone with paint or markers, selecting a color that complements your roll's design. Apply a thick layer of hot glue in a circle inside the cone and place your toilet paper roll inside. Adjust the cone so that not only does the glue adhere to the roll but also so the tip of the cone is parallel with it.

STEP 3

With the cone securely attached, let's use different materials to create the illusion of a firework bursting out of the container. I'm drawing inspiration from old-timey cartoons, which adds a fun touch as it doesn't have to be realistic. Twist some pipe cleaners in various ways to make it look like they're exploding. To do this, wrap a pipe cleaner around your finger and secure the end inside the toilet paper roll with hot glue. Allow it to dry, and then add another. I used various shades of red, orange and yellow to imitate the fiery colors of sparks and flames. I also added silver stars by cutting them out from a sheet of paper, painting them silver, and then gluing them onto a pipe cleaner, sandwiching them together. If you want, run a few pieces of curl ribbon across the blade of your scissors to make them curl and secure them by attaching the ends inside the toilet paper roll. To spell out "Baby, You're a Firework!," we are going to recreate the cartoon explosion design. It should resemble something like this:

Once you've created this explosive effect with all these different materials, glue a skewer inside the toilet paper roll, and voilà!

Romance or Revenge? - 51

Instagram IRL

♥💔♥💔♥💔♥💔♥💔♥💔♥💔♥💔♥💔♥💔♥💔♥

In today's digital era, flaunting your boo thing on social media platforms like Instagram is almost a requirement. But what if you're not an Insta-enthusiast or prefer keeping your love life a bit more low-key? Well, here's a nifty craft that lets you showcase your affection without resorting to PDA on the 'gram.

MATERIALS

Paper (any kind)

3" x 3" (7.5 x 7.5–cm) photo of you and your significant other

TOOLS

Ruler

Scissors

Craft knife (I use X-Acto)

Markers or colored pencils

Black and gray fineliners

Foam tape

STEP 1

This craft might come in handy, especially for those fellas who often feel the pressure to share their relationships with the world. So, let's dive right in. Begin by cutting a 4 x 5½-inch (10 x 14–cm) piece of paper. Within this rectangular piece of paper, we're going to draw out a square. Leave a ½-inch (1.3-cm) border along the top and both sides, ensuring you've got a generous 2-inch (5-cm) margin at the bottom. Place the 3 x 3-inch (7.5 x 7.5–cm) picture featuring you and your lover in the same spot where you drew the square. Set this piece aside for now as we work to prep the next sheet of paper.

STEP 2

In this age of digital aesthetics, Instagram posts come in a couple different shapes and sizes, but for that classic Instagram look, we're going to focus on a central square, precisely 3 x 3 inches (7.5 x 7.5 cm). Hold your paper vertically and mark a ¼-inch (6-mm) border from the top and both sides of the square. To carve out the square, employ your trusty ruler to guide your craft knife.

STEP 3

Just above this freshly minted square, add a teeny tiny circle to mimic an Instagram profile picture, and don't forget to throw in an Instagram username at the top margin. Directly beneath the square, sprinkle in those symbols that we associate with an Instagram post: the heart symbol, the comment symbol and the share symbol. Then, write a caption that spills the beans on your affection for your partner or any message that tickles your fancy. You can even simulate the number of likes this "Instagram post" has, and for extra flair, toss in comments from adoring fans, raving about how you are such "couple goals." Feel free to get a tad creative here, perhaps including a comment from your partner's favorite celebrity. For that polished look, grab a black fineliner for the Instagram symbols and usernames, and a gray fineliner for the caption and comments.

STEP 4

Now to put these two sheets of paper together: To add dimension to this craft, stick the pieces of foam tape along the border of the picture. Line the sheets up so the picture is seen through the second sheet's cutout and press them together like a perfectly curated Instagram feed.

Ta-da! You've just whipped up your very own, real-life Instagram post, ready to impress your partner. Whether they're an Instagram sensation or a social media novice, it's a fun and clever way to express your love without resorting to those oh-so-public social media gestures.

Machine Claw Game

♥ 💔 ♥ 💔 ♥ 💔 ♥ 💔 ♥ 💔 ♥ 💔 ♥ 💔 ♥ 💔

I've spent an exorbitant amount of money trying to win a 50-cent prize from a claw machine. The dazzling lights, catchy music and competitive spirit cloud any rational thought, leaving me fixated on winning that prize. But what if we could recreate that excitement for a partner? Imagine, instead of a trivial prize, they receive a piece of your heart. To me, that sounds like a much more meaningful exchange. So, let's begin crafting.

MATERIALS

Templates (pages 223–227)

Clear plastic sheet

10 Tiny Love Letters (page 12)

Jump ring or thin ribbon

2 skewers

Paper clip or earring hook

TOOLS

Scissors

Paint

Paintbrushes

Craft knife (I use X-Acto)

Ruler

Hot-glue gun and hot-glue sticks

Superglue (optional)

Acrylic markers (optional)

Pliers (optional)

STEP 1

Let's start with the upper base template provided on page 223. After cutting the template out, but before folding and assembling it, paint or color one or both of the sides with your desired colors. Feel free to embellish with designs or patterns for a more personal touch. You'll notice that, for this template, there are large gray rectangles within the cut lines. These must be cut out because they are going to act as our little windows. Do this with a craft knife along with a ruler to get nice smooth lines.

STEP 2

Now to make them functional windows, we'll need a piece of flexible plastic sheet to create the "glass." Cut the plastic to be slightly bigger than the cutouts on the template, and with hot glue, adhere the pieces to each of the cutout window sections on the template. With your "glass" windows prepared, assemble the craft but make sure you fold the exposed plastic edges inward. Leave the top tab unglued for now. You'll notice there is an "X" shown on the ceiling. For right now, just cut on the X lines with your craft knife.

STEP 3

Once the upper base template is completed, go ahead and cut out the lower base template on page 225. Paint or color the template to match the upper base. You will notice there are two rectangular holes missing from the base. One hole will act as the exit for the prizes, and the other will act as the opening to get the prizes once they have been won. Just so we make sure no prizes escape through this hole when they are not actively being removed by the claw, we need to build a small wall. To do this, take some of the excess clear plastic sheet, heavyweight paper or another sturdy flat material and cut it into two ¾ x 3⅕-inch (2 x 8-cm) rectangles.

Make sure the larger of the two rectangular openings is positioned on top and press the rectangles against both of the sides that do not touch the exterior corner. Add a small bit of superglue in place if they do not feel secure enough on their own.

(continued)

STEP 4

To connect the upper and lower bases, cut out the connecting strip template on page 227 and fold along each of the designated lines. Feel free to color this to match your base or provide some decorative contrast if you so choose. (I opted to keep it white.) Line up the upper and lower bases and hot glue this strip around the points where the bases connect to combine the two into one.

STEP 5

Make at least 10 Tiny Love Letters (page 12), but feel free to add more if you are so inclined. Before you go ahead and place them in the crane machine, attach a small jump ring or a loop of thin ribbon to each item so that our "claw" will have something to grab onto. Once each item has a ring or ribbon attached, place them inside the crane machine by flipping the machine claw game upside down and shimmying the letters through the bottom opening.

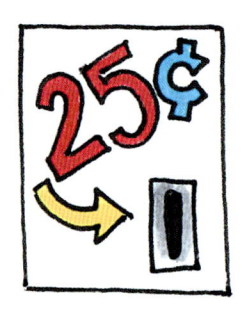

STEP 6

Now let's add some detail! Cut one of the skewers, into two ¾-inch (2-cm) pieces. Add a dab of hot glue to each to resemble knobs. After the glue dries, paint the skewers to resemble levers. Then, attach them to a ¾ x 1¼-inch (2 x 3-cm) piece of cardboard. Glue this assembly right next to the prize slot. This is also a great opportunity to include a small illustration for the token slot, which I did using some acrylic markers.

STEP 6

Let's make the claw machine functional (finally!!). You can make the claw a few different ways. I started with the second skewer, and wrapped an unrolled paper clip around the skewer. On the bottom of the skewer, I let the unrolled paper clip extend 1¼ inches (3 cm) past the skewer and curled it up with my pliers to make it into a hook. If you do have an earring hook on hand, you can opt to secure that to the skewer instead of the paper clip. Squeeze your "claw" through the "X" we cut into the upper base of our craft and you're ready to gift!

Have your giftee try their hand at securing one of the letters by looping the claw though one of the ribbon loops or jump rings. Once it's through, they can take it out through the opening in the bottom template and read your tiny love letter. This way, you not only get to tell your partner you love them through all of the love notes inside the machine, but you also get to play a little game to provide both of you with memorable entertainment.

Puzzle to My Heart

I'm realizing midway through writing this book that I use matchboxes A LOT. (Keep going . . . you'll see.) In fact, I use more matchboxes than matches! I really can't help it. It's so easy to transform one of these little guys into the perfect little token of affection. Just add a little paint and a little bit of love and BAM, you got yourself the perfect little gift. This craft is no different. It uses the little matchbox as a perfect substitute for a puzzle box. This is great for any puzzle lover in your life, or really any lover (unless they absolutely despise puzzles).

MATERIALS
Matchbox

Watercolor paper

TOOLS
Pen or pencil

Colored markers or pencils

Scissors or craft knife (I use X-Acto)

Paint

Paintbrushes

Acrylic markers and decorative supplies (optional)

STEP 1
First things first: Ditch the matches. The size of the matchbox doesn't matter much; it just dictates the scale of your puzzle. Draw a heart shape on a piece of watercolor paper. Inside this heart, create little puzzle pieces that will fit in the matchbox.

STEP 2
Keep the design relatively simple, as we don't want our partner to struggle too much putting it together. Color your heart, add a little love note and then carefully cut out each puzzle piece, ensuring you keep the heart shape intact. Small scissors are your best friend here for precise cutting, but for those tricky little details that scissors can't handle, a craft knife might come in handy.

STEP 3
Let's now give some love to the matchbox. You're free to decorate it in any style that speaks to you. A good starting point is to paint the box first and then add details with acrylic markers for a personal touch. I went for a classic black paint job and then glued a piece of watercolor paper on it with the words "A Puzzle for You." (I wanted to leave a bit of mystery as to what the puzzle inside entails.) And there you have it, the perfect addition to a Christmas stocking, a Valentine's basket or something to simply sneak in during game night.

Romance or Revenge? - 57

A Cozy Cup of Love

If your loved one is a particular tea snob, then I may just have the ultimate gift idea. Let's transform a typical tea bag into a pocketful of love. While this will not make your tea taste any better, I can guarantee you that it will make it far more *lovely*.

MATERIALS

Tea bag

Construction paper

White string

Plain paper

TOOLS

Staple remover (optional)

Scissors

Washable nontoxic markers (optional)

Coloring utensils

Stapler

Glue

STEP 1

Let's start by getting a packet of tea. Make sure the tea is prepackaged in those paper tea bags—get out of here with that fancy loose-leaf tea. Remove the staple from the bag. For some tea bags, you may need a staple remover to remove the staple without damaging the tea bag. So, be careful, because we want the tea bag in as pristine condition as possible. Once the staple is removed, unfold the top and the middle of the tea bag until it's in a tube shape that you can remove the tea from. Put the loose-leaf tea aside for a cozy cup later.

STEP 2

Now, cut out up to 20 small hearts from the construction paper that fit inside the tea bag. Hearts in a few different colors are ideal. One easy way to make hearts is to fold a piece of paper and cut half a heart a few times.

TIP: If you really want this craft to blow minds, consider coloring your hearts with washable nontoxic markers, so when dipped in water, the colors disperse from the tea bag, like a magic potion!

STEP 3

Place the hearts into the unwrapped tea bag and fold it back up along all of the original creases. Place an 11-inch (28-cm) piece of white string along the top fold, and then staple the tea bag back into its folded position with the string attached.

STEP 4

Now we are going to want to recreate the paper tag that is commonly attached to the end of the tea string. Cut out two ½ x ½-inch (1.3 x 1.3-cm) squares from the plain paper. On these squares, draw a design that you think accurately represents your love. It can be simple, plain, striped, complex, however you choose. Here are some paper tag designs that cover all spectrums of love:

STEP 5

Apply glue to the back side of the tags, and sandwich the other paper square between them. Yay! Your tea bag is done! Now let's create the perfect packaging to fit this packet of love into. Cut out two 3 x 2½-inch (7.5 x 6-cm) rectangles from the plain paper. On at least one of the rectangles create some tea + love-related illustration. You can get as creative as you want with this, but I am drawing a cup with hearts, calling it "Love Tea" and including the tagline "Soak up my love." Here are some more tea bag design ideas you can use to inspire your very own tea company!

STEP 6

Once at least one rectangle is colored, either recreate the same design on the other rectangle, or simply color it to resemble the base color of the first rectangle. Put a small amount of glue at the sides and the bottom of the uncolored side of each of the decorated rectangles and attach them together so they line up properly and make a pocket. In the pocket, place your tea bag and finally, glue the top of the pocket closed. A perfect way to give this craft is to sneak it with your other teas. Your loved one will notice the peculiar design of the packaging and begin their investigation. When soaked in water, the hearts will become ever so apparent (especially if you used washable markers) as well as the thoughtfully designed paper tag and packaging.

Love: Delivered to Your Door

♥💔♥💔♥💔♥💔♥💔♥💔♥💔♥💔♥💔♥💔♥💔♥💔

A mailbox is truly an unsung hero of every good love story. Just think of the love letters that sit within, waiting to reveal the innermost thoughts of their writer's affection. Or consider gift packages sent during the holidays, carefully thought-out and delivered with care and love. The mailbox truly holds some of the most valuable objects of love one can find, so it only makes sense if we take the concept of a mailbox and turn it into a loving gesture in and of itself.

MATERIALS

Toilet paper roll

Heavyweight paper, such as bristol paper, watercolor paper or thick cardstock

Plastic straw

Cardboard

TOOLS

Ruler

Scissors

Pencil

Hot-glue gun and hot-glue sticks

Paint

Paintbrushes

Coloring utensils (optional)

STEP 1

Begin by flattening the toilet paper roll in half. Measure ¾ inch (2 cm) from the width of the toilet paper roll and cut it off. Keep in mind that you are technically cutting off 1½ inches (4 cm) because the roll is folded in half. Measure the length of the toilet paper roll and cut it to measure 6 inches (15 cm). Now that the tube shape of the toilet paper roll is cut open, we have a dome-like shape, which is exactly what we need for this craft. Set your dome aside for now.

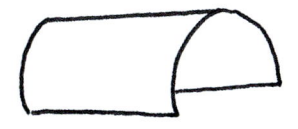

STEP 2

Cut a piece of heavyweight paper measuring 6 x 1½ inches (15 x 4 cm), but with ½-inch (1.3-cm) tabs on opposite sides, like so:

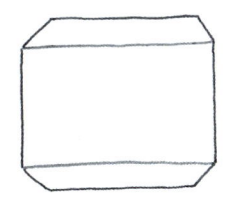

Fold the tabs up and glue them underneath the dome, creating a flat "floor." Now it should look like those tunnels you drive through that always have really cool graffiti inside for some reason. Trace the two open ends onto a piece of heavyweight paper, but don't cut them out just yet. Given that it is an ambiguous shape, each of us will have slightly different measurements, but it should have the same shape as a mailbox door (you should have two of these). Here's the diagram for mine:

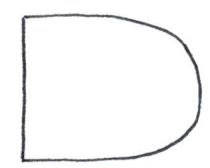

STEP 3

For the first drawing, add a ½-inch (1.3-cm) tab at the flat end. Cut it out and etch where the mailbox door shape ends and the tab begins ever so slightly, and glue the tab to the flat side of the toilet paper roll dome. You should be able to move this dome open and closed now, like you would an opening of a mailbox.

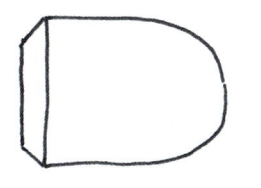

(continued)

Romance or Revenge? - 61

STEP 4

For the second one, which will be the back of the mailbox, draw a ½-inch (1.3-cm) border around the entire drawing and cut it out.

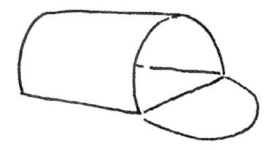

Cut slits every ¼ inch (6 mm), but do not cut past the original mailbox door shape. Add a small amount of hot glue to each of the slits and put it inside the toilet paper tunnel. Put your finger through the roll and hold the slits down to make sure they dry securely. (Just try not to burn your fingers.)

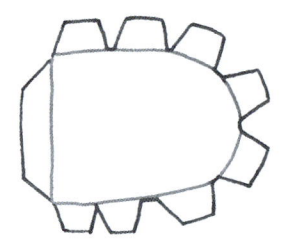

STEP 5

You now have the basis for your mailbox! Paint your mailbox whatever color you choose. I decided to reference one of my favorite Pixar movies and added small handprints to mine. (Ten points if you can guess the movie.) Once your paint has dried, let's add the little lever. Draw the lever on a piece of the heavyweight paper, and cut it out. Here are some various lever designs you can use as a reference:

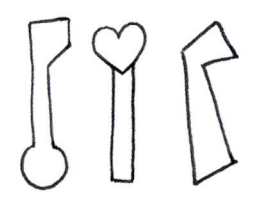

STEP 6

Color your lever with either paint or coloring utensils, add a small bit of glue onto the end and attach it to the base of the mailbox. To make the stand, cut a plastic straw from your kitchen to 2¾ inches (7 cm) long. I am also adding five little slits going down ½ inch (1.3 cm) on either side of the straw. Fold the slits down and add a small amount of glue to each slit. Hold both the straw and the mailbox down and wait for the glue to fully dry. Make sure the straw is secured to the very middle of the bottom of the mailbox.

STEP 7

Cut out a 4½ x 2¼-inch (11.5 x 6-cm) piece of cardboard. Secure the other end of the straw to the center of the cardboard square. If your mailbox has trouble balancing, cut out a 5 x 2¼-inch (13 x 6-cm) piece of cardboard, and glue it to the cardboard base as well as the back of the mailbox. Now the cardboard will have an "L" shape around the mailbox. Paint the back cardboard to look like a fence or simply a continuation of the backdrop like a nice blue sky or something along those lines. Either draw the ground or make some paper grass (You're Dead to Me. . . Literally, step 2 [page 200]).

STEP 8

With the mailbox mounted and able to stand up on its own, open the mailbox up and fill it with An X-Small Delivery (page 30) and Tiny Love Letters (page 12) for your partner. If you want to add an adorable touch, add your partner's mailing address on the tiny letters or packages. Now for an ultimate love/mail paradox, leave this in your loved one's mailbox! How crazy would it be to find a miniature mailbox within your mailbox! What a fun way to find out how loved you are!

You Make My Heart Bounce

When I fell in love for the first time, every moment felt like my heart was going to beat out of my chest. It is an incredibly thrilling yet terrifying feeling to let someone have so much power over your heart, but yet, because of this, it is truly the best gift you can give someone. Your heart, your love, your vulnerability. So, let me teach you an adorably metaphoric way to give your heart to someone and let them know it beats only for them.

MATERIALS

Large matchbox

Heavyweight paper

Small spring or one from a retractable pen

TOOLS

Pink or red paint

Paintbrushes

Coloring utensils

Scissors

Glue

STEP 1

For this craft, give a large matchbox a makeover by painting it a lovely shade of pink or red. Don't forget to add your personal touch with some decorations. Feel free to add glitter or stripes or whatever you fancy. Over the top of your decor, write, "You make my heart bounce," setting the tone for the surprise inside. Feel free to decorate the interior of the matchbox. You can design it to match the exterior or simply paint it white.

STEP 2

Now, on to the heart of the matter (literally). Draw a heart on a piece of heavyweight paper. Whether you prefer a realistic or stylized design is entirely up to you and your artistic capability. Before placing everything inside the matchbox, write, "Literally!" in big bold letters in the interior box. Make sure it is bold and large enough to capture everyone's attention. Glue one end of your spring to the heart drawing and the other end inside the matchbox. If you do not have a spring, go ahead and take apart a retractable pen. You'll find a spring within the mechanics that you can use for this. Press down the spring and corresponding heart drawing and close the box. This is the secret ingredient that will make the heart bounce when the box is opened.

Romance or Revenge?

My Favorite Sweet Treat

Ah, the nostalgia of childhood summers encapsulated in the simple joy of clutching an ice cream cone after a long day at the beach. That feeling of magical contentment is unmatched, until perhaps, it's rivaled by the rush of falling in love. If you're fortunate enough to have someone in your life who brings back that child-with-an-ice-cream-cone happiness, then you should let them know before that ice cream melts! Here's a craft that channels that pure childhood joy and directs it right back to your partner.

MATERIALS

Template (page 229)

Heavyweight paper, such as bristol or watercolor paper

Thick craft stick

TOOLS

Scissors

Hot-glue gun and hot-glue sticks

Black marker

Watercolors or other coloring utensils

Paintbrushes

STEP 1

For this *sweet* project, you'll need to first cut out all the necessary pieces. If you're looking at the template for this craft on page 229 and feeling a bit puzzled, don't fret. I'll guide you through transforming these quirky paper shapes into an endearing ice cream pop.

After cutting, start by etching along the indicated lines on the two main pieces. Fold back these edgy spikes, preparing them for their transformation. Next, cut out the long strip. This will act as the connecting piece for our pop. Apply hot glue to the folded slits of one main piece and gently wrap the strip around the template, ensuring a snug fit, but refrain from attaching anything to the bottom. Any excess paper that peeks out can be trimmed off to maintain a clean look. Fold the spikes back for the second dome piece, add hot glue along them and place the spikes inside the previous dome and strip pieces. Again, make sure nothing is glued to the flat bottom.

STEP 2

You may have noticed an extra strip template with a small oval inside. This will act as the bottom of our ice cream pop. Cut this out along with the inner oval big enough so your popsicle stick fits through snugly.

Add glue to the spikes that extend from the flat bottom of the template and line up this small strip to the bottom of both of the main pieces.

STEP 3

Get out your thick craft stick and cut a bit off the top to remove the rounded edge. With a black marker, write, "You're such a sweet treat!" on the stick, and insert it into the popsicle. This hidden message remains a secret until the stick is pulled out, adding an element of surprise to your craft.

Now, the fun part: decoration! I opted for a chocolate-covered ice cream bar theme, using a touch of watercolor, but feel free to use any coloring utensils you have on hand. You can even cut out small strips of multi-colored construction paper to add "sprinkles." This is the perfect way to let someone know that they feel like summer without saying it!

Romance or Revenge?

You Rock My World

♥💔♥💔♥💔♥💔♥💔♥💔♥💔♥💔♥💔♥💔♥💔♥💔

I have a very serious question: What is inside a guitar? It's hollow, you say? Well this guitar isn't! This tiny guitar doubles as the perfect place to store any little trinket, and if you're planning on gifting this neat little container, it also doubles as the perfect way to let someone know that they strike a chord in your heart.

MATERIALS

Toilet paper roll

Heavyweight paper, such as bristol or watercolor paper

Cardboard

Thread (optional)

TOOLS

Ruler

Scissors

Hot-glue gun with hot-glue sticks or superglue

Pencil

Coloring utensils

STEP 1

First things first, let's start with the heart. Trim a piece of toilet paper roll to ¾ inch (2 cm) in height. Gently mold it into a heart shape, pinching the bottom and bending the top. At the top of the heart where the two domes curve into each other, apply hot glue into the crevice and squeeze it together until it has cemented the toilet paper roll into a heart shape. This heart will serve as the base of our musical creation. Next, lay the heart onto a piece of watercolor paper and trace around it, capturing its silhouette. Cut out two of these watercolor-paper hearts, leaving one a plain heart and the other with an extra rectangle attached to the side. Here is an example of what I mean by an extra rectangle:

STEP 2

Using your hot glue or superglue, glue the plain paper heart along the rim of the toilet paper roll, lining it up the best you can. If there is some paper extending past the toilet paper roll, feel free to do a little trimming.

STEP 3

For the heart with an extra rectangle on the side, glue the extended rectangle to the interior of the toilet paper roll, allowing the heart to open and close atop the toilet paper roll.

STEP 4

Measure the length of the heart from its bottom point to the crevice and add 2¾ inches (7 cm). Draw a neck for the guitar using this measurement as the length. Here are some ways to design your guitar neck:

STEP 5

Color your guitar neck and cut it out. To reinforce the delicate guitar neck, hot glue a piece of cardboard matching the dimensions of the guitar's stem. Attach small strings of thread to mimic guitar strings, and use tiny dabs of hot glue colored black to represent the tuners.

STEP 6

Finish coloring or painting the entire craft to give it a harmonious appearance. Feel free to layer paper on top and add buttons, glitter, all the works to make your tiny guitar truly rock! Finish with either a Tiny Love Letter (page 12), a piece of jewelry or simply a note letting them know they rock your world!

You Are a Snack!

If you're lucky enough to have a partner who is an absolute snack, then what are you waiting for? You gotta let them know! With this in mind, I made this gift so you can easily and thoughtfully let them know how delicious and addicting they really are.

MATERIALS

Toilet paper roll

Red and yellow construction paper

Foil

Thin paper

TOOLS

Ruler

Scissors

Glue

Coloring utensils

Pencil or pen

STEP 1

Let's start with our toilet paper roll, but let's try to make it look like it did not just come from the bathroom. Start by measuring the height of your toilet paper roll, and then wrapping a piece of red construction paper around the entire roll. Mine measured 4½ x 6 inches (11.5 x 15 cm).

STEP 2

Put a bit of glue onto the roll, and slowly roll your sheet of paper around it, covering it entirely. Take your time with this to ensure it doesn't end up crooked.

Use the hole of the TP roll to trace over a piece of foil. Cut around this outline, but add an extra ½ inch (1.3 cm) of space. Line up the piece of foil onto the toilet paper roll opening, folding the excess along the opening to enclose it completely. Do this for the top and bottom of your toilet paper roll.

STEP 3

On the sheet of thin paper, color the logo for your favorite chip company. I'm going for a playful take on Lay's® with "Wanna Get Lay'd" because who doesn't get a little hot and bothered while gorging on our favorite chips? However, feel free to choose a normal chip logo for a wholesome touch.

Cut out your logo design and glue it directly to the center of the toilet paper roll.

TIP: Alternatively, if you had a bad one-night stand, simply switch up the wording to read, "You're a horrible Lay."

STEP 4

To make the chips, trace the toilet paper roll onto a folded piece of yellow construction paper to get a general idea of the size of your chips. Within this tracing, draw an oval smaller than your toilet paper roll opening. Cut out the oval but leave a section of the crease so you can open and close the chip. Curl your oval slightly with your fingers in the middle to give it a chip-like appearance. Write a little note inside each one that follows the chip theme. For example: "You're such a snack," "I crave you" or "You're so yummy." Remove the top foil and fill up your toilet paper roll with these chips. It's okay if you don't fill it all the way up; what chip company actually does? It just makes it more realistic. Put the foil back on top and gift away. The end result is a funny, cheeky gift for your partner or crush—a truly yummy way to flirt.

I'm So Glad You Popped into My Life!

♥💔♥💔♥💔♥💔♥💔♥💔♥💔♥💔♥💔♥💔♥

While my partner and I dabble in adventuring and traveling, some of my fondest moments with him are simple movie nights spent cuddling on the couch. If you take pleasure in some of these more low-key moments, then for your next movie night, ditch the popcorn. You won't be needing it. Instead, let's feed our partners kernels of our affection. (I'm kidding. Please don't actually feed your partner crafts. They could get a bellyache.)

MATERIALS

Template (page 231)

Yellow construction paper

TOOLS

Scissors

Red chisel-tip marker

Ruler

Hot-glue gun and hot-glue sticks

Pen or marker

STEP 1

If we're going to make popcorn, then obviously we need something to put it in. So, start by cutting out the template on page 231. If I'm being honest, this one is a tad tedious because of the scalloped edge, but trust that this little detail will pay off in the end.

STEP 2

Once the template is all cut out but before you assemble it all together, let's add some classic popcorn box vibes. Draw a few red lines that go vertically through the template. I drew mine with a chiseled red marker and ruler to make sure the lines were straight. I added three of these red lines on each of the four sides of the template. This will give it that classic popcorn box look that we're going for.

For flawless folds, consult page 9 in Craft Basics—it's pretty much my secret to achieving a truly perfect fold. With the template colored and folded, glue it all together to craft the perfect popcorn vessel.

STEP 3

Now that the popcorn box is ready for action, let's infuse it with some love. Grab your yellow construction paper and cut several 1 × 1-inch (2.5 × 2.5–cm) squares. For an organic popcorn edge, skip the straight cuts. I found that ripped squares at the approximate length do the trick. (No need to stress about getting it to the precise measurement.)

STEP 4

On each square, jot down what makes your love "pop." Keep those love notes on theme, whether it's related to a movie night or the popcorn itself! Here are a few examples to help spark inspiration:

- ♥ You're the pop to my corn.
- ♥ Our love is poppin'.
- ♥ You make my heart pop.
- ♥ Life with you is butter when we're together.
- ♥ You're my favorite kernel of joy.

Once each "popcorn" piece is filled with a burst of love, crinkle the notes in your hand and delicately place them inside the popcorn container. Pair this delightful gift with your partner's favorite romantic comedy, and watch as your partner unravels each popcorn piece for an adorable yet undeniably "corny" moment.

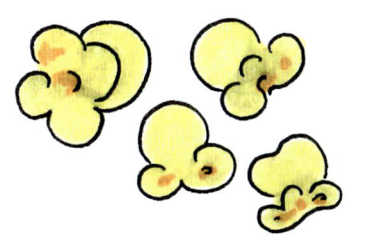

Romance or Revenge?

Tootsie Rolls® for My Tootsie

♥💔♥💔♥💔♥💔♥💔♥💔♥💔♥💔♥💔♥💔♥💔♥💔

Tootsie Rolls often get a bad rap, and I realize not everyone appreciates them; it's a rather controversial candy, if I do say so myself. So, before attempting this craft, it might be a good idea to check in with your partner to gauge their feelings regarding this gooey candy. However, if they happen to love them, this craft could become your new go-to way of expressing your affection.

MATERIALS

White tissue paper

Printer paper

TOOLS

Ruler

Scissors

Green and orange markers

White gel pen or acrylic marker

STEP 1

Cut out a 5 x 3½-inch (13 x 9-cm) piece of the white tissue paper. Use markers to design the tissue paper into the outer covering of your candy. Maintain a ¾-inch (2-cm) margin on either side of the rectangle. At the very top of your tissue paper, inscribe either "Tootsie" or a playful variation expressing your adoration for your giftee, such as "You are my Tootsie." (Okay, super cheesy, but some folks are into these pet names.) Or keep it simple and do not add any words at all.

STEP 2

If you do decide to write "Tootsie" onto your tissue paper, strive to replicate the font used in the original packaging for added realism. With your green marker, create a vertical green rectangle going down the middle of the tissue paper. To prevent the marker bleeding into the words, use a white gel pen or a white acrylic marker. Exercise caution when coloring on the tissue paper due to its thin nature. Add an orange stripe on either side along the margins outside the newly colored green rectangle. Now that the wrapper is complete, let's fashion the little note that will go inside.

STEP 3

Cut a 2½ x 4-inch (6.5 x 10-cm) rectangle out of printer paper. Color it green and with the white gel pen, compose your love note. This could range from a sweet message like "You're so sweet" or "You're my favorite candy" all the way to a heartfelt note tailored to your loved one.

STEP 4

Roll up your note tightly and place it at the end of the tissue paper rectangle, flipped to the side of the paper you did not directly color on. Now, roll up the note with the tissue paper. Once you reach the end, twist the ends of the tissue paper and present it to your partner. If you're looking for creative places to stash this note, hiding it in a Halloween candy stash or a snack closet is a great way to let them know your adoration without making too big of a fuss!

Romance or Revenge? - 73

Map of Our Love

♥💔♥💔♥💔♥💔♥💔♥💔♥💔♥💔♥💔♥💔♥💔

Looking for a gift that's guaranteed to evoke all the feels? Well, look no further! This craft has been tried, tested and yes, it even made my partner shed a couple tears (the good kind). I too got emotional making it just because my heart was filled with so much love for my partner as I reminisced about our favorite experience. This craft is special because it isn't only meant to make your partner feel good; it should make you feel more bonded and connected with your loved one as well. So, if you want something special that you or your partner can potentially frame and keep forever, then try your hand at this better-than-treasure map.

MATERIALS

8½" x 11" (22 x 28-cm) or larger printer paper

Rice

Twine

Melted red candle wax (optional)

TOOLS

Black pen

Coffee, tea or watercolors

Paintbrushes (optional)

Blow-dryer (optional)

STEP 1

So before we create anything, it's up to you to think about what special memories you have had with your partner that you would like to commemorate. If you need some help, here are a few ideas that you can sift through:

- ♥ Your first kiss
- ♥ Where you first knew you loved them
- ♥ Where you said "I love you"
- ♥ Engagement spot
- ♥ Where you met their family
- ♥ First date
- ♥ Favorite date
- ♥ Favorite dinner spot
- ♥ Fun vacation together
- ♥ Where a funny memory happened
- ♥ Every other memory that has made your relationship what it is today

Think of the little moments that made you fall deeper in love. Gather seven to twelve memories you want to plot on the map. Create a simple visual for each memory—lips for the first kiss, a fork and knife for your favorite dinner spot . . . you get the gist.

STEP 2

Now that we have done all the prep work, let the mapmaking commence! The map should measure somewhere between a standard sheet of printer paper or bigger. In fact, the bigger the better! Holding your paper horizontally, pour a cup of dry rice directly on top of your paper. The rice will create random and various clumps of all different sizes. I know it sounds weird, but with the black pen, outline the larger segments of rice to create "continents," and add some smaller rice pieces to create "islands." Yes, I realize this map is not accurate to the world map, but this is a map of your love, not a map of the world!

STEP 3

Once everything is outlined and you like how your little fantasy world is looking, remove the rice and pour a cup of coffee or tea directly on top of the map. Or if you don't want to waste your precious beverages, you can also generously apply tan/brown watercolor all over the map. Embrace any sort of ink smearing—it adds that "old pirate map" vibe we're aiming for. Dry your map, either in an oven preheated to 250°F (120°C), while checking on it every 10 minutes until it is dry, or with a blow-dryer. Feel free to go over any areas where the lines smudged or disappeared more than you'd like with the pen you used earlier.

STEP 4

Now, using the memories that we brainstormed earlier, begin adding your symbols all around the map. Underneath each of them, write a title that references the memory in question, such as "Kiss Island" to indicate when you shared your first kiss in Hawaii or "The Love Cafe" to indicate when you said "I love you" for the first time while in a coffee shop. Do this all around your pretty little map, and feel free to add other old map designs such as mountains, trees, sea monsters, etc. in any of the negative spaces.

STEP 5

Write in a big pirate-y font, "Map of Our Love," as well as a little compass wherever you can squeeze it. Either rip or burn the edges for that ever-so-classic pirate map feel, wrap it up like a little scroll and tie it with a piece of twine. You can even add a red wax seal to keep the twine connected if you really want to go above and beyond, but that is totally up to you. Present this to your partner and brace yourself for the waterworks. They'll be weeping like a baby, relishing every special moment you've shared and marveling at just how much they love you. Ahoy, matey! We've found the treasure!

Matchbox TV

Imagine you are watching a show with your partner after a long day. You're snuggling on the couch when it cuts to a short commercial break. You begin to let your mind wander, all until BAM!, a commercial comes on with a video montage of you and your partner while the voice of your partner repeats how much they love and adore you. While that would be cute and all, that's not what this craft is. But it may be the closest thing we can get to it. For this craft, we will be making a miniature TV using pictures of you and your loved one to express your love.

MATERIALS

Matchbox

Match, skewer or toothpick

Heavyweight paper

Printer paper or photo paper

Fairy lights (optional)

TOOLS

Ruler

Scissors or craft knife (I use X-Acto)

Paint

Paintbrushes

Hot-glue gun and hot-glue sticks

Printer

STEP 1

Let's begin with a large matchbox. While the exact measurements of your matchbox may vary by brand, the one I used for this project measures 4¾ x 2½ x 1¼ inches (12 x 6.5 x 3 cm). Make sure to measure your particular matchbox and adjust the measurements accordingly.

Cut out a 3 x 1¾-inch (7.5 x 4.5-cm) rectangle from the left-hand side directly out of the matchbox, leaving a ½-inch (1.3-cm) border on the left and 1¼-inch (3.5-cm) border on the right. I recommend curving the edges ever so slightly while cutting out your rectangle just to give it an extra detail to make it look like a TV screen.

TIP: Make sure you only cut the exterior matchbox

STEP 2

Now is a good opportunity to paint over any matchbox advertisement on the cardboard. I decided to paint my matchbox mauve, but I added a few different details to give the TV a rustic appearance, such as a brown border around the newly cutout rectangle.

STEP 3

To add even more detail, use the leftover piece of matchbox that we just cut out. Cut it to 2 x 1 inches (5 x 2.5 cm) so it fits nicely within the right margin of your matchbox. This is where you should add little buttons and gadgets on your TV, imitating any sort of volume or channel buttons. Paint the rectangle a color of your choosing and paint on some buttons. And if you want a slightly more dimensional appearance, add small dollops of hot glue to give the look of buttons popping out of the TV. Once all of the buttons are to your liking, glue the rectangle to the right-hand side next to the rectangular cutout.

STEP 4

To add the extra details to make this look like a real vintage TV, we need to add the legs and antennae. To create the antennae, you can use either skewers, toothpicks or even some matches. Whatever you decide to use, cut them into two 2-inch (5-cm) pieces. Add a small hot-glue bulb to each end and paint it to your liking. We want to attach them to our matchbox, but it is a little bit tricky given there isn't a ton of surface area on the end of our antennae. To solve this, I added a dollop of hot glue, stuck the matches in at an angle and held them until the glue dried throughly and the matches stood up on their own.

(continued)

STEP 5

Now that our antennae are secure, we need to add the legs so the TV stands on its own. Cut four ¾ x ¾ x ¾–inch (2 x 2 x 2-cm) triangles out of the heavyweight paper. Create a crease down the center of the triangles and round off the bottom edges. Color the legs to match your matchbox, and glue each of them directly onto the matchbox at each corner, lining up the crease with the corner leaving ½ inch (1.3 cm) sticking out from the matchbox. Now your matchbox should stand up on its own. If normal-looking legs aren't your style, you can also use toothpicks instead of paper. (This is what I did in the project shown here, but be warned that they gave me a very hard time and tended to break off as I transported it.) Cut four 1-inch (2.5-cm) toothpicks, add a little hot glue to the bottom of the matchbox, position the legs at an angle and allow the glue to dry.

STEP 6

Now that the TV looks like a TV, it is up to us to add the magic! Theoretically, you can add any image and either keep the project for yourself or give it to whomever you choose. But to wrap this craft up with a romantic and loving touch, I printed a 3 x 1¾–inch (7.5 x 4.5-cm) picture of me and my partner on glossy photo paper. Instead of cutting this picture down to size, I kept some of the excess white of the paper and simply cut it to fit snugly within my matchbox. Measure the length and width of your matchbox's inner box and cut it to match. Feel free to print out a few different pictures of you and your partner or even include a heartfelt drawing as well, all as long as you maintain the same measurements between the size of the paper and the margin of negative space. To place the image to act as the TV screen, place the image inside the matchbox before sliding in the inner box. The inner box will push the image forward right up to where the TV screen should be.

STEP 7

To add an extra touch that will really bring it all together, crumple up a string of fairy lights and place it within the box behind your printed image. This will illuminate the image from the back, making it appear to be a real TV. Now give this to your partner while binging your favorite Netflix show.

iLove Your iMessages

iPhones are the present day's love letters. They're what we use to communicate with the world, whether that be with our friends, parents, siblings, coworkers or (especially) our partners. While a simple text may not spark the same exhilaration as an old-fashioned love letter (or let's face it, any of these crafts in this book!), it is still an incredibly valuable way to check in with your partner, giving them reassurance that they are loved, cherished and appreciated. So, if your phone is the first means of communication with your partner, and you want your future texts to feel just a little bit sweeter to them, look no further than this iPhone craft.

MATERIALS
Cardboard
Bristol paper
Printed pictures of you and your partner

TOOLS
Smartphone
Ruler
Pencil
Scissors
Hot-glue gun and hot-glue sticks
Paint
Paintbrushes
Markers
White gel pen

STEP 1

Okay, so I realize that this book may be around longer than the iPhone 14, but whatever the go-to cellular device is in the future (hello, future humans!), feel free to use this craft as inspiration when recreating this device. (Because paper crafts will NEVER go out of style!)

Measure the length and width of your smartphone. Cut this measurement out on three separate pieces of cardboard. I am rounding the corners of each of the pieces and gluing them one on top of the other with hot glue, matching them up so they sit together perfectly. Because I am a perfectionist, and I love little details, I am adding a 1¼ x 1¼-inch (3 x 3-cm) piece of cardboard to the upper left-hand corner to act as my camera. Feel free to opt out of this step if you choose.

(continued)

STEP 2

Now that the base is created, we want to cover up those ugly cardboard edges. Cut a ½-inch (1.3-cm)-wide strip of bristol paper. Apply a generous amount of hot glue to the cardboard edges and drag the slice of bristol paper along it to cover up the cardboard sides. Once all of the cardboard sides are smoothed out, trace your cardboard on another sheet of bristol paper, and cut out two of these phone-sized pieces. Hot glue these pieces to both the front and back of your cardboard to give us a nice clean base to draw up our smartphone. If you opted to add a camera, make sure you cut out a little square from the back piece of paper so you don't end up covering up your camera.

STEP 3

Now for the fun part—turning this hunk of cardboard into a realistic-looking phone. Paint the back of the phone black, gray or the color of your choice. (You know Apple® is always coming out with new phone colors.) Add circles over the square camera in the back to resemble the camera lenses. My phone has three cameras, so I drew three circles, but feel free to match it up with the number of cameras on your phone. For extra pizzazz, I also add blobs of hot glue to accentuate the lenses, but again, that isn't super necessary unless you're extra like I am. Flip the phone over and draw a black outline around the borders of the phone. Feel free to also draw the little speaker and front camera for added realism.

STEP 4

Now we design the screen. While this can be an opportunity to add anything you want in a variety of ways, I decided to create a text conversation with my partner. I started by designing the front and bottom of the phone to match the look of texting my partner. I opted to change my partner's name to simply read "<3," and I printed a very small photo of my partner and I together, cut it into a circle and glued it right above my partner's contact name. I also added all the toggles and symbols that are present underneath the messaging text box. Here is a better visual for you to recreate:

STEP 5

In the blank space between the top and bottom illustrations, draw two text bubbles. For the first one, draw a blue text bubble. Within this text box, use a white gel pen to write, "I <3 you."

STEP 6

Directly underneath this text bubble write a few reasons why you love your partner. Do this in pencil to get an accurate measure of how long your message will be, and then go over it with the same blue coloring utensil used to create the first text bubble as well as the white gel pen to go over the words. Measure this second text bubble and create a blue or green text bubble that shares the same measurements as the list on a separate sheet of heavyweight paper. On the outskirts of the message, add an additional ¼-inch (6-mm) tab and cut it out. Fold down this tab and line it up with the list. Once it is lined up perfectly, add a bit of glue to the tab and glue it to the phone on the right of the list. Once the glue is dry, in white gel pen, write, "Here's why . . ." at the very beginning. With these two components, your phone will now represent you saying to your partner, "I love you" and "Here's why" with a list of reasons hidden underneath the second text.

STEP 7

Your smartphone love letter is complete. Instead of directly giving it to your partner, I recommend getting just a bit more devious with it. Hide the phone screen side down in-between couch cushions or other common places you typically lose things. Tell your partner that you have lost your phone, but it died and you can't call it. Ask them to help you find it and direct them to the area the phone is hidden. When they look, they will think it is your actual phone (given your incredible artistic ability), but after a little examination, they will see the heartfelt message and be overwhelmed with joy.

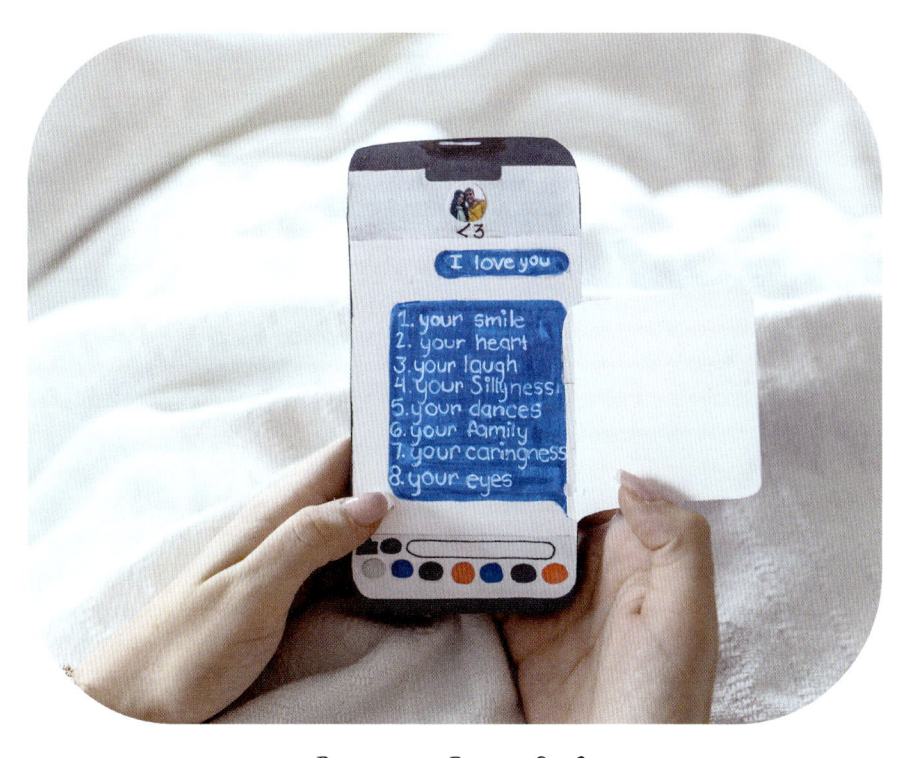

Romance or Revenge?

Listen When You Miss Me

♥ 💔 ♥ 💔 ♥ 💔 ♥ 💔 ♥ 💔 ♥ 💔 ♥ 💔 ♥ 💔

Hopefully this project will bring you back to the tummy full of butterflies kind of love, the goosebumps you get from them holding your hand for the first time kind of love, the final scene at the end of an '80s movie where they're holding a boombox outside your window kind of love. Well, this is a lot lighter than a real boombox and a ton more effort, but I think it still gets that cheesy, gooey affection across.

What is it about certain songs that just makes you want to squeeze the person you love, but then the very next song makes you want to scream at the top of your lungs? Here is a gift that will encapsulate this variety of musical emotions in a beautifully enclosed container. I am going to show you how to make this adorable boombox and accompanying mixtapes. This is a cute little way to give someone exactly the song they need exactly when they need it.

Remember, anything handmade is sure to get big smiles from your loved ones, so I encourage you to go for this project even if you do not have special supplies or artistic tools on hand. But if you're really trying to blow them away, like the kind of surprise that will make them feel bad about their own gift (isn't that always the goal??), then use the materials I recommend below.

MATERIALS

Templates (pages 233 and 241)

Cardboard, ideally as flat and sturdy as possible

Heavyweight paper

TOOLS

Scissors

Hot-glue gun and hot-glue sticks

Ruler

Coloring utensils

Active Spotify® online music account

Printer

STEP 1

Let's start by making the boombox that will house our little mixtapes. To begin, cut out the template on page 233. Make sure to fold it nicely. Glue the tabs together with your hot-glue gun, but make sure the front tab opens and closes freely. Cut out the handle on page 241 and fold it along the fold lines. Glue it to each side of the boombox.

The mixtapes are where the love language really comes across. Think of high school sweethearts sharing mixtapes to confess their love in the cafeteria. (Clearly, I am very jealous of the love affairs of the '80s.) These mixtapes need to be big enough to fit snugly in the boombox while also small enough not to add unwanted tension to the box. So, for each mixtape, cut one piece of cardboard and one piece of heavyweight paper, each 4 x 3⅕ inches (10 cm x 8 cm). Use your hot-glue gun to adhere the paper to the cardboard. This adds much more dimension and structure to the mixtapes than using paper alone.

STEP 2

Phew! We did all the hard stuff. Now you can relax, shake it off a bit, because it only gets more fun from here! This is where you can really explore your own creativity. Here are some images for inspiration on how you can make your boombox look. Let your imagination soar! Feel free to play with patterns, colors, textures, the whole works! Here are a few of my designs:

Just like we did with the boombox, color the mixtapes however you prefer, but you know I'm not gonna leave you high and dry! Here are some examples of styles that I have used for this project:

STEP 3

Once the boombox and mixtapes are decorated and ready to go, write, "Listen When" on the outside of the boombox. Now think about songs that your partner would enjoy when they are experiencing different emotions. For example, I chose songs that my partner and I listened to when we first started dating, and I put these songs in the mixtape labeled "When You Miss Me." Label the different mixtapes with different emotions or circumstances where these songs will resonate with your partner.

> **NOTE**: Spotify has a very nifty application where you can print out a barcode to any song. To use this feature, go to Spotify on your desktop, find your song and click the three dots next to the heart icon and copy the link. Exit out of the Spotify website and go to spotifycodes.com, enter your song link and get the Spotify code. Print the code that the website generated and attach the corresponding song codes to each of the mixtapes, and voilà! You're finished!

If in the future, Spotify is totally obsolete, you can also simply write the songs and the artist on the back of each mixtape. I love this craft because it can be as meaningful as you decide to make it. I think it even tops the real boombox-outside-your-window trope!

Romance or Revenge? - 83

Mine to Be Mine

This craft is dedicated to all the gold miners out there. We see you, we feel you and we didn't actually know that you were still around, but keep slaying. Of course, I'm joking. This craft is for the lovers who want to let their partner know how they feel in a way that is a tad more engaging than a note (but make it forty-niner themed). For this interactive way to say "I love you," we will be recreating a mineshaft, but minus all of the dust, debris, rocks and, well, danger. But it maintains the same spirit!

MATERIALS

Heavyweight paper

TOOLS

Pen or marker

Ruler

Alcohol markers or other coloring utensils

Gold pen

Scissors

Double-sided tape

Hot-glue gun and hot-glue sticks

STEP 1

Begin by sketching out the exterior of a mineshaft on your heavyweight paper. Make the mineshaft 6 x 4¼ inches (15 x 11 cm). Ensure a distinguishing separation between the ground and the rock mineshaft, because it will be folded later, and you don't want the foreground of the drawing to be folded into the background. Here is a little drawing so you can reference what I mean:

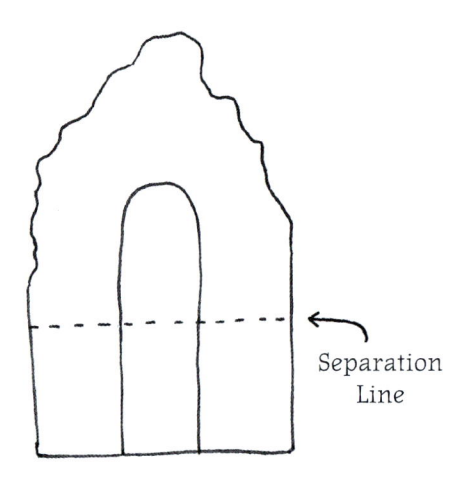

← Separation Line

Now let's do some coloring. I used alcohol markers (my fav coloring utensil!), but use whatever you have on hand. Color in the rocks, and for some added spice, add little gold nuggets with your gold pen because a gold mine seems a lot more romantic than a coal mine (if one of them had to be romantic).

STEP 2

Now that your mineshaft is looking fab, it's time we add the love. On the heavyweight paper, draw smaller rocks and cut them out. Again, I wouldn't leave you high and dry. Simply try to recreate these little rock drawings below:

Color them in with the same color or colors that you used for the rest of the mineshaft, and write little love notes or words of affirmation on the backs. Some examples that match the theme of this craft are:

- ❤ You're my rock.
- ❤ You're MINE.
- ❤ Our love is golden.
- ❤ I've hit gold with you.

Use double-sided tape to attach them to the mineshaft, specifically placed to cover some of our previously placed gold nuggets. Fold from where the foreground ended and the mineshaft began. Here's a little drawing that you can reference:

STEP 3

On the back of the mineshaft, create a support using heavyweight paper measuring 4 x 1½ inches (10 x 4 cm). Create a ½-inch (1.3-cm) crease down from the top and glue it onto the back middle section of your mineshaft. This should allow the mineshaft to stand up on its own.

STEP 4

To complete the craft shaft and make it officially interactive, use the scraps of the heavyweight paper and create a small pickaxe as well as a signpost with your chosen phrase (mine being "Mine to Be Mine"). This provides instructions and a cute little pun because, fun fact: Love is all about the cute little puns. I colored my sign to have an old wood post kind of vibe. Fold a small section of the bottom of the sign and adhere it with hot glue to the foreground of the craft so it stands up on its own. This will be a very fun way to remind someone you love them because, if you're going to play games with their heart, at least make it interactive!

Instant Love (Ramen Noodles)

So, not to expose myself or anything, but I did come up with this craft while munching on dry ramen noodles in bed because cooking them seemed like too much effort. But to be fair, most of my best ideas come from when I am lying in bed doing something relatively unhinged . . . so it is only fitting. This craft takes inspiration from every college freshman's dorm room, because after a long night of drinking, there are only two things I want: my partner's love and ramen noodles.

MATERIALS
Photo paper or printer paper

Cardboard

Aluminum foil

TOOLS
Ruler

Scissors

Tape

Coloring utensils

Hot-glue gun and hot-glue sticks

Yellow paint

Paintbrush

Silver chrome marker (optional)

Pen

STEP 1
Let's begin with a sheet of paper that measures 6 x 8 inches (15 x 20 cm). Opt for thin, flexible paper (avoid watercolor paper or cardstock). I'm using photo paper for its shiny resemblance to the ramen noodles packet, but if you don't have that, printer paper will work just as well.

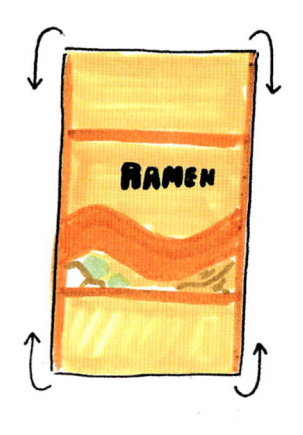

We will not be creating any sharp folds on this paper; instead, hold the paper lengthwise and connect the edges together using tape or glue. Lay the paper down flat on the table and choose a front and back. Recreate a ramen noodles package with your coloring utensils. Replace words like "chicken flavor" with "love flavor" and "cooks in 3 minutes" with "fall in love in 3 minutes." Try to mimic the styles used for the packaging. If drawing isn't your forte, print off ramen noodle packaging from online and trace it on your paper using a lightbox or a window. Color it in completely, replicating the colors in the original packaging. Flip the package over and color the back the same colors used on the front. Once you are happy with how the packaging looks, put it aside.

STEP 2

Let's go on to make the noodles. Glue three 3½ x 5-inch (9 x 13-cm) pieces of cardboard on top of each other, and use a hot-glue gun to create swirly noodle patterns on top of the cardboard. Wait for each side to dry before moving on to the next, layering them up so they really look like a dry brick of noodles. For an extra touch, use hot glue to write a hidden message in the noodles, like "I love you" or a heart sneakily hidden within the other chunks of noodles. Once every layer of the glue is dry, paint on top of the cardboard and the noodles. Ensure you get in between all the crevices with a nice ramen yellow color, which is essentially a light-yellow hue.

STEP 3

With the noodles done, let's move on to the seasoning packet. Because I love a nice realistic effect, I am using aluminum foil, but you can opt for paper colored with a silver chrome marker as well. Cut a 3 x 2¼-inch (7.5 x 6-cm) rectangle out of the foil, and fold it in half. Glue the right and left edges to create a little pocket. Add a little note for your loved one and fold it so it fits inside the seasoning package. Feel free to get cheesy with expressions like, "You're the seasoning in my life" or "You're the Ramen to my noodles." Add a little dab of glue to the top to fully enclose the note inside the seasoning packet. On the left and right side of the packet, cut a chevron pattern to make it extra realistic.

STEP 4

Now let's bring everything together. Put the seasoning packet on top of the noodles, and slide the packaging over them. Add a little glue to the top and bottom of the package to secure it inside and gift away! This is a perfect gift to give a loved one if they just moved to college and will be living off of these cheap noodles or simply to give to anyone who always has ramen noodles stocked! It's a fun way to say "I love you," because of all the little ways you can customize this project while still maintaining a very realistic look.

Ticket to My Heart

♥💔♥💔♥💔♥💔♥💔♥💔♥💔♥💔♥💔♥💔♥💔♥💔♥💔

If you have ever been in a long-distance relationship, you know that love knows no borders. (And as someone who has been in one for three years, I feel your pain!) In fact, even if you are 1,000 miles away, the love does not stop. So, if you are in a relationship where love simply knows no distance, then this may be a great gift to send your loved one, which in this economy may even be more accessible than an actual plane ticket. So, let's begin making our "plane" ticket.

MATERIALS

Printer paper

TOOLS

Ruler

Scissors

Pen or marker

Coloring utensils

STEP 1

Let's start with formatting our plane ticket. Cut out a 6½ x 3¼-inch (17 x 8-cm) piece of paper. Write the following on it:

- Passenger name: (either your partner's name or both of your names)
- From: Loneliness Island
- To: Endless Love
- Date: (current date)
- Flight: LOV3
- Gate: <3
- Time: 11:11
- Seat: Bmin3
- Boarding class: First Class Love
- Love Airlines

Use the photograph on the previous page for a better idea of where to include everything. Put in effort to make the appearance of the writing look like text printed from a computer. Refrain from cursive or sloppy handwriting (sorry for calling you out if you have messy handwriting!), and do your best to maintain the same size for each of the letters. We want this to look as similar to a printed plane ticket as possible.

STEP 2

Along the top and bottom of the ticket, create simple illustrations to make it look more like a plane ticket. I am simply going with a red-and-white checkered pattern, but here are some other simple illustrations you can add to your plane ticket to add some personality:

STEP 3

To finish it off, either draw or print an illustration of an airplane, cut it out and stick it to the top right-hand side.

While there are many ways to give this craft, even if you are not in a long distance relationship, a very special one is to take a photo of the ticket in the midst of travel, capturing the travel surroundings in the background, such as with your suitcase or with the airplane window in the background.

TIP: If you want to be extra with this, use a barcode as an opportunity either to attach a Spotify code (see page 83), or create your own barcode to direct your partner to a specific website, picture or voice message.

Romance or Revenge?

> To my Love,
> I miss you so much I can't stand it. I can't help but think about that week you were here. It was probably the happiest week of my life. I can't get the taste of your lips out of my mouth. I don't know when I'll see you next but I hope that it's soon.
> All my Love
> XOXO

Antique Love Letter

♥💔♥💔♥💔♥💔♥💔♥💔♥💔♥💔♥💔♥💔♥💔♥💔

Romeo, Romeo, why haven't you written me any letters, Romeo? Or something like that. I mean, it's been like 600 years. It could have gotten lost in translation. But could you imagine being a princess galloping in the forest and finding a beautiful handwritten letter? Now I feel like I'm lucky to even get a text back! So here is a step-by-step to make your partner feel like that princess (or prince) galloping in the woods out of excitement from receiving a handwritten letter from their lover.

MATERIALS

Printer paper

Envelope

Decorative supplies, such as lace, pearls, gold leaf, flowers, etc.

Dried rose petals (optional)

Perfume (optional)

TOOLS

Coffee or tea

Blow-dryer (optional)

Lighter

Pen or marker

Hot glue and hot-glue gun (optional)

Gold metallic pen (optional)

STEP 1

You know that extra cup of coffee that you probably shouldn't have bought? Yeah, pour it all on top of a sheet of printer paper, like literally all over. I recommend pouring it over a dish so coffee doesn't spill all over everything, but hey, this is your home, so don't let me tell you what to do. You can dry off the paper by placing it in the sun, but this will take some time for it to fully dry. If you want to get this done now, use a blow-dryer and get all the excess coffee out.

STEP 2

After your paper is completely dry, tear off the edges to give it a more organic appearance, and slightly burn the edges of the torn paper with a lighter. Make sure you're in a safe, well-ventilated space. (Emphasis on safe. DO NOT BURN YOUR HOUSE DOWN! Seriously, a lawsuit would be oh so inconvenient right now!) The torn edges will burn quicker and easier than the rest of the paper, but make sure you have some water that you can quickly dump over the fire in case it gets out of hand. It may also ride up the sides of the paper farther than you were expecting, so spray the embers of the fire with some water to completely stop the burning process. Although this is way more dangerous than I like my crafts to be, the burnt edges give it a nice touch that really captures the antique style we are going for. Now that that's done and we got out alive, go ahead and handwrite your note.

The envelope can be any color, but if you are going for a simple white envelope, I recommend also soaking it in coffee to keep the cohesion with the letter. How strange would it be if you found an 18th-century letter in a perfectly white envelope?

STEP 3

To really wrap this all together, I got a little strip of lace from my sewing kit and hot glued it to the inside flap of the envelope so that when it is closed you cannot see any hot glue, just the lace poking out of the inside. I also added a gold border with a metallic pen as a lining to the envelope. At this point, I was really getting into decorating my envelope, and I put down a whole big fat glob of hot glue, stuck some dried flowers in it and waited until it dried. Once it was dry, I went over with my gold metallic pen to match the gold paper border. I encourage you to add whatever you can think of: pearls, gold leaf, flower petals, you name it! Make it your own!

Finish up this adorable gift with some dried rose petals inside and a spritz of your favorite perfume, and you have immediately got yourself a date. Who wouldn't fawn over something like this?? This gift feels like it would be suitable to hand-deliver to a princess. Doesn't everyone deserve to feel like that at least once?

PASSPORT

TO MY HEART

Passport to My Heart

So, you know how people get passports to jet off anywhere they fancy, as it allows them to have unique experiences that you simply cannot even begin to experience without traveling? Well, love is like that too, minus the airport security lines. Falling in love opens doors to emotions and intimacy that are like a VIP lounge for your heart. With that in mind, let's turn this whole passport concept into a lovey-dovey symbol, giving your partner the ultimate freedom to explore their feels anywhere you are.

MATERIALS

Heavyweight paper, such as bristol or watercolor paper

Printer paper

Photo of you and your loved one

TOOLS

Ruler

Scissors

Paint

Paintbrushes

Gold marker

Stapler

White glue

STEP 1

To begin, decide whether you want your passport to be realistic or stylized. It would be incredibly adorable to go with a red or pink color scheme for Valentine's Day, but I decided to go the realistic route for this one!

To do this, begin by cutting out a 7 x 5-inch (18 x 13-cm) piece of heavyweight paper. Paint it to match your passport's color scheme. Because I am American, I color-matched my faux passport to my real passport: navy blue. When the paint is dry, fold your paper in half horizontally so it looks like a little card.

(continued)

Romance or Revenge? - 93

Now that it is all folded, take the front of your faux passport and let's decorate it to look like the front cover of a passport. The American passport has a gold eagle embossed on the front cover, and while I love my country and all, eagles don't necessarily scream romance, so I am recreating this logo design with a gold marker:

STEP 2

Now that the front cover is done, let's add the pages. Cut out three to five pages of printer paper measuring 7 x 5 inches (18 x 13 cm). Fold each of the pages in half and stick them inside the passport. Staple the pages along the crease to make it into a booklet.

Using very light colors, such as pastels, create a design over each of the pages. This is to mimic the various patterns typically found in a real passport, except, why not make yours just a little more lovey-dovey. You can also cover your page with little kisses used from kissing each of the pages with lipstick, but here are some passport page designs to take inspiration from if you need some more to reference:

STEP 3

Now that each page has a cute little design on it, open up your booklet to the third page. Typically, when you open the passport to page three, you have the picture of the passport recipient. Inspired by this, flip the booklet to open vertically and put the pictures of you and your loved one inside. This is where you can get all cutesy with your message. Write about how you want to explore the world with your lover, or how their love allows you to explore more of yourself. Deck out this page to be a collage of your loved one and yourself as well as the dreams you hope to accomplish with them. While you can continue to do this to the rest of the passport pages, you can also imitate the passport stamps that one collects as they travel to write either words of affirmation for your partner or all the places you hope to travel with them. Extra points if you make these sentiments look like real travel stamps!

Hand this love passport to your partner. For bonus points, surprise them during a trip. Just make sure not to forget the real passports–airport security doesn't appreciate arts and crafts. Safe travels in love, explorers!

You Are My Favorite Song

♥💔♥💔♥💔♥💔♥💔♥💔♥💔♥💔♥💔♥💔♥💔♥💔

This is another craft that is sure to bring up some nostalgia, if you are even old enough to know what a record player is! We are going to make a miniature record player to let your partner know that their voice is music to your ears!

MATERIALS
Template (page 235)
Scrap piece of watercolor paper
Heavyweight paper

TOOLS
Craft knife (I use X-Acto)
Ruler
Coloring utensils
Glitter and glue (optional)
Hole puncher
Chrome marker (optional but recommended!)
White pen
Hot glue and hot-glue gun

STEP 1
Cut out the template on page 235. Once everything is all cut out and beautiful, lightly take the edge of your blade and follow along the dotted lines with a ruler—not enough to make an actual incision, but just enough to release some of the tension of the paper fibers and give it a clean, beautiful fold.

Color one side of the paper with a coloring utensil of your choosing. Like always, I am going to go for my trusty alcohol markers and acrylic paint, but I don't want to dim your light—choose what materials you like! I chose to color one side of the paper red. This will be the outside of the record player, so keep that in mind when coloring.

I personally decided to go with an old Hollywood look because I am just dramatic like that, but you do you! The reverse side of the template will be the inside of the record player. I kept this part black with a layer of acrylic paint so it would not bleed. If you want to go above and beyond, cover this side of the template with some glue and then some glitter matching your interior color to give a bit of va-va-voom and to blind whoever takes a peek without your permission. Once the glitter is dry and secure, fold the template and hot glue all of the tabs together to create the three-dimensional record player.

STEP 2
After the base of your record player is complete, take the scrap piece of watercolor paper and draw a cute heart-shaped record that's small enough to fit in your record player. Feel free to take a peek at this little illustration for some guidance, or simply create streaks of gray, black and white at certain highlight points to get the appearance of a record.

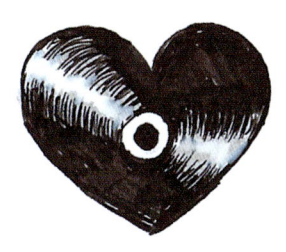

This does not have to look perfect, so please don't stress. Cut the heart out and put it aside for now.

STEP 3
You are also going to want to include two small rectangles out of the heavyweight paper. The one on the left measures 3/8 x 3/4 inch (1 x 2 cm), and the one on the right measures 3/8 x 1 inch (1 x 2.5 cm). These will act as little music panels. I painted mine black to match with the interior of the box. I used a little hole puncher to get perfectly sized circles where I then glued them on top of the rectangles. I recommend coloring them with a little bit of metallic chrome. It's a little detail that will really make these mechanical record pieces take the appearance of metal, but this isn't something you should be too concerned about. To make the needle, use that same metallic marker and recreate the following shape. Glue the circle down to the left rectangle while the other end lays atop the record.

On the right rectangle, I mimicked the little notches one would find in a record player. I replicated the little buttons simply with some small strokes of a white gel pen, nothing too complicated!

STEP 4
Glue both the record and the music panels inside the record player in the spots of your choosing and finish it off by writing something cool at the top inside of the player. I wrote, "You are my fav song," but "Your voice is music to my ears" is also a cute quote that would match the theme of this gift. This gift is as timeless and dramatic as your love, so give it to your partner with the utmost confidence!

WILL YOU BE MY MUSE?
YES
NO

I LOVE LEARNING ABOUT YOU

Devyn has a crush on you, do you like her back?

you give me BUTTERFLIES

Confessing Your Love

HE LOVES ME, HE LOVES ME NOT

If you're looking to tell someone special that you have an interest in them, then you may want something that will allow you to stand out from the pack. While there's a certain perceived allure in maintaining an air of nonchalance when it comes to someone you are romantically interested in, this book is not about playing the hard-to-get game. We're romantics over here! So, instead of pretending that you are not a born and true lover girl/boy, let's embrace the love through every aspect of our being and provide the most memorable creative love confessions the world has ever known.

Of course, this isn't a fantasy world. You may get rejected—we all do. But you know what? Showing up with love, devoid of fear and insecurity, puts you miles ahead of those adopting a nonchalant facade. There is no shame in getting rejected; there is only shame in not trying!

2000s Flip Phone

♥💔♥💔♥💔♥💔♥💔♥💔♥💔♥💔♥💔♥💔♥💔♥💔

Alright, darlings, we're about to create that iconic pink '90s flip phone that every "it girl" had in the early 2000s. This craft not only oozes the mean girl–esque charm but also embodies the fabulous essence of Barbie® and unapologetic girlhood. Let's take a trip down memory lane with this craft, back to an era when mixtapes ruled and frosted lip gloss was a must.

But here's the twist: This paper flip phone has a secret up its sleeve. Bring it to a club and ask for some numbers, and you are guaranteed to leave with some digits. So, grab your craft supplies and channel your inner Regina George, because we're about to craft a mini pink flip phone that'll make you feel like you're living in a 2000s chick flick.

MATERIALS

Templates (pages 235 and 247)

Heavyweight paper

TOOLS

Scissors

Ruler

Acrylic markers or other coloring utensils

Glitter (optional)

Glue

Foam tape (optional)

Tape

STEP 1

We're going to start with the templates on pages 235 and 247. Begin by cutting out each of the shapes. You'll notice that the templates are in either a top or bottom category. This is in reference to what part of the flip phone each element will correspond with, so we don't get it mixed up.

For the top section of the phone, take the dome piece with the flat bottom and draw a square in the center of the dome measuring 1¼ x 1⅗ inches (3.5 x 4 cm) and color it black. Over the top of the black square, write a message. I kept mine simple by writing, "Text me." I used an acrylic marker, but you can use whatever you have on hand. A little tip: If you really want to cement the 2000s aesthetic, try to recreate a pixelated font! Once this is done, you can color the rest of the template pieces pink and add glitter if you want to go that extra mile.

STEP 2

Once everything is colored, take each of the longer spiky strands of paper and fold down the spikes. These will help us glue each of the pieces together. Add a little glue to the flat-bottomed top pieces, and glue them to the uncolored side and hold the spikes against the dome pieces, adhering them together. Make sure you do this around the entire perimeter of the dome, including the flat bottom. Let it dry, and add a little glue to the remaining spikes and line up the second top dome to the first one. Disregard the excess on the bottom for now. Do this again with the bottom pieces.

We are going to want to glue these pieces together so it opens and closes just like a flip phone. To do this, take the excess on the top outer dome, add glue to the inside of the excess piece and press it down to adhere to the sides of the phone. Take the bottom section, align it so the flat side is facing the excess piece and glue the excess to the side of the bottom section as well. Now you should be able to open and close the phone.

STEP 3

Now that the base of the phone is created, all we need to do is add the details. Create a keyboard using heavyweight paper; feel free to create your own or try to mimic the ones shown in the picture. In terms of what I put on the keyboard, I went as simple as possible, simply writing 0 through 9, but this is also a perfect place for you to secretly write in your phone number! Add this keyboard to the bottom section of your phone, and add the circular keyboard just above it. To give it just a bit more dimension, I recommend using a small amount of foam tape so it ever so slightly lifts off the phone.

To finish the screen, add a small piece of tape directly over the cutout to give it the same shimmer that a phone screen has. After this, feel free to decorate the rest of your phone however you like. You can add realistic details such as antennae and speakers, or go full drama queen and add rhinestones, pearls and more glitter! Now, I dare you to go to the club and ask random people for their number. Before they can answer, hand them this phone instead!

Lemon Juice Secret Letter

♥💔♥💔♥💔♥💔♥💔♥💔♥💔♥💔♥💔♥💔♥💔♥💔

I don't know about you, but when I was a child, one of my favorite things to do was set things on fire. I realize this is me confessing to a bit of a pyromaniac streak, but don't worry, I never ventured into anything "major"—just some harmless papers and such. But let's face it: Fire has always held a mesmerizing allure for most of us, right? (Please tell me I'm not alone in this.)

With that being said, this craft is dedicated to those who share a fascination with flames. Here's your chance to channel that fiery energy into an act of love. Hopefully, it sparks more than just passion and ignites a special connection. And if not, at least it provides a safer outlet than contemplating arson as a pastime. However, before we proceed, a crucial disclaimer: Never attempt this craft indoors, and do not gift it unsupervised. Remember, we're here to spread love, not wildfire!

MATERIALS

Lemon juice

Printer paper

Empty tin mint container

1 matchbox

10–12 matches

TOOLS

Jar or cup

Fine-tip paintbrush

Scissors

Tape

Pen or marker

STEP 1

To begin this fiery endeavor, place some lemon juice in a container such as a jar or cup, and have a fine-tip paintbrush at the ready. Instead of writing a note to confess your love, we will be painting one, with lemon juice of all things! With your paintbrush, carefully write your heartfelt message on a piece of printer paper cut to fit inside the tin container. Keep in mind that once the lemon juice dries, your message will become invisible, so it's best to keep it short to ensure you can remember what and where you wrote. Let your note dry thoroughly without smudging any of the lemon juice, and then place it inside your tin container.

Cut the matchbox striker out of your matchbox and glue it to the outside edge of the tin container. Take out 10 to 12 matches and secure them to the inner lid of the tin container with a piece of tape.

To guide the giftee to uncover the secret message, I wrote this riddle on a sheet of paper and secured it to the top of the tin container:

On this page a message lies, with a fiery touch it shall arise.

Once the paper is heated from the bottom, the words written out in lemon juice will reveal themselves, and with them, your feelings to the giftee. Enjoy this unique and intriguing way to confess your feelings. Just remember, this craft is all about kindling affection, not conflagration, so be careful!

You're My Muse

♥ 💔 ♥ 💔 ♥ 💔 ♥ 💔 ♥ 💔 ♥ 💔 ♥ 💔 ♥ 💔 ♥ 💔 ♥ 💔 ♥ 💔 ♥ 💔

This is an adorable craft, especially if you or your giftee is an artsy person, but it doesn't take a Picasso to make it. In fact, if you simply follow the instructions, you could probably complete this craft even if you don't have a drop of artistic ability within you.

MATERIALS

5 craft sticks

Watercolor paper

Cardboard

Paper

Paintbrushes

TOOLS

Scissors

Ruler

Hot-glue gun and hot-glue sticks

Watercolor pencils

Pencil

White crayon

STEP 1

In this craft, we will need to create three distinct elements: the easel, the art palette and the canvas. To make the easel, you'll need to cut 5 craft sticks with the following measurements:

- ♥ 3 sticks measuring 4¼ inches (11 cm)
- ♥ 1 stick measuring 2¾ inches (7 cm)
- ♥ 1 stick measuring 1½ inches (4 cm)

Position two of the largest sticks facing each other in a slight diagonal shape. Next, connect the smallest stick at the top of the two sticks where they come together. Hot glue to keep it in place. This will serve as the top part of the easel.

(continued)

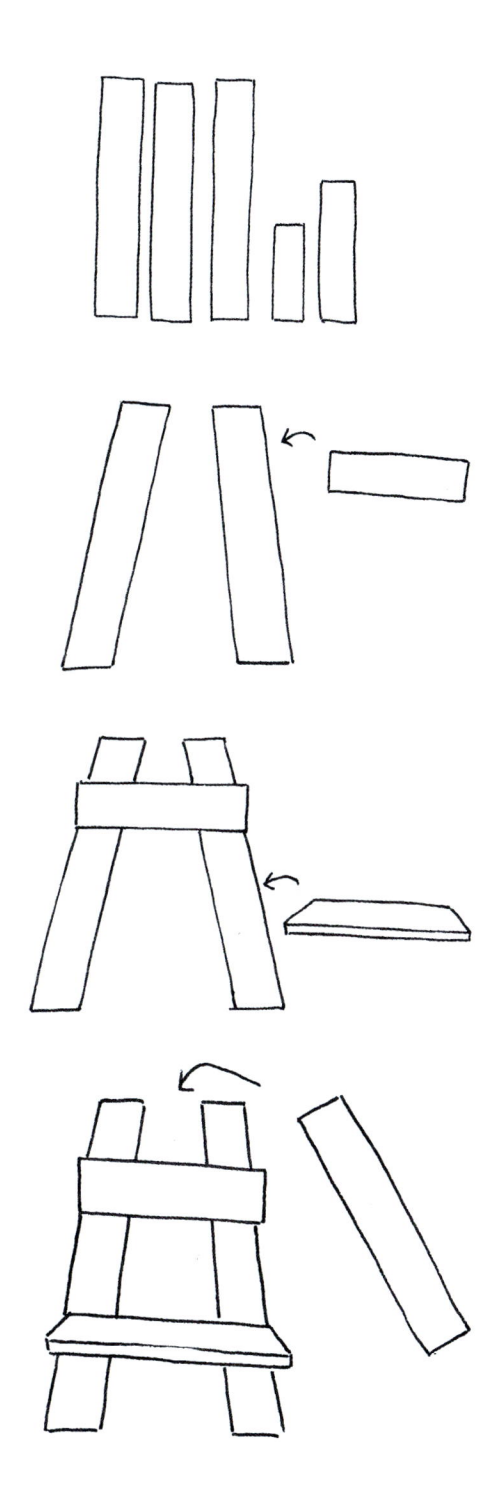

STEP 2

Take the 2¾-inch (7-cm) stick and turn it on its side, and then glue it to the other 4¼-inch (11-cm) sticks approximately 1½ inches (4 cm) from the bottom. This additional stick will hold your paper in place. To complete the easel, stand the entire easel up and attach the remaining large stick diagonally, connecting it to the center of the smallest stick. This diagonal stick will serve as the easel's stand. Once all the pieces are securely glued together, your easel should be able to stand on its own and hold a sheet of paper with ease.

STEP 3

Now, let's move on to creating the art palette, and yes, it will actually work! Begin by cutting a piece of watercolor paper into the shape of an art palette. We are going to create small sections of "paint" with our watercolor pencils. Color them to look like small paint blobs while layering up a few layers to ensure there's enough to paint with later.

STEP 4

To add support to our palette, trace it over a piece of cardboard, cut it out and glue it to the back of the art palette to make it sturdy. Now dive into the craft's "gimmick." To do this, cut a 3 x 3–inch (7.5 x 7.5–cm) sheet of watercolor paper, and use the white crayon to write something along the lines of "Will you be my muse?" with checkboxes for "yes" and "no" underneath. Place the watercolor paper on top of the easel with the art palette and a paintbrush next to it. Instruct your giftee to use the palette to paint a picture. When they are painting, the watercolor will avoid showing up where the white crayon was placed, revealing the message as they paint.

TIP: Watercolor pencils are essentially a mix between colored pencils and watercolor. When dry, they act as colored pencils, but once water is placed on them, they turn into watercolor. If you don't have access to watercolor pencils, you can opt for tube watercolor, placing a dollop of each color on the palette, or you can add multiple thick layers of normal watercolor.

Decipher Your Love

Imagine this scenario: You're an international spy, embarking on a mission to uncover the world's most closely guarded secrets. You've been on this challenging mission for a while now, but it has become evident that this task is impossible to accomplish alone. Your mission? Love.

But hold on. You've suddenly stumbled upon the missing piece of your puzzle: the one individual who possesses the key to unraveling the secrets of the universe. And, recruiting this person is crucial to unlock the mysteries that lie ahead.

Here's the twist: This isn't just pretend; this is the real deal. Your heart has been stolen, and the time has come to disclose your feelings before it's too late. While I can't help you in catching international spies, I can certainly assist you in capturing the attention of your beloved. Grab your scissors, and let's uncover the ultimate prize. This craft will take all of the essence of your favorite spy movie and turn it into a real-life way to ask your crush out.

MATERIALS

Heavyweight paper

Clear plastic sheet

Brass paper fastener

Yellow envelope

TOOLS

Protractor

Scissors

Pencil

Marker

Pen

Craft knife (I use X-Acto)

STEP 1

To uncover this secret, we will be creating a special cipher that will be used to create (and ultimately reveal) the contents of our hearts. Begin by using a protractor to draw a 6-inch (15-cm)-diameter circle on the heavyweight paper. Cut it out either with normal scissors or patterned scissors. Inside this circle, with a pencil, lightly draw two smaller circles: one with a 4⅛-inch (10.5-cm) diameter and a second with a 3¾-inch (9.5-cm) diameter.

STEP 2

With your pencil, lightly draw a line down the middle of the circle. Then draw a line perpendicular to the first one. Finally, draw lines between these two lines until you have divided the circle into eight equal-sized wedges. Between the border of the outer circle and the 4⅛-inch (10.5-cm) diameter circle, write out all 26 letters of the alphabet with your pencil. Make sure they are evenly spaced around the circle. Use the pencil-drawn wedges to help gauge the spacing. Below the alphabet, between the two drawn circles, create arbitrary symbols below each letter. Make sure the symbols are easily replicable, because we will need to recreate them in our note. These should also be evenly spaced, using the same distance between each symbol as there is between letters.

STEP 3

With the protractor, draw a 6-inch (15-cm)-diameter circle on the plastic sheet and cut it out. Cut a line through the circle slightly off center. Keep the larger of the two slices and line it up with the circle we have just jotted down letters and symbols on. Through the sheet, you will be able to see the center of the circle where all of the eight wedges connect. Poke a hole directly through the plastic sheet and the center of the circle. Attach the plastic and the cipher with a brass paper fastener. You should now be able to rotate this plastic sheet around and access all of your paper circle. On one side of the plastic, place a box around a letter with a marker and on the other side, place a box around one of the symbols.

Rotate the plastic sheet to make sure that all 26 letters of the alphabet line up with a different symbol within the boxes we created with our marker. If there are any that are slightly off, erase either the symbol or letter to make sure they align. Once you notice that each symbol aligns with its corresponding symbol, take off the plastic sheet and go over each letter and symbol with a pen or permanent marker. This is also a great opportunity to add any sort of colors or designs as well (as long as they aren't too distracting).

STEP 4

Cut a piece of heavyweight paper to match the plastic sheet. Line them up and draw and cut out the two boxes with the craft knife. Replace the plastic piece with the paper version, and discard the plastic. Decorate the top of the cipher however you want. Fasten the cipher with the brass fastener. If done correctly, your square cutouts will show a letter with its corresponding symbol, just as it did on the clear sheet. Now when the paper is spun around, a new letter and symbol will be revealed within each of the boxes.

STEP 5

Finally, you can use this tool to create a message made entirely out of symbols. Simply spell out your message, but instead of writing down each of the letters, replace them with the symbols that appear in the other square. Do this for each letter of your message. When it is completed, only the one with the cipher will have any access to your note.

Once you are happy with the contents of your note and cipher, sneak both into a yellow envelope conveniently titled "TOP SECRET" and hand this to your love interest. While this is certain to intrigue them, let's just hope that the curiosity will surpass deciphering the note and ultimately lead to you two deciphering each other's hearts.

> **TIP:** This can be used in many different ways, from a baby reveal to a proposal, or simply exchanging it with friends to pass secret notes while in class. It's the perfect way to keep the mystery alive for any occasion!

You Give Me Butterflies

♥💔♥💔♥💔♥💔♥💔♥💔♥💔♥💔♥💔♥

Falling in love is one of the worst feelings. In fact, someone please explain to me why it is so glamorized? That stage before you know whether or not your feelings are reciprocated? Absolute torture. Having butterflies stuck in your stomach? It actually kind of sucks! Why do we call them butterflies when they actually feel more like wasps stinging and poking at our insides? That's why I drafted up this craft. I mean, if we are going to feel like we're being tortured, we might as well craft it out.

This craft takes inspiration from all of that pain. If we could take out all the butterflies in our stomach and give it to the person who is inciting that feeling, what would it look like? Well, I imagine it would look a little something like this fun project.

MATERIALS

8 cotton swabs

Toilet paper roll

Jewelry clasp (optional)

Printer paper (optional)

TOOLS

Scissors

Ruler

Hot-glue gun and hot-glue sticks

Wax paper

Paint

Paintbrushes

Coloring utensils, including watercolor paints

Protractor

STEP 1

First up, let's prep our cotton swabs by cutting off the cotton ends. Just slide open scissors under the cotton and nudge it off. Moving on to the toilet paper roll, cut a ¾-inch (2-cm)-wide band. Glue the cotton swabs evenly inside the band with the hot-glue gun, making sure the bottom ¾ inch (2 cm) of the swabs is attached to the roll, leaving no exposed edges at the bottom. Bend the top of each swab so it curves inward.

Create a hot-glue dollop on a piece of wax paper and allow it to dry. Squeeze the top of the cotton swab tips together, add some more hot glue to each top of the cotton swabs and place the dried hot-glue dollop over each of the cotton swab tips. Hold them in place like this until completely dry and the cotton swabs are adhered together with the dollop on top.

STEP 2

Cut a ¼-inch (6-mm)-wide band from the toilet paper roll. Place it in the middle of your "cage," below where the swabs bend. A dab of hot glue will keep this in place. You can also add a bottom to the "cage" by cutting out a paper circle matching the diameter of your toilet paper roll, adding hot glue to edge of the bottom of the "cage" and adhering them together.

STEP 3

Now to move on to paint. I'm going for gold, but feel free to pick any color that tickles your fancy. Spray paint is great for covering all angles, but regular paint does the trick too. For an optional detail, pop a jewelry clasp into the top glue bulb as a makeshift cage handle.

STEP 4

Now, on to the butterflies. Fold a few sheets of paper in half, and draw wings against the creases. Cut out and unfold to reveal symmetrical wings. Paint a black stem along the fold, and then color the wings in various shades and patterns. Aim for five or six butterflies, each with its own little personality. Arrange some inside the cage and some fluttering around and at the bottom.

STEP 5

Finally, the love note. Cut out a 2 x ½-inch (5 x 1.3-cm) strip of paper, and age it with brown watercolor. Roll the paper between your fingers for an even more aged scroll-like effect. Write either, "You give me butterflies" or "The butterflies I collected from my tummy." Glue the paper to the outside of your cage and give it to your crush.

This craft is a whimsical take on the fluttery feelings of a crush. It turns that anxious energy into adorable pets you can cherish. And who knows—your crush might just be harboring similar "butterflies," so sharing this craft might lighten both your hearts!

Secret Bookmark

For those of us who are a bit more reserved in expressing love and affection, I've got the perfect solution for you. It's a subtle approach that will catch them off guard in the most delightful way. They'll catch a glimpse of your affection without it being too direct, sparing you the awkwardness of a blatant confession—because let's face it, the fear of someone reacting with a "What the heck, you like me?" is a little too real.

There are many creative ways to use the technique I'm about to share, but we'll focus on making a bookmark because it's an incredibly easy item to gift. You can casually offer it saying, "Hey, need a bookmark?" Or you can sneakily slip it into one of their textbooks. There are plenty of excuses to use that won't give away your intentions too much—that is, until the message is revealed.

MATERIALS
Colored paper
White paper
Ribbon

TOOLS
Ruler
Scissors
Marker
Glue
Hole punch

STEP 1
Cut the colored paper in two identical pieces, both measuring 6½ x 3 inches (17 x 7.5 cm). Cut the white paper slightly smaller, 6 x 2¼ inches (15 x 6 cm). Write your feelings on the smaller white piece of paper with the marker. If you're giving this bookmark in a casual way and they might not remember who it's from, you might want to hint that it is you specifically that has a crush on them. For example, write something like, "Devyn has a crush on you, do you like her back?"

STEP 2
Next, sandwich the small white sheet between the two larger pieces. Carefully glue down the sides of the larger pieces, ensuring all three are securely attached. Just be careful not to get glue on the white paper, as it might show when the message is revealed. Punch a hole at the top of your bookmark, thread the ribbon through the hole and tie it off.

STEP 3
Now, the big reveal. When the bookmark is held up to the light, your hidden message will become visible. But be warned. You might find yourself in limbo, not knowing whether or not they've figured it out. However, let's hope they reciprocate your feelings and show it in some way. And let's also hope that if they don't, they never bring it up and spare you any potential awkwardness!

Confessing Your Love

I Love Learning about You

♥💔♥💔♥💔♥💔♥💔♥💔♥💔♥💔♥💔♥💔♥💔♥💔

If the mere smell within a bookstore sends a wave of dopamine through your body, then chances are, you're a book lover. Books, for us, are more than bound pages; they're treasures that hold our hearts. They are the silent companions in our moments of solitude, the mirrors reflecting the depth of our emotions. And when you find someone who stirs within you the same profound affection that a cherished book does, you know you've found something truly special. Just as a favorite book becomes a part of who we are, so too can the right person. If you're fortunate enough to discover a person who kindles the same warmth and wonder as a beloved story, it's essential to let them know. After all, just like a rare first edition, such connections are to be treasured and celebrated.

But to make sure this person is still around next chapter, you may want to make a move. Here is a way to confess your love inspired by your love of books.

MATERIALS

Heavyweight paper or cardstock, or any thick paper material

Printer paper

TOOLS

Scissors

Stapler

Pen or marker

Coloring utensils

STEP 1

Let's begin by selecting our base material. We need this material to be slightly thicker and sturdier than everyday printer paper. I am using watercolor paper, but feel free to cut up an old cereal box or use something similar that's lying around the house. This is going to act as the front and back cover of your book. Cut your material into one piece measuring 2¾ x 1¾ inches (7 x 4.5 cm). Turn it to lay horizontally and fold it in half.

Next, prepare the pages. Cut five sheets of printer paper, each measuring 2¾ x 1¾ inches (7 x 4.5 cm). Fold these in half and place them inside to sit within your cover.

STEP 2

Staple two staples along the crease of the folded pages. Ensure the staples are vertical along the book's crease to avoid any issues when opening the book. Feel free to add any cute little design to the front cover. I kept mine simple, just adding a swirly border with a black pen along with the text, "I love learning about you."

Now it's time to get sentimental. On each page, write what you love learning about your special person. This can be how their nose scrunches when they smile or how they talk really fast when they're excited. There is no need to paint them with a perfect brush. People adore when they are loved for who they are, peculiarities and all, so make sure you let them know what it is exactly that stole your heart.

STEP 3

On either the cover or on the very first page of your book, write the phrase, "I love learning about you." Just like how our favorite books take us on a journey through our wildest fantasies, so too could this happen with this special person if you let them know how you feel.

Read between the Lines

Imagine this: You've got a crush, and your heart flutters whenever they're around. The moment has arrived to pluck up the courage and ask them out, but you're not one for ordinary gestures. You're on the hunt for something special, something that perfectly matches the unique connection you share. This craft offers you the chance to add a touch of mystery to your heartfelt message. It's a brilliant mix of creativity and simplicity, allowing you to create a concealed love message that will pleasantly surprise your crush. And guess what? You can finish it in just a few minutes, ensuring your effort is both thoughtful and time efficient.

I'll guide you through the process of crafting a note that hides your true feelings between the lines. This creates a charming and memorable way to ask your crush out. So, let me teach you the steps of revealing your hidden love message and ensuring your words remains etched in their memory.

MATERIALS
Lined notebook

TOOLS
Pencil

Pen

STEP 1
Number the lines on the first page of the notebook as follows:

- Line 1: Leave blank
- Line 2: Start your love note
- Line 3: Leave blank
- Line 4: Continue your love note
- Line 5: Leave blank
- Line 6: Finish your love note

STEP 2
On the first page of your notebook, write your love note on lines 2, 4 and 6. While writing your secret note, use a pen or pencil with firm pressure. The idea is that the pressure will transfer to the next page without any ink, making it a challenge to read unless uncovered. I recommend writing something quick and to the point, for example: "I like you, do you like me?" or a simple "Would you like to go to the movies with me?" Just make sure to allow a place for their response with two squares followed by "yes" and "no."

STEP 3
Once your love note is written, remove the first page of the notebook. Write, "Remember to always read between the lines" in bold letters on the lines that don't have your secret message (lines 1, 3 and 5).

To present this to your crush, hand them the notebook with a pencil. If they possess the quick wit needed to be the one for you, they'll notice the etched words between the lines you wrote in pen. They can then use the pencil to shade over the hidden words and check off the box with their response. It's a clever way to ask out your crush without exposing too much of yourself or making a public scene.

Will You Wear Your Bow Tie (Pasta)?

♥💔♥💔♥💔♥💔♥💔♥💔♥💔♥💔♥💔♥💔♥💔♥💔

Bow tie pasta, also known as farfalle, is a type of pasta that is characterized by its distinctive bow tie or butterfly shape. (Farfalle is actually derived from the Italian name for butterflies. How cute is that?!) In my opinion, these little edible bows are really the perfect way to ask any man or masculine-presenting person to a formal occasion where they can break out that bow tie for real! So, using adorable carbs as inspo, let's create a craft perfect for asking your crush to prom, homecoming or even a wedding!

MATERIALS

Template (page 221)

Clear plastic

Yellow construction paper

TOOLS

Craft knife (I use X-Acto)

Hot-glue gun and hot-glue sticks

Coloring utensils

Sheer pattern scissors (optional)

Bow tie (optional)

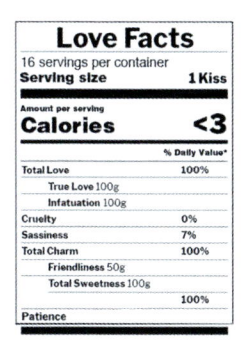

STEP 1

Let's start with the box. Cut out the template on page 221. You will notice the big hollow rectangle on one side of the template—make sure you cut it out completely with the help of a craft knife. Cut a sheet of clear plastic either from a clear plastic bag or a paper protector that fits in the hollow rectangle. Add glue to the border around the hollow rectangle and secure your clear plastic onto it. Flip the template over and all the gluing imperfections should be out of sight and out of mind!

STEP 2

Now that we have the window in place, let's begin creating our packaging. While you can certainly design your own packaging based off of a real-life pasta box, you can also look to some of my designs for a little extra inspiration. Just make sure that you curate your design to fit around the window we just created. Of course, I am adding my cheesy tagline to the exterior packaging, simply stating, "Will you wear your BOW TIE?"

(continued)

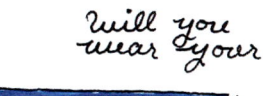

For an extra way to flirt, fill out the "love facts" as a romantic rendition of a typical nutrition fact tab. Add in your favorite qualities of your special person, such as sweetness (100 g) or cruelty (0%). Once everything is colored, assemble the box with your trusty hot-glue gun. Just be sure to keep the top of the pasta box unglued for easy access to the inside.

STEP 3

Now that our box is finished and looking fabulous, it's time to make the little pasta pieces. I am starting the pasta-making process by cutting out a 2 x 1½–inch (5 x 4–cm) piece from the yellow construction paper. I took my sheer pattern scissors and cut on the longer sides to give it a chevron pattern, but this can also be done by hand. (Tedious, I know, but it really adds that extra detail!)

Stay with me here because this may get a little confusing. Hold the paper horizontally, and fold the paper in half. Once there is a crease, unfold the paper and bend the outer edges to meet in the middle at the crease.

Flip the paper over and put a small dot of hot glue in the center of the paper and fold back the sheet so the hot-glue sticks the middle of the paper together. Gently, without agitating the hot glue, push out the outer edges and fluff out those bows. You may have to try this a few times before getting the hang of it, so just be patient with yourself and watch pasta-making videos online if you need to! Make enough of these to fill your box.

STEP 4

Now, just because I am extra, I also sneakily added a real bow tie inside the box using the paper bow tie pieces to hide it from the outside. I also added one purposefully placed piece of "pasta" and wrote "@ prom?" to signify my specific intentions. When my giftee opens this craft, not only will they have my cute little rendition of a box of pasta but also have a new bow tie, perfect to wear on our date (assuming they say yes because . . . c'mon . . . how could you say no to this craft?). Once you're done, fold up the top of the box and get ready to impress your crush with an invite that is cute, quirky and a bit saucy!

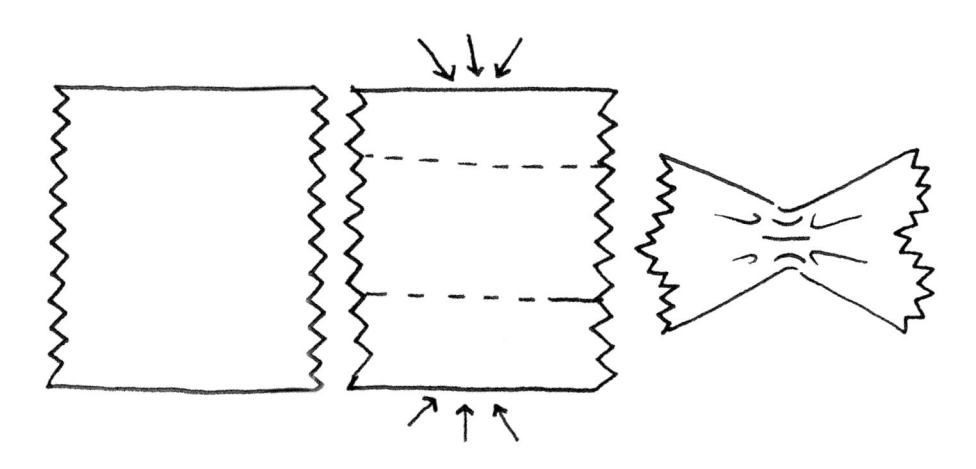

The Love Equation

Let's say your crush or partner is quite the smarty-pants. How about instead of using words, crafts or art to confess your feelings, why not use a language they already understand?

Even if you are not a math whiz, we can still make it easy to slide in your feelings with this little trick.

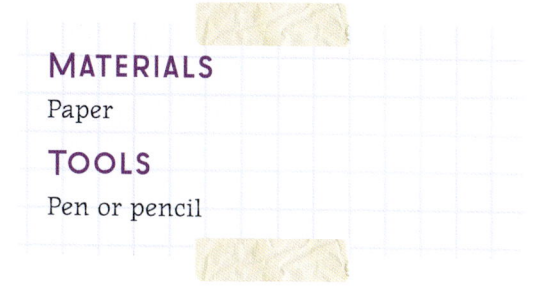

MATERIALS
Paper

TOOLS
Pen or pencil

STEP 1
The equation **9x–7i < 3(3x–7u)** might look like any typical math problem, but it holds a secret message. When solved, it spells out **I <3 u**, which is classic text-speak for "I love you." So, how do you use this equation to confess your feelings? I have two sneaky ways to approach it.

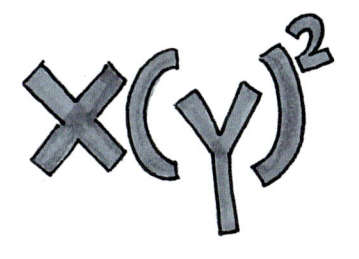

STEP 2
The direct approach: Casually compliment their intelligence and ask for help with this specific math problem. As they guide you through it, they'll unravel the hidden message. Once you reach the end and the secret message is revealed, it's your chance to share your feelings. Their realization of the message hidden in the math will make for a sweet and memorable moment.

The subtle approach: For those who aren't math enthusiasts, write out the equation and solve it yourself. Make sure to show all the steps involved. At the end, circle the solution to draw attention to it. Ask your crush or partner to double-check your work, subtly leading them to the answer. The surprise in discovering the message at the end can be the perfect segue into expressing your feelings.

This crafty method combines intellect with romance, creating a unique and memorable way to confess your love. Whether they're a math geek or not, this approach adds a playful and thoughtful twist to the age-old challenge of saying "I love you."

Confessing Your Love

Mirror Writing

🤍💔🤍💔🤍💔🤍💔🤍💔🤍💔🤍💔🤍💔🤍💔🤍💔🤍💔🤍💔🤍

If you've ever prepared for a spicy date by bringing a pack of mints with you, then you're probably familiar with the convenient tins they come in. But these tins aren't only an essential for PG-13 one-offs, they're also a must-have for craft enthusiasts, even for those of us who aren't particularly fond of mints. In fact, I have seven mint containers stashed away in my craft closet, and I don't even like mints! For this craft, we will be utilizing these versatile little containers as the perfect discreet packaging to declare our love.

MATERIALS

Printer paper

Tin mint container

Small mirror

TOOLS

Scissors

Pen or marker

Hot-glue gun and hot-glue sticks

Decorative materials (optional)

STEP 1

Let's focus first on your secret love letter. Write a note to your crush on a piece of printer paper. Make sure to end your note with a simple yes or no question they can answer. Snap a photo of your note, and use any basic editing software (like on the Apple photos app) to flip the image. Then, on a new piece of paper, cut slightly smaller than your tin, recreate what you see in the flipped photo. The message will magically become legible in front of a mirror if done correctly. Place your cleverly coded note inside the tin. Then, hot glue a small mirror to the inside of the lid. You might be surprised how tricky it is to find a mirror small enough to fit, but an old makeup palette can be a great start.

STEP 2

Now you've got two options for presenting this craft: Keep the tin's exterior plain for a casual, "Hey, want a mint?" approach, or decorate it to fit your or your crush's personality. Totally up to you!

When they open the tin, it might take them a moment to figure out the puzzle. But once they do, they'll discover your message and can check off their response. Sure, those few seconds of waiting might be a heart-racing experience, but remember, you miss 100% of the shots you don't take. And just in case things don't work out so well, you can always use a project from Never Mind. You Suck. (page 185) as a backup plan. Good luck!

Conceal to Reveal

♥💔♥💔♥💔♥💔♥💔♥💔♥💔♥💔♥💔♥💔♥💔♥💔♥

Say you've had this best friend for a long time, and while you know that it is platonic, you can't help but smile thinking about their laugh and your heart skips a beat whenever they text you. I have some bad (or good?) news for you. You are not simply friends; you are slowly falling in love with this person more and more every day. While this can be incredibly nerve-wracking, especially because you don't want to ruin your friendship, when and if you decide to tell them, I got you covered on a way to break the news that they will never forget!

While this little surprise announcement tool may seem simple enough, it brings a creative twist that makes it far superior to slipping any regular old note in someone's locker.

MATERIALS

Heavyweight paper

Thick paper, cardstock or recycled material

Small envelope

TOOLS

Scissors

Ruler

Pencil or pen

Craft knife (I use X-Acto)

Black marker

STEP 1

Firstly, let's cut a piece of heavyweight paper to 3½ x 5 inches (9 x 13 cm). Get a second piece of thick paper in any other color, and cut it to the same size. Keep in mind that this is a perfect time to recycle! I am using an old rigid mailer I had laying around. On the first sheet of thick paper, start by measuring out the paper in perfect ½-inch (1.3-cm) increments down from the top. Once that's done, do it again vertically, creating a perfect grid. While you can use pen or pencil for the first sheet, do it again with a lighter touch on the second sheet so we can erase it later. With the craft knife, cut out one of the grid squares from the cardstock. Do this again sporadically until you have eight holes in the cardstock. Place this directly over the first sheet of paper, lining it up perfectly. Within the squares we cut out, write, "I love you," putting it in order going from the top row from the left to right and so on. Leave spaces or even go in various rows to mix up the placement of the letters—just make sure that it remains legible.

STEP 2

Take away the cardstock and fill the rest of the boxes on the first sheet of paper with letters from the alphabet. Color the upper left square on both pieces black to indicate the orientation. Completely erase the grid on the cardstock (the one with the cutout squares in it). When the giftee is presented with this puzzle, they should line up the two black squares and reveal the message. Stick these into a little envelope, and either stuff it into their locker at school or their mailbox. It's an easy little puzzle that allows you to show your affection in a way that is a tad more interactive than a typical note.

Confessing Your Love

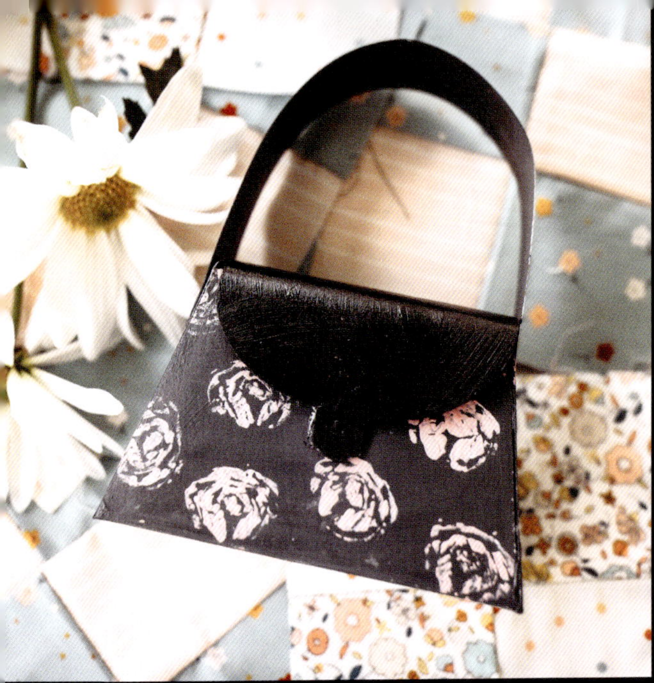

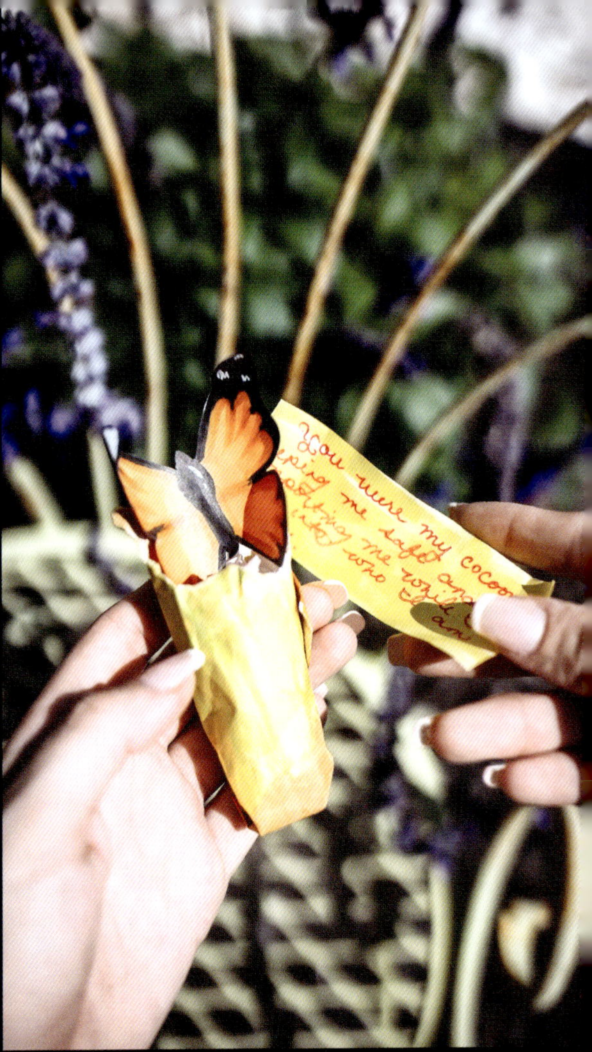

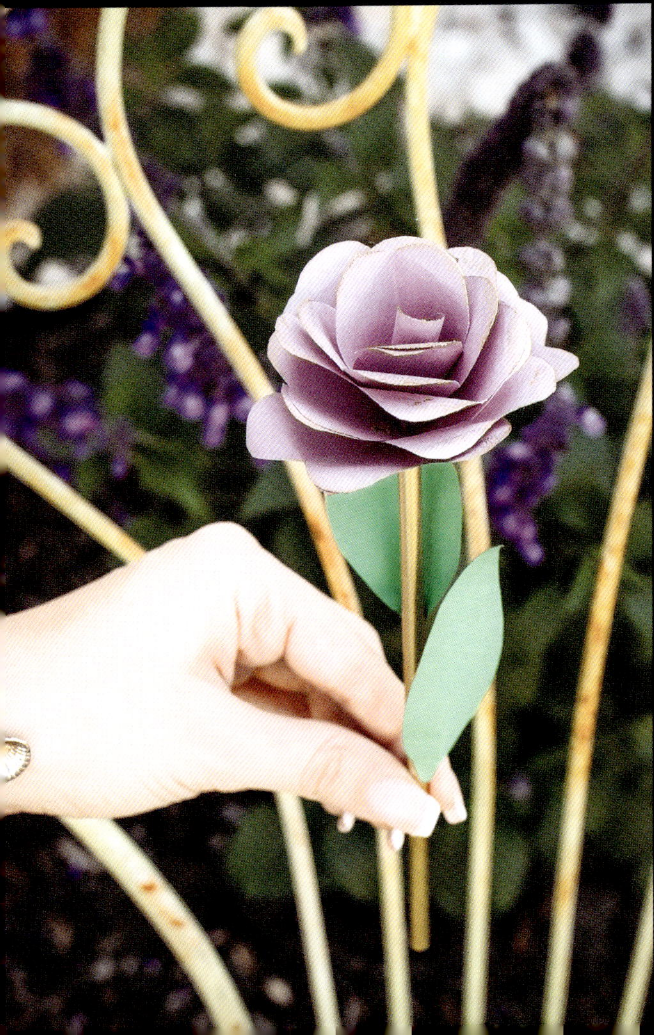

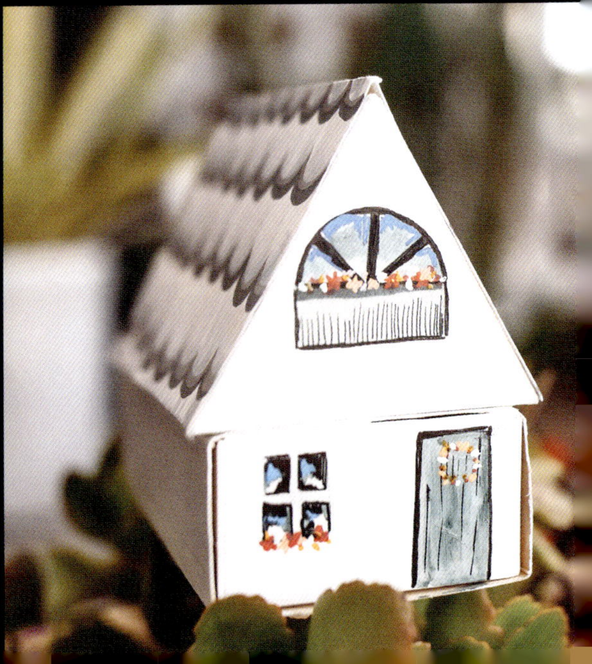

Family Is Forever (?)

Home is where the heart is, or at least that's what they say. While I can say for most that our families do love us, that doesn't necessarily mean they are capable of showing it in a healthy way. I mean, consider this: People can't teach what they do not know themselves. We look up to these big adults when we are small and dependent, but after taking time to grow up for ourselves, we realize how simply human they have always been. While that isn't to say this "humanness" is very capable of causing us pain, if you can, take the opportunity to celebrate the humanity of your family. And if you are lucky enough to relate to the opening quote, then revel in the fact that you are surrounded by love even on the darkest of days, and do your best to honor your luck by showing a little appreciation—maybe with some of these sweet (or not so sweet) crafts.

Home Is Wherever My Family Is

♥💔♥💔♥💔♥💔♥💔♥💔♥💔♥💔♥💔♥💔♥💔♥💔

The concept of "home" is more than just bricks and mortar; it's a feeling of belonging, warmth and connection. At the heart of every home is the family, the people who make any place feel like you belong. For this craft, we are going to contemplate the idea of what home is, using an old matchbox to convey this feeling only family can provide.

MATERIALS

Matchbox
Heavyweight paper
Craft sticks (optional)
Family photos
Ribbon/twine (optional)

TOOLS

Ruler
Pencil or pen
Scissors
Hot-glue gun with hot-glue sticks
Coloring utensils

TIP: Not everyone feels this way about genetic family. It is up to you to decide who your family is. This gift can be given to non-biological family and still hold the same sentiment.

STEP 1

To begin, get your hands on a matchbox. Measure the length, width and height of your matchbox. Mine measured 4¾ x 2½ x 1¼ inches (12 x 6.5 x 3 cm). Make sure you write your measurements down because we will be referencing them throughout this project.

Let's begin by making two triangles on heavyweight paper where each of the sides are the same length as the width of your matchbox. Add little tabs to each of your triangles so it looks something like this:

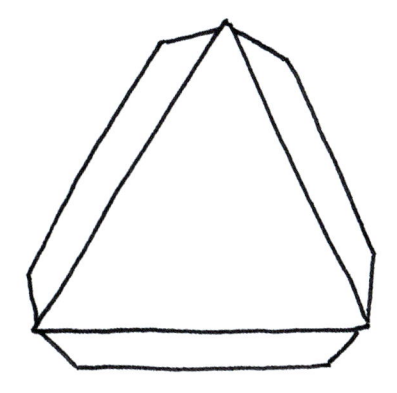

(continued)

STEP 2

Cut out your triangles and fold down each of your tabs. Secure each of the two triangles to either side of the front and back of your matchbox (decide which is which). The pointy part should be sticking directly up. Now draw a rectangle on a piece of heavyweight paper that measures the same length and twice the width of your matchbox. Again, add little tabs to the width sides. Fold this sheet of paper in half vertically, and while you're at it, fold down the little tabs as well.

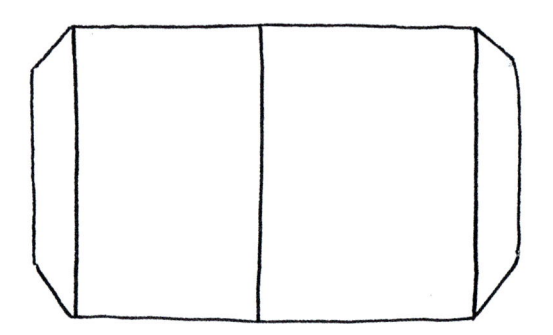

STEP 3

Add some glue to the remaining tabs on each of the triangles as well as on the rectangle's tabs we just created. Put this new little "roof" on top of your matchbox and let the glue dry. Decorate your matchbox house to resemble either your dream home or your childhood home. You can also add craft sticks to the top to create realistic-looking shingles.

STEP 4

Once your home is decorated to your liking, gather a bunch of family photos and cut them to fit inside your matchbox house. You may have to stalk your family's Facebook or Instagram and print them out. If you do, just be sure to opt for photo paper so it looks more professional. Once you have a bunch of pictures that are sure to trigger nostalgia, write a note that says "Home Is Where My Family Is," or simply, "You Are My Home."

> **TIP:** You can also specify this for a singular person, such as a parent or sibling if you prefer.

Wrap the note and pictures with a piece of twine or ribbon and place them inside the matchbox. Give this to your family as a thoughtful sentiment that will be sure to warm their hearts and brighten their days.

Thank You for Helping Me Grow

♥ 💔 ♥ 💔 ♥ 💔 ♥ 💔 ♥ 💔 ♥ 💔 ♥ 💔 ♥ 💔 ♥ 💔 ♥ 💔 ♥ 💔

In my perspective, a beautiful analogy for a loving family is akin to nurturing flowers and plants. Much like these living beings, a family requires love and care to flourish. It necessitates constant attention, affection and nourishment, for neglect can yield obvious consequences. However, when we invest our time, energy and love into our family, the results can be remarkably beautiful and life-giving. To me, this craft serves as a symbolic representation of a loving parental figure, much like a watering can that nourishes life from the ground up. Therefore, in this craft, we will ingeniously construct a watering can using readily available household items.

MATERIALS
Heavyweight paper

Toilet paper roll

TOOLS
Ruler

Scissors

Hot-glue gun and hot-glue sticks

Protractor

Paint

Paintbrushes

Coloring utensils

STEP 1
Cut out a piece of 4½ x 12-inch (11.5 x 30-cm) heavyweight paper. Leave ½ inch (1.3 cm) on either side of the width and mark these areas, leaving 3½ inches (9 cm) in the middle. Fold down both of these tabs and make slits ½ inch (1.3 cm) wide, ensuring not to cut beyond the marked lines.

STEP 2
Apply a small amount of glue to one edge of the paper and wrap it around to connect with itself, forming a tube. Measure the distance between one end of the opening circle to the other end, finding the diameter.

(continued)

Use a protractor with this same diameter to create two circles. (My circle's diameter measures 1¼ inches (3 cm), which should be similar to yours, though it may vary slightly.) On one of these circles, use the protractor to create another inner circle with a 1-inch (2.5-cm) diameter. Cut out this circle, leaving one circle intact and the other with a circular hole through it. Place the circle with the opening to the top of your watering can, and attach the other circle to the bottom. To do this, make sure all of your slits are bent inwards, and apply glue. Hold the circles securely to the slits until the glue is dry.

STEP 3

Cut the toilet paper roll in half lengthwise (the long way). Then, carefully roll one half of the toilet paper roll into itself, securing one end farther into the roll than the other to create a "spout." Use hot glue to secure the roll in this position, ensuring that one side extends 1½ inches (4 cm) into itself, and the other side just ¼ inch (6 mm).

Now, notice that one end has a larger opening than the other, holding it horizontally. Apply extra glue to any areas that need further securing. From the larger opening, cut the entire toilet paper roll at a 45-degree angle. Add glue to the edge of the toilet paper roll cut at an angle and attach it to the watering can, making sure the spout is facing upwards. Press firmly to ensure a secure bond. You may need to apply glue a few times due to the limited surface area.

STEP 4

Cut a 2¾ x ½-inch (7 x 1.3-cm) strip of heavyweight paper. Fold a ½-inch (1.3-cm) crease on both ends, add a small amount of glue to each of the folded edges, and place one at the top and one at the bottom of your watering can to form the handle. Paint and decorate your watering can however you like. I kept mine incredibly simple by spray-painting it a shiny white, but feel free to paint it any color of your choosing.

Your craft is now complete, resembling a charming miniature watering can ready to symbolize the nurturing love within your family. Pairing this gift with a seed packet and flowers would make it a perfect gift for anyone in your family, but if you want to continue with the homemade theme, check out Everlasting Flowers on page 136.

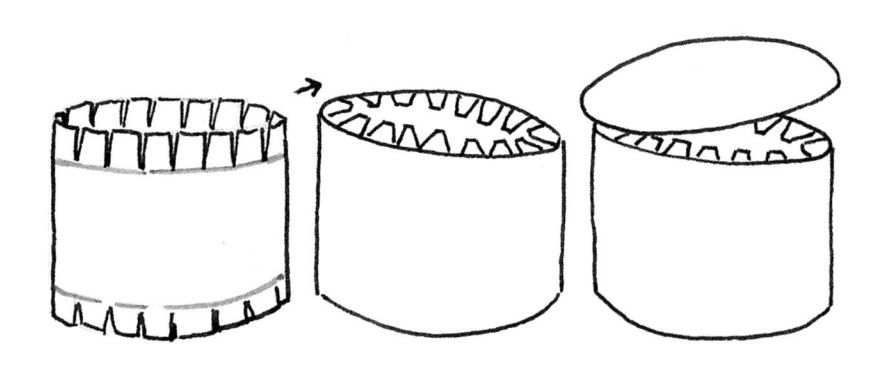

My Family's Cookbook

This gift is a truly heartfelt and adorable craft to give to any family member. While it shouldn't cost a lot in terms of dollars, it does require some extra time, research and detective work. While most of this book is centered around crafts you can simply make out of paper or such materials, we will need to recruit some family members for this one. But trust me, it will be incredibly worth it.

MATERIALS

Cardboard

Fabric

Printer paper

Textured paper

All of the recipes you gathered

Ribbon

TOOLS

Ruler

Scissors

Pencil

Hot-glue gun and hot-glue sticks

STEP 1

Let's begin with the most valuable part of this gift: getting the info. Since the bulk of this gift is the recipes, you'll have to do a little digging to find them. Begin by asking all the family members you know (except the giftee). Some of the recipes may be written on little postcards or sticky notes—don't worry about it; these will do just fine.

If you're super lucky, you'll be able to find Grandma's old set of recipes or a favorite cookbook with their favorite recipes marked. You may have to do a little attic digging to really find some substantial recipes, but once you have contacted the proper relatives from all different generations, you should have the information you need.

(continued)

Family Is Forever (?) - 133

STEP 2

Separate each recipe by relative to keep it organized. Create names for each of them following the relative in question, such as "Grandma's Favorite Stew" or "Auntie Maria's Childhood Green Soup." Make sure to credit the recipe owner for an added sentimental touch.

Now that we have all the recipes at our disposal, we can begin assembling them into a little book. If you are keen on doing this professionally, you can, of course, send the information off and get it printed and published in a proper journal. But if you are a crafter at heart and love the sentimentality of a handmade gift, let me walk you through the steps of creating your own cookbook with minimal headache.

STEP 3

Cut out a 15 x 8½-inch (38 x 22-cm) piece of cardboard. Holding the cardboard horizontally, measure from the right, and draw a line at 6¾ inches (17 cm) and 8¼ inches (21 cm). This will give you a 1½-inch (4-cm) center or spine. Crease both lines running down the center of your cardboard using the edge of the ruler to help you. Fold the cardboard over, and now you have yourself a makeshift binder.

Unfortunately, cardboard is not the most aesthetically pleasing material in the world, so to not only add further structure and support but also beautify it so it looks nice and professional, we'll cover it in fabric. Start by cutting your fabric to match the shape of your cardboard but be sure to leave 2¼ inches (6 cm) extra around the entire perimeter.

Wrap the fabric to cover the entire outside cover and flip it over to the reverse side. You will notice there is extra fabric but not enough to cover the entire inside. For each of the four corners of the cardboard, take the excess fabric corner and glue it into the center as far as the fabric extends. Cut a 1-inch (2.5-cm) strip in the center on either side, lining it up with the spine. Glue these extended pieces of fabric as far as they go directly over the spine on both the bottom and the top. Cut a 2½ x 8½-inch (6.5 x 22-cm) piece of fabric and glue it to the center of the binder to cover up the rest of the spine. Stretch the rest of the main piece of fabric on all of the sides over the cardboard and glue each secure to the interior.

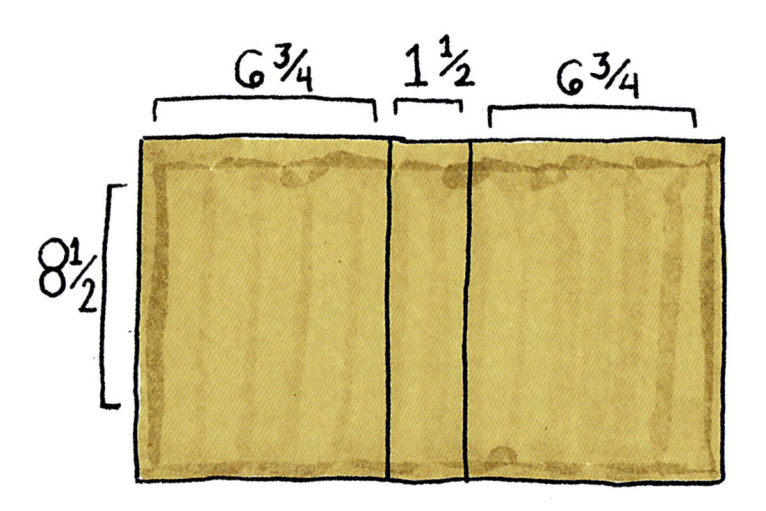

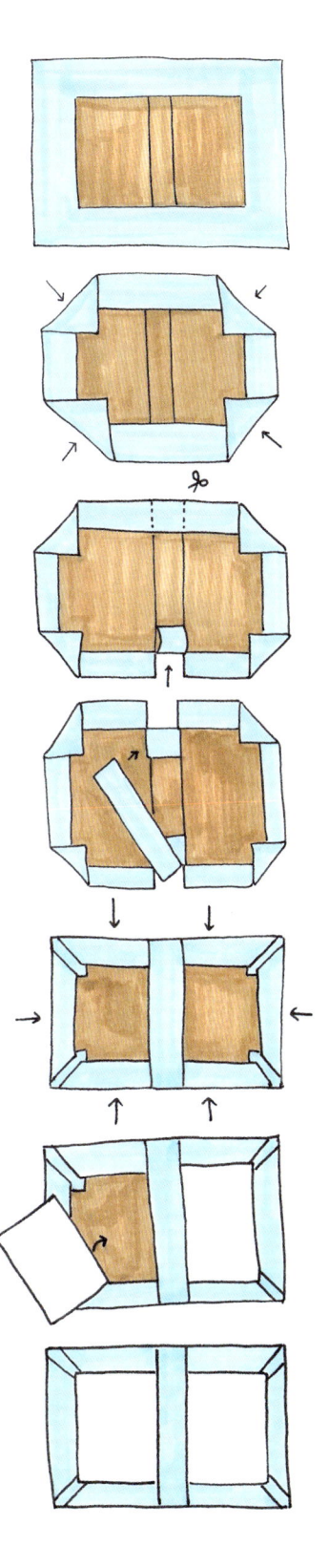

STEP 4

At this point, the exterior of the binder looks nice and clean, but the interior is kind of a mess. To clean it up, cut a 7 x 5½-inch (18 x 14-cm) piece of paper, add some glue, and place it on the back of the front and back cover where the fabric doesn't cover up the cardboard.

Now that our book is created, cut pieces of textured paper that you like to 14 x 8½ inches (36 x 22-cm) and fold them down the middle. On this paper write down each of your recipes. Feel free to add little illustrations that correspond with the recipes or simply little cooking illustrations in general. Here are some illustrations I added to my recipe book on both the front cover and the recipes themselves:

Once you have assembled all the paper you like, along with the corresponding recipes, take a piece of ribbon of your choosing and tie it into a bow through the folded lines of the paper along with the spine of the book base. Tie it in a big beautiful bow, and voilà! You have a sentimental yet useful gift ready to give to any family member. Bon appétit!

Everlasting Flowers

♥💔♥💔♥💔♥💔♥💔♥💔♥💔♥💔♥💔♥💔♥💔♥💔♥💔

For me, there is something incredibly tragic about flowers. They are so beautiful (and let's be honest, they aren't on the cheap side either), yet after two days they begin to wilt, and after a week they are dead! It makes me feel incredibly guilty and so sad--so much so that I have instructed my loved ones to not buy me any. But yet, they make the perfect gift! I realize that my dramatic response to the death of flowers may not be the norm, but if you share this sentiment even a little bit, here is a way to still gift flowers without their tragic demise.

MATERIALS

Construction paper

TOOLS

Ruler

Scissors

Glue (any kind)

Pencil

Plastic straw

Paint (ideally green or brown)

Paintbrushes

STEP 1

Cut out a 3½ x 3½-inch (9 x 9-cm) square from the construction paper. Fold one of the corners to the opposite corner to form a triangle, giving it the appearance of a bandanna. Then, take either of the pointed sides of the bandanna and fold it in half again. Then, fold the triangle in half one more time for a total of three folds. Now you have a triangle where one point is connected to the crease and the other is not. Just below the point that is not connected, near the center, round out the edge and cut it off. Here is an illustration to help you visualize:

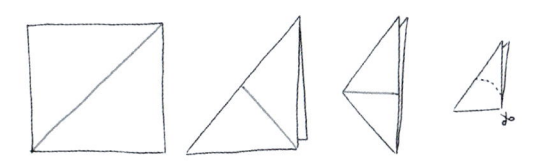

Open up all of the folds. You now have a flower-like shape with eight petals. Create five of these eight-petaled flowers.

STEP 2

For the first eight-petaled flower, cut a slit from one petal crease up to the center, but do not cut beyond the center. Take the petal beside the slit and add a little glue to it and connect it to the petal on the other side of the slit.

Proceed similarly with the second flower, but this time cut a full petal and then connect the petals together on either side of the missing petal. Do this again to the next flower shape, except take away two petals. Continue on decreasing the number of petals, creating smaller and smaller flower cones until you use all five of your flower shapes. Take one of the excess cutaway petals and set it aside.

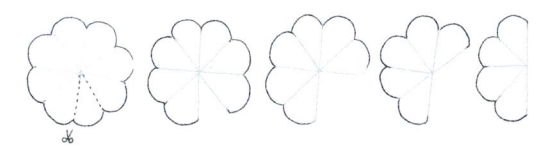

STEP 3

Assemble these flower cones by adding a touch of glue to the pointy center of each and fitting them within the next larger cone. For example, nest the seven-petal cone within the eight-petal cone, the five-petal cone within the four-petal cone and so on, until you reach the single petal. Roll this single petal into itself, securing it with a small amount of glue at the pointed edge, and then place it at the center to complete your flower. Once the glue dries, use a pencil to gently curl the petals outward, giving the rose a fuller, more blossomed appearance.

STEP 4

To add a stem, measure ½ inch (1.3 cm) from one end of your straw and cut slits up to this mark. Paint the straw green or brown for a realistic look. Apply glue to the slits and attach the straw to the bottom center of the rose, holding it steady until the glue sets. To make the leaves, cut a leaf shape into a piece of green construction paper. Apply glue to the bottom of the leaf and attach it to the straw. You can now make an entire bouquet of these roses.

Family Is Forever (?)

My Mother's Purse

I find this craft not just adorable, but ridiculously so. My mother's purse is like a treasure trove, an ever-expanding collection of the most random yet essential items. Have a little bit of a sniffle? BAM!, there's a tissue. Got a sunburn? She's already whipping out the sunscreen. Her purse is more than a fashion statement; it's a testament to her beauty and self-sacrifice, always having everything her children might need within the confines of its leather walls.

This craft is a heartfelt homage to mothers or any purse-carrying guardian—a way to show them that their efforts are noticed and deeply appreciated.

MATERIALS

Templates (page 237 and 245)

Fabric (optional)

Ribbon (optional)

Chain (optional)

TOOLS

Ruler

Scissors

Coloring utensils

Spray adhesive (optional)

Metallic markers (optional)

Glue

Double-sided tape

Pen or marker

STEP 1

Let's start by selecting a template. Purses come in countless shapes and sizes, so I have assembled two different templates to choose from on page 237. Of course, you can base this craft on your giftee's real purse or create something totally unique—it's up to you!

If you want to keep it simple, cut and fold your template, but color the entire paper before gluing it together, just to make sure you get within every crevice. For an even more realistic effect, adhere fabric using spray adhesive, trim any excess and fold as usual (though the fabric's thickness might require adjustments). To mimic the look of alligator skin leather, I placed a piece of printer paper over my template and sketched an alligator skin pattern. The pencil left an imprint on the template, which I then colored over as normal. Once you like the texture of your purse, assemble it. As always, refer to the template for where to fold and glue. Once you have the basic shape of your purse, we can start adding additional decorations.

STEP 2

Metallic markers are great for adding metallic accents, but to avoid absorption into the paper, use a bit of water-based glue first. For my purse, I drew a hollow rectangle to replicate the metalwork on one of my mom's actual purses and attached it to mine, lending that special detail that makes this craft stand out. Here are some metal embellishment ideas to consider adding to your purse craft:

STEP 3

Now to mimic a real purse's clasp, I used a piece of double-sided tape on the reverse side of the main flap. This ensures the bag stays closed but can still be easily opened when gifting.

Of course, now we need to add the bag's handle. Use the template on page 245. Again, handles are all different depending on the bag. Paint it to match your purse and attach either end of the handle to the sides of your bag. If you want a different look, you can also use real ribbon, adhering the ends of the ribbon to the side of your bag, or you can even add a chain. Once your purse is decorated to your liking, write a card to your guardian, addressing how much you appreciate them (and their fashion sense!) and stuff it inside the paper purse. Gift away knowing you are giving them a gift they will never forget.

Opening Doors

♥💔♥💔♥💔♥💔♥💔♥💔♥💔♥💔♥💔♥💔♥💔♥💔♥

This craft holds a special place in my heart, as my family is my absolute ride or die. But I must admit, it's often harder to come up with gifts for family than for a romantic partner. So, to address that challenge, I've come up with a unique card idea perfect for any family member who has been a significant support in your life. Because trust me, if it wasn't for my family opening doors for me one way or another, I would not have gotten the opportunity to pursue my dreams and ultimately be able to write this book. (I realize this makes me sound like a nepotism baby, LOL!)

MATERIALS

Watercolor paper

Cardboard

TOOLS

Ruler

Scissors

Hot-glue gun and hot-glue sticks

Paint

Paintbrushes

Markers

STEP 1

For this card, you can adjust its size to your preference, but I chose to make it a bit smaller because I have a fondness for tiny things—something you've probably noticed by now.

Cut a 6 x 4½-inch (15 x 11.5-cm) piece of watercolor paper and fold it in half. Cut out a 3 x 4½-inch (7.5 x 11.5-cm) cardboard rectangle. If you decide to adjust the size, ensure that the cardboard rectangle matches the dimensions of your paper folded in half.

Hot glue the cardboard rectangle to the front cover of the card, and with the help of some paint and markers, transform it into a miniature door. You can choose whatever door style you like. Here are some examples of door designs to inspire you.

STEP 2

Once everything is colored and designed to your liking, add a tiny dab of hot glue near the opening of your door to serve as a door handle. Once it is dry, paint it gold or silver to look like a real door handle.

On the inside of your card, write the following message: "Thank you for opening doors for me." This phrase, of course, refers to the metaphorical doors that a parent, mentor or supporter opens for their children or mentees. When gifted, the door will be opened to reveal the message inside, adding an adorable twist to this classic phrase.

TIP: On the other hand, if you are in the market for a card for a family member you are not so fond of (someone who has negatively impacted the opportunities in your life), you can opt to switch the words around just a tad: "Thanks for closing all the doors in my life" is enough to get the message across, in my opinion!

Family Flowers

I'm particularly fond of this craft idea for a multitude of reasons. It's versatile enough to double as a thoughtful gift for family members or a cherished keepsake for yourself. Moreover, it captures the essence of family beautifully, which holds a special place in my heart. Just like flowers and plants that require care and attention to bloom and grow, it perfectly symbolizes the nurturing nature of a good family. (And let's be honest. If you've ever tried keeping a houseplant alive, you know it's not always a walk in the park.)

MATERIALS

Heavyweight paper, such as bristol or watercolor paper

Tissue paper or kraft paper

Ribbon

TOOLS

Access to cooperative family members

Ruler

Scissors

Pencils

Coloring utensils

STEP 1

Cut out several 2 x 5–inch (5 x 13–cm) boxes out of the heavyweight paper. You'll need one for every family member you plan to include. (Yes, even the ones you don't really like . . . I know, I know. But we need all hands on deck!)

STEP 2

With pencil and boxes in hand, bravely approach each family member and have them draw a flower within their box. It's up to you whether they get to color it in or if you'll take over later. (This decision might depend on how much you trust their artistic skills.) If you want to go above and beyond, invite your relatives to jot down why they cherish the family member you intend to give this craft to on the front or back of the flower.

As you collect these floral masterpieces, you'll see the unique ways each person interprets the prompt. These varied flowers reflect the diverse personalities and viewpoints in your family (or at least how they fare with a pencil).

If the artistic prowess of your relatives doesn't quite hit the mark, take the reins and add your own colors. This could add a harmonious uniformity to the bouquet that might have been missing. Once satisfied, cut out each flower and set them aside.

STEP 3

Cut out a 4 x 4–inch (10 x 10–cm) piece of tissue paper. Fold it in from each corner to the middle to create a shape reminiscent of a bouquet.

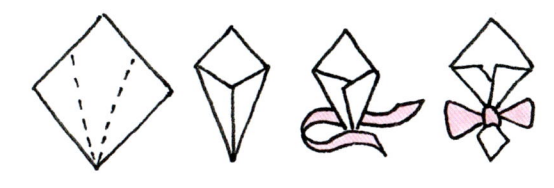

Tie it all together with a ribbon, fashioning a neat little bow and tuck the flowers inside to finish the bouquet. Present this bespoke floral ensemble to a family member of your choosing, or keep it as a personal token of familial love.

> **TIP:** And if your family dynamics are, well, a tad more complicated, feel free to use grays, blues and browns for your flowers. It's a subtle way to represent your feelings toward your family, indicating that your relationship isn't necessarily "blooming."

Family Is Forever (?)

You Were My Cocoon

♥💔♥💔♥💔♥💔♥💔♥💔♥💔♥💔♥💔♥💔♥💔♥💔♥💔

A butterfly symbolizes so many different things: rebirth, transformation, hope and much more. In many ways, we can compare the symbols of a butterfly to what our family represents as well. We all begin as little caterpillars and slowly transform into beautiful, full people. I like this gift idea because it represents the process of growing up within your childhood home, symbolized as the cocoon. The cocoon is meant to keep us safe and nourished as we begin our transformation from child to adult. Let's use these motifs to create the perfect gift for any family member who was particularly helpful during your transformation.

MATERIALS
Printer paper

White tissue paper

TOOLS
Pen or pencil

Ruler

Scissors

Coloring utensils (markers for me, duh!)

Glue (any kind)

STEP 1
Draw a butterfly on your printer paper with a 3-inch (7.5-cm) wingspan. You can use the project photo here as a reference or print out a template online. Color the butterfly whatever color or style you choose, but make sure the butterfly is fully colored on both sides. Cut it out and set it aside.

STEP 2
To make the cocoon, cut out a piece of paper measuring 5 x 5 inches (13 x 13 cm). Color the cocoon either green or brown on both sides and crumple it up just a tad to give it some texture. Take a corner and wrap the cocoon around itself, forming a tube-like shape in the middle, and secure it with glue. Squeeze the bottom of the cocoon together, fold it upwards and glue this cinched end to the base of the cocoon. Currently, the cocoon should act as a small tubular pocket. Cut a 5½ x 4-inch (14 x 10-cm) piece of white tissue paper and stuff it into the cocoon, focusing on filling out the sides. Curl up your butterfly drawing, place it inside the cocoon. Write your note on a 1 x 2-inch (2.5 x 5-cm) piece of paper. An adorable note that maintains the theme of the butterfly and cocoon duo is "You were my cocoon, keeping me safe and supporting me while I was growing into who I am today."

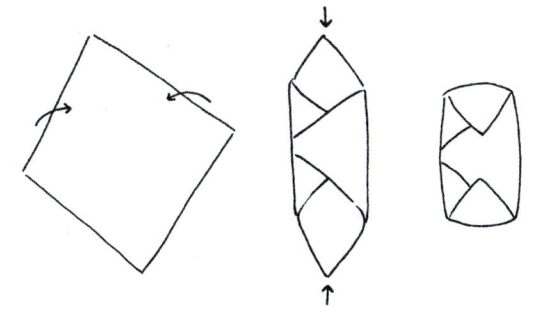

STEP 3
Curl up the note and place it inside the cocoon in between the butterfly wings. Finish this craft by cinching the top of the cocoon, folding it down and gluing it to the base just like the bottom. When it is gifted, they will be able to rip open the cocoon to reveal the butterfly and the corresponding note.

> **TIP:** With a slight change of wording, this is also a very sweet gift for a child in your family, such as a daughter, son, niece or nephew. Adjust the quote to read, "I love watching you grow into a beautiful butterfly," and gift away!

My Father's Wallet

♥💔♥💔♥💔♥💔♥💔♥💔♥💔♥💔♥💔♥💔♥💔♥💔

Wallets, in many ways, are symbolic of fatherhood. Much like a wallet, a father often holds the essential pieces of the family—providing security, identity and a sense of belonging. Fathers carry the weight of responsibility, protecting the family such as a wallet protects the valuable assets inside. While some may see wallets as a mere vessel used to store money, a wallet, just like a father, is much more complex in their purpose. A bad wallet, like a bad father, will spill the valuable assets, leaving us vulnerable and unequipped within the world. If you're searching for a heartfelt and special way to let your father or father figure know their value in your life, why not embark on the following craft?

MATERIALS

Heavyweight paper, such as bristol or watercolor paper

Clear plastic sheet

TOOLS

Ruler

Scissors

Coloring utensils (specifically browns and tans)

White charcoal (optional)

Water-based glue (I use Mod Podge) or white glue

Hot-glue gun and hot-glue sticks

STEP 1

To begin making our faux leather wallet, cut out the wallet's pieces, following each of the sizes listed in my illustration:

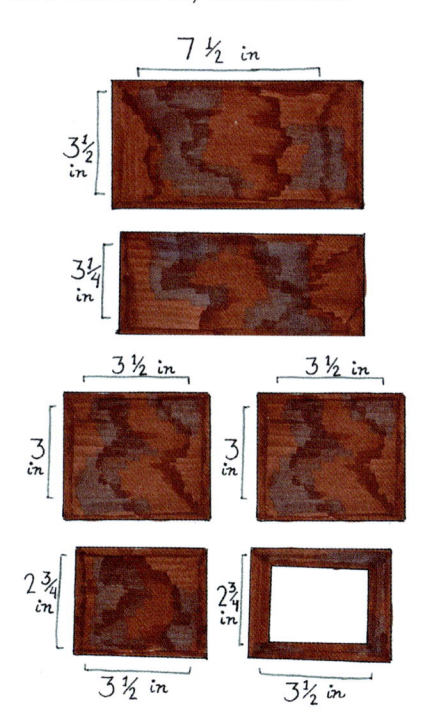

- 7 ½ in × 3 ½ in
- 7 ½ in × 3 ¼ in
- 3 ½ in × 3 in (×2)
- 3 ½ in × 2 ¾ in (×2, one with window cutout)

The key to achieving a leather-like appearance lies in the coloring phase. I recommend using a mix of browns, tans and a hint of white charcoal for that vintage, worn-in effect. While markers are a great choice, experimenting with watercolors or acrylic paints can also create interesting textures that will mimic the appearance of leather.

STEP 2

After you have colored the wallet, apply a layer of water-based glue to each piece for a shiny finish, reminiscent of polished leather. I highly recommend finishing the coloring and finishing process before assembling anything to ensure complete coverage and an overall more realistic appearance.

STEP 3

With your hot-glue gun on a low-heat setting, start constructing your wallet. Use the diagram to help you put everything together. You see the piece of wallet that has a square cutout? This will serve as the "wallet window." Cut out a "window" from the clear plastic sheet, and attach it to the piece with the square cutout. Carefully glue the smaller rectangles (at the very bottom of the diagram) onto the larger ones (just above them), focusing the adhesive on the edges to maintain the pockets' functionality.

Assemble the wallet by attaching one set of pockets to the second largest rectangle (second one from the top), placing the pocket at the bottom corner, either right or left. Repeat the process with the second set on the opposite side. Finally, attach the larger rectangle (the very top piece on the diagram) to the smaller one (just below it), again, applying glue only along the edges. You can now fold your wallet in half.

Your paper wallet, now complete, is a testament to your creativity and ingenuity. Fill it with personal notes or surprises like Dollar Bills (page 148), making it a thoughtful and unique gift.

Family Is Forever (?)

Dollar Bill

If you just finished My Father's Wallet (page 146) and you're poking around at what you could include inside, look no further. This craft is a sweet way to further symbolize your love and appreciation. A unique and playful addition is a special dollar bill, designed to emphasize that your love and appreciation are as valuable as any currency.

MATERIALS

Printer paper

Photo of father figure

TOOLS

Scissors

Coloring utensils

STEP 1

This part of the craft invites a touch of artistic flair. If you're confident in your drawing skills, you can create a customized dollar bill from scratch. For those who might want a bit of assistance, please feel free to work off of my own illustration. Feel free to scan it, print it out and then color it in to bring your creation to life.

To personalize this dollar bill, add a small photo of your father in place of George Washington. This whimsical touch transforms the bill into a fun and affectionate tribute, drawing a comparison to the Founding Fathers. For an extra dash of creativity and humor, draw a stylish George Washington–style wig onto the photograph. (If your dad is a history buff like mine, he will certainly get a kick out of this.) Color your dollar bill completely with a nice money green color and write, "In Dad We Trust" just above your father's picture.

STEP 2

Now crumple it up between your hands to mimic that worn dollar bill look. Unravel it and place it in My Father's Wallet (page 146).

Placing this customized dollar bill in the wallet you've created adds layers of meaning to your gift. It's a playful yet heartfelt reminder that while the material value of money is transient, the value of a father's love and guidance is priceless and ever-lasting.

NOTE: Or, if you do not see your father as a strong leader comparable to George Washington, there is a very simple way to turn this craft sour without much adjustment. Instead of, "In Dad We Trust," write, "You are Just a Wallet to Me." I'm not going to lie; it is very mean, but if that's how you feel about your father, I won't invalidate your feelings!

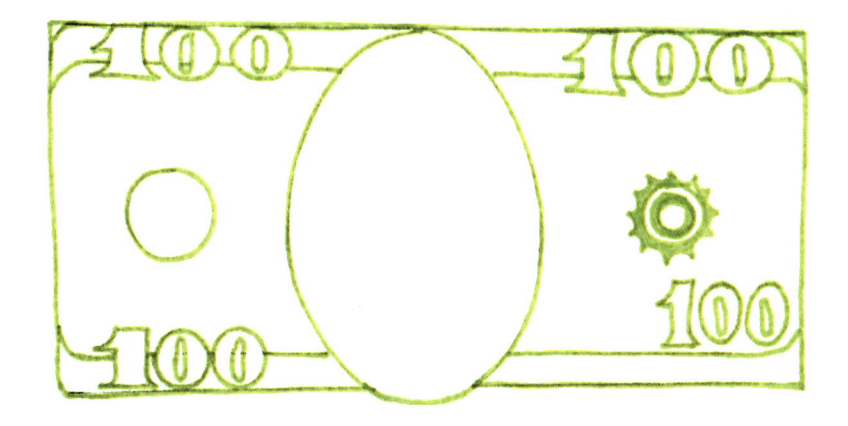

Family Is Forever (?)

Surprise Party in a Box

♡💔♡💔♡💔♡💔♡💔♡💔♡💔♡💔♡💔♡💔♡💔♡💔♡

As a self-diagnosed holiday lover, I love hosting surprise parties for my family. It's like giving a gift, but the gift is all of the people they care about celebrating them! The only problem is, just because you may be up for a party doesn't mean your giftee is quite so fond of sudden social obligations. So, if your family is more of the introverted type, but you still want to surprise them, then maybe opt for a surprise party in a box rather than a real social function.

MATERIALS

Cardboard

Cardstock

2 rubber bands

Skewer

Template (page 239)

Confetti, flowers or an additional present (optional)

Ribbon

TOOLS

Ruler

Scissors

Glue (any kind)

Packing tape

Coloring utensils

STEP 1

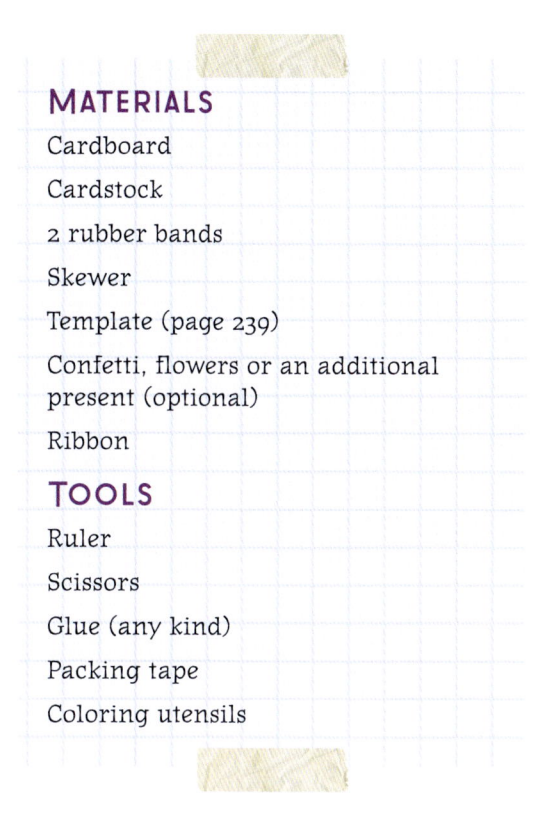

Let's make a box! Cut out five 6 x 6-inch (15 x 15-cm) cardboard squares. Now, let's give this cardboard a makeover by gluing on some cardstock.

Attach a piece of packing tape connecting the cardboard pieces to look something like this:

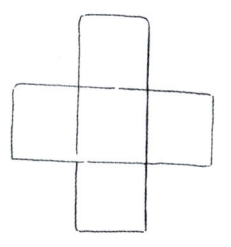

Only add tape to one side. When finished taping, do not flip over all five pieces and tape the other side, as this will affect its flexibility.

STEP 2

Now we need to find the center of each cardboard piece. To do this, take your ruler and draw two lines straight through the cardboard, connecting the opposite corners. Poke a hole through the center where the two lines meet for all the cardboard pieces except the one in the center.

Fit a rubber band through one of the holes we just created. I used a small ½-inch (1.3-cm) piece of skewer to keep the rubber band in place outside the box. Stretch out the rubber band, and pull it through the hole of the cardboard opposite to the one you originally put the rubber band through. Now do the same thing connecting the top to the bottom. Put your box aside.

STEP 3

To create a lid, cut out the template on page 239. Attach the tabs together to form a lid that is able to contain our creation. Paint or draw on the lid if you choose. Fill up the inside of the box with either flowers, confetti or a special present for your family.

> **TIP:** This is a perfect time to add a second craft from this book to fit inside!

Now, carefully twist your box so that the rubber bands are extended on the exterior of the box. Remember how we only added tape on one side? That allows the creases of each cardboard piece to be flexible. This means you can quite literally flip the box so the inside walls are on the outside. Just make sure you put the lid on once you do! Wrap everything up with a ribbon and gift it! The ribbon adds an element that makes this seem like a normal gift, but once you take off the lid, the box will extend past its walls, pop up and reverse—shaking out all the confetti and popping up the hidden treats within it.

It's Been a Bumpy Road

♥💔♥💔♥💔♥💔♥💔♥💔♥💔♥💔♥💔♥💔♥💔♥💔♥💔♥

This craft is dedicated to family because God knows those are some of the most complicated relationships in our lives. But ultimately, they are also the most enduring to any roadblocks we cross along the way.

MATERIALS

Heavyweight paper

TOOLS

Coloring utensils

Scissors

Ruler

Pen or pencil

Hot-glue gun and hot-glue sticks

Protractor

STEP 1

Start by drawing a car on a sheet of heavyweight paper. If you're no Van Gogh, either try to recreate this illustration of mine or print one from the internet and trace it onto your heavyweight paper. Color your car, adding all the little details like doors, windows, lights, etc. Cut out your car once you like the way it is colored and designed.

STEP 2

Start by cutting out two pieces of heavyweight paper each measuring 9 x 4½ inches (23 x 11.5 cm). For the road, draw a squiggly pattern on one piece of paper, making sure the width of the road measures no bigger than ¾ inch (2 cm) wide and no smaller than ½ inch (1.3 cm) wide. Cut out your road and place this sheet of paper directly over its twin. Use a pencil to sketch out where the road will be exposed on this base piece of paper and color it to look like a typical road or highway. Set the colored sheet of paper aside for now.

On a separate sheet of paper, cut out a circle with at least a 1½-inch (4-cm) diameter. Flip over your car, line up the cutout road in the general middle area of the car and add a little dollop of hot glue on the car through the road's cutout, making sure it doesn't get on the road paper whatsoever. Attach the circle. Now that the car is secured to the circle you are able to move it up and down through the swirly road.

STEP 3

Use the colored sheet of 9 x 4½-inch (23 x 11.5-cm) paper and secure it to the back of the piece with the road cut out. Add glue along the edges, avoiding adding glue near the "road."

On your road paper, write, "It's been a bumpy road, but I wouldn't want to do it with anyone else." Or, if you have a little more vengeance toward your family, erase the positivity and simply write, "It's been a bumpy road with you and now we're at the end of the line."

Now, leave it with your family or a specific family member to let them know that any adverse situations you've gone through together do not affect the love you have for them. (Unless, of course, they do. LOL.)

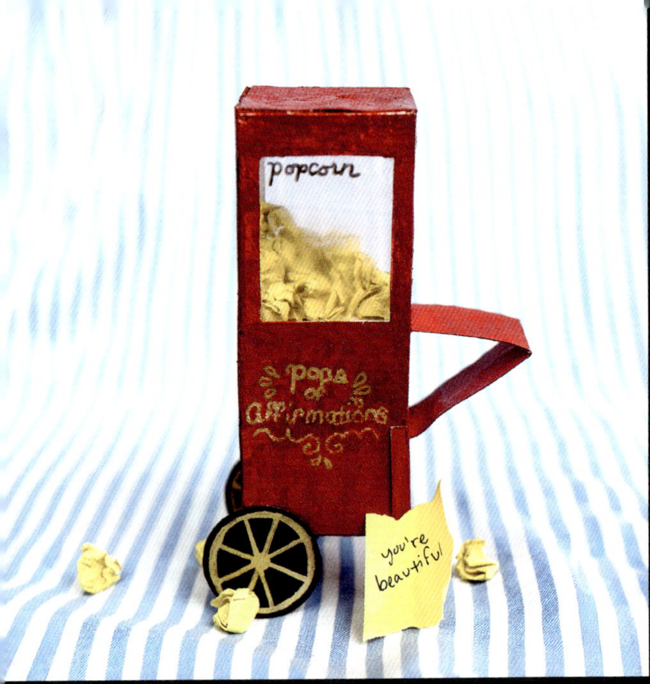
popcorn
Pops of Affirmations
you're beautiful

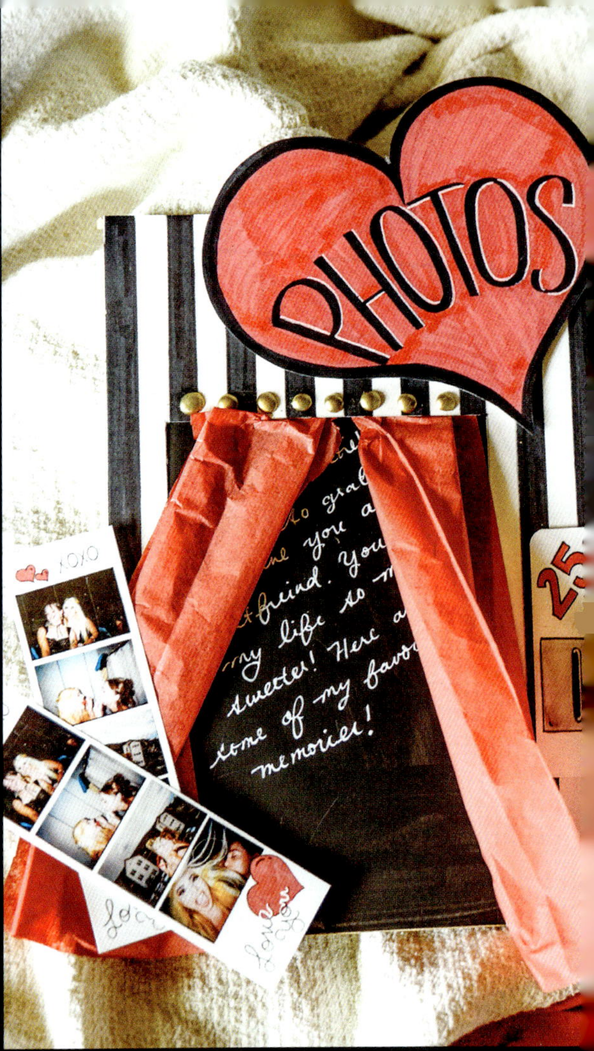
PHOTOS
XOXO

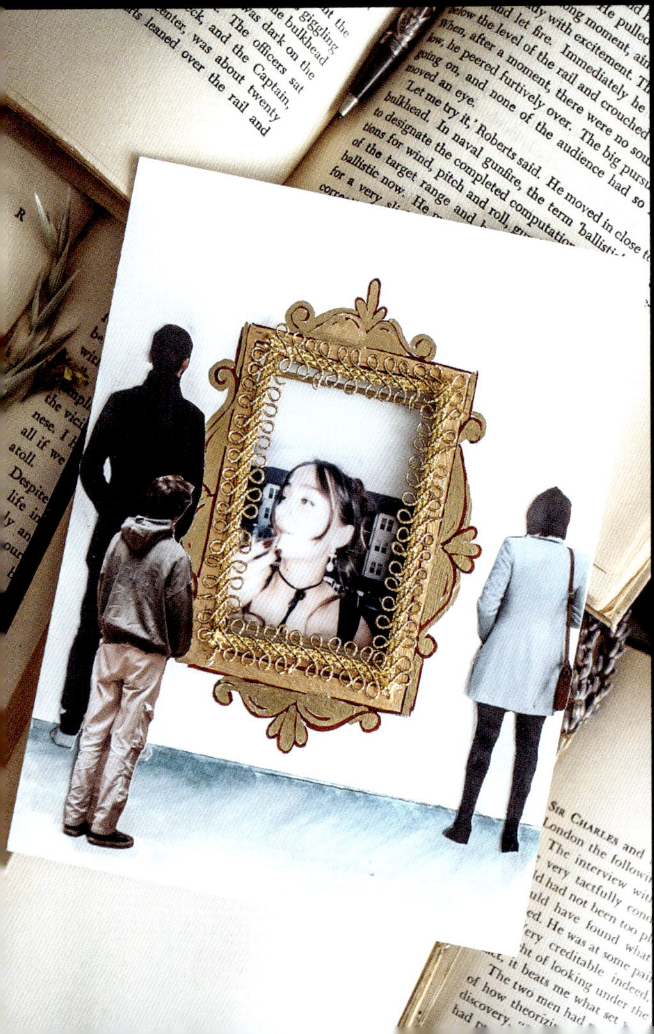

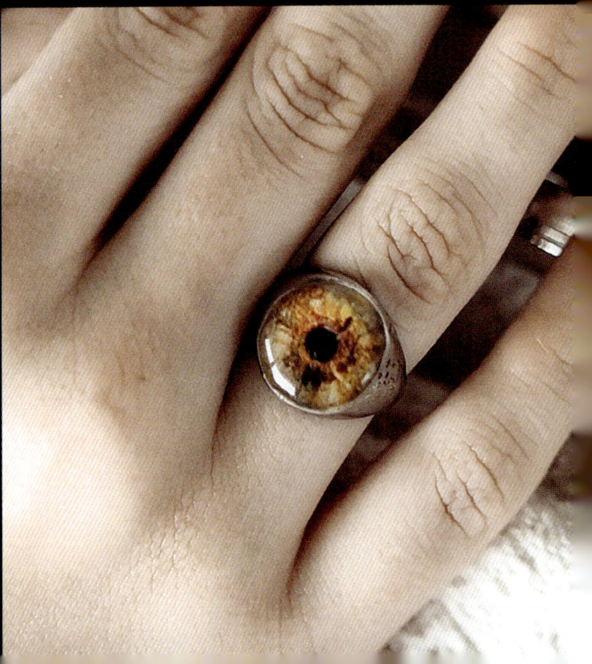

For Your *BFFs* or Your Frenemies

While romantic relationships hit you with an intense feeling of adoration and love, don't forget it's the besties that really need the extra appreciation! Our friendships are the basis of who we are, and who we have become, especially through their companionship, their (sometimes shitty) advice and our late hungover mornings. Our friends love us without condition, and I highly recommend fostering these relationships in all the special ways that you can—such as the ideas I outline in this chapter.

The great thing about besties is there's a much greater chance they will keep your little tokens of appreciation for the long term because there is no messy breakup coming your way. (And if there is a messy breakup, at least we have the crafts in this chapter for them too!)

For the Record, You're My Best Friend

Record players have made quite the comeback in recent years, with all different artists creating their own vinyl records. Just like there was back in the '50s. Whenever I can add a little bit of nostalgia to a gift, I take that opportunity and run with it. In this case, we are going to make a miniature version of a record sleeve.

MATERIALS

Heavyweight paper

1¾" x 1¾" (4.5 x 4.5-cm) photo of you and your bestie

TOOLS

Ruler

Scissors

Glue stick

Protractor

Coloring utensils

Pen or marker

STEP 1

To kickstart your very own miniature record sleeve, cut out a 3½ x 1¾-inch (9 x 4.5-cm) rectangle out of heavyweight paper. Additionally, we need a second rectangle that measures 1¾ x 1½ inches (4.5 x 4 cm), but with additional ¼-inch (6-mm) tabs on three sides. These tabs will help you create a pocket to hold the record. Refer to the illustrations I made for you to assist you in this process.

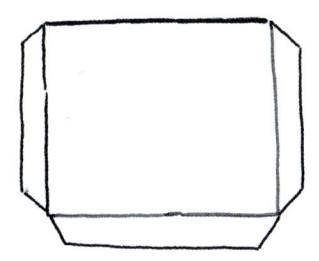

Crease each of the tabs on the smaller rectangle. We also need to fold the larger rectangle in half completely. Create a crease in the center while holding it horizontally at the 1¾-inch (4.5-cm) mark.

Crease each edge of the smaller rectangle and fold it down the middle longways. Once both your papers are neatly creased, place the square with the tabs on one side of the larger rectangle. Fold the tab over the rectangle and secure it with your glue stick. Allow the tabs to dry, and you'll have a tiny pocket ready to accommodate your record.

STEP 2

To create the record, create a ¾-inch (2-cm) circle with your protractor. This size allows it to fit snugly within the pocket while leaving enough of the record poking out for easy access. Color the circle to resemble a real record. I used white, gray and black to recreate the highlights that a genuine record would have. Just be sure to leave a small white circle in the middle. Refer to my doodle for some extra guidance.

Complete this on both sides of the record and let it dry. Now, returning to your sleeve, you have plenty of creative freedom. Record sleeves come in various colors and designs. I chose to make mine look like cardboard (boring, I know, but I was aiming for realism). However, you can opt for a more vibrant design or even print out a real album cover if you prefer.

STEP 3

Fold the rectangle back onto itself on the side where the tabs are hidden; this will serve as our front cover. On the cover, write, "For the Record . . ." Over the pocket on the inside, write, "You're My Best Friend." On the left side, apply a bit of glue and attach the picture of you and your best friend.

And there you have it, a nifty little craft that's as cool as a vintage vinyl record. What makes this craft special? Well, it's got a sentimental touch with that personal picture, and it's not just a tiny masterpiece—it's a heartfelt keepsake that can fit right into your wallet or wherever you fancy. It's like a little secret between you and your bestie—a reminder of the fantastic bond you share.

TIP: Now if your "bestie" is more of an annoying frenemy, then you can use a particularly unflattering picture of said person, scratch out their eyes or draw silly faces over their face. On the cover, write, "You're as annoying as . . ." and write, "A broken record" on the inside pocket.

Paper Dolls

The memories we share with our besties are unparalleled. Some of the best moments I can recall are simply going over to each other's houses and sharing memes with each other, or maybe a specific time when we went on a trip together. Either way, commemorating these memories and special moments deepens my bond with my besties and makes me eager to create more. So, for this craft, we are going to celebrate these moments with a truly personal whimsical gift: paper dolls.

Paper dolls may seem pretty juvenile, and I mean technically they are made for and by children, so by definition of course they are. But they are also the perfect medium to dive directly back into a memory in a way that is much more engaging than a simple photograph. So let's recreate our favorite moments and memories in the most nostalgic way possible.

MATERIALS

Templates (pages 239–241)

Heavyweight paper, such as a cardstock or watercolor paper

TOOLS

Pen or pencil

Coloring utensils

Scissors

Double-sided tape

Glue (any kind)

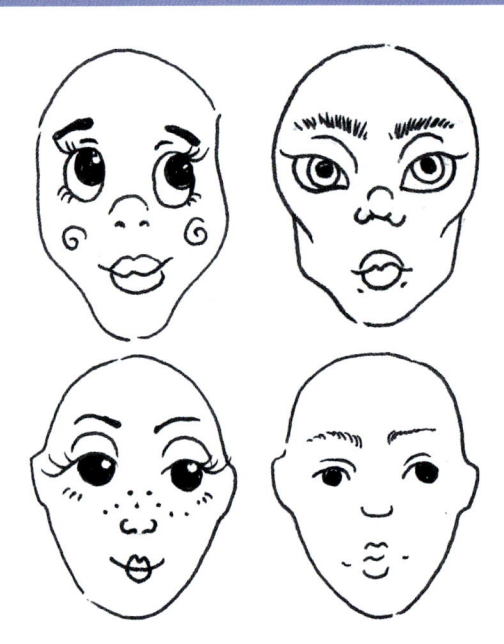

STEP 1

Let's start with the dolls. We want each doll to not only resemble the physical likeness but the essence of you and your bestie. Begin by brainstorming what exactly you and your bestie exude into the world. Are you a goth while your bestie is an artsy hippie? Look through your closet and find what aesthetic you feel would most fit your paper doll.

Now onto the doll creation. We are going to draw the dolls using a template we can build on. Go to pages 239 and 241 to find some fresh bases to start your dolls off with. Of course you should customize your dolls to you and your bestie's ethnicity and physical attributes. Keep in mind that we are not trying to make it realistic; just be sure to choose features that you personally identify with the most!

STEP 2

Once the base, hair and face of each doll are drawn and colored, carefully cut them out. To allow the dolls to stand up on their own, cut out the additional rectangle on page 239. Cut along the designated slit and fasten your paper dolls inside this crease. Now, trace the bodies on more heavyweight paper to create a base for clothing. Think of you and your bestie's favorite outfits. Look through your camera roll if need be. Always keep in mind the overall aesthetic you are hoping to exude through each of the dolls.

Once you have made a few different outfits for each of the dolls, as well as colored and cut them out, add a small piece of double-sided tape to the back of each of them. Double-sided tape is strong enough to allow the clothing pieces to stick onto the figures but loose enough that we can remove it easily when we want to exchange outfits. Put your dolls and corresponding outfits aside for now, because now we are going to recreate your home bases.

By home bases, I mean places where you two go together. This could be either of your bedrooms, your favorite coffee shop or a favorite teacher's classroom—anywhere you guys spend a lot of time catching up. Since my bestie and I used to be roommates in college, I made our old college dorm my home base.

STEP 3

Cut a piece of 8 x 14–inch (20 x 36–cm) heavyweight paper. Fold it in half so one half is your floor and the other a wall. Using some more heavyweight paper, cut out a large triangle and fold it in half. Glue the folded half of the triangle to the back of the wall near the center to allow the wall to stand on its own.

Take out a photo reference to recreate your chosen scenery to the best of your ability. I realize that we all have different skill levels, but feel free to opt out of any unnecessary details such as wall decor, light fixtures, furniture, etc. that you do not think you will be able to recreate very well. Simply draw the floor, the wall and a window if you must.

Now this is where you can really hone in on your special relationship. Do you constantly laugh at the same meme or have the same catchphrase? Are you both obsessed with cats, or do you both love to play guitar? Whatever the thing is that makes your relationship special, draw it.

This could be a speech bubble or a tiny phone with your favorite meme. Try to draw as many of these friendship references as you can and put them in the room using a small bit of double-sided tape. Set up you and your bestie's dolls in the room and give it to them. When you gift it, make sure they know how special all the little moments you have with them are.

Pops of Affirmation

♥ 💔 ♥ 💔 ♥ 💔 ♥ 💔 ♥ 💔 ♥ 💔 ♥ 💔 ♥ 💔 ♥ 💔 ♥ 💔 ♥ 💔

When I think of a girls' night, I envision popcorn and an ice cream sundae, all of us gathered around to watch a movie while we keep each other up laughing and talking through the whole film. Yes, my perfect girls' night out is pretty much the same as a typical middle-school slumber party, and I have no shame about that. So, if you're thinking of a way to show some appreciation to your bestie, doing so with a little bit of popcorn and craftiness can never go wrong. For this craft, we are going to sneak in little notes of affirmation in a handcrafted popcorn cart.

MATERIALS

Templates (pages 241–243)

Clear flat plastic

Yellow construction paper

TOOLS

Scissors

Craft knife (I use X-Acto)

Hot-glue gun and hot-glue sticks

Coloring utensils

Paint

Paintbrushes

Ruler

STEP 1

Cut out the base template on page 243. Now you'll begin the base. Cut your clear plastic for each of the windows, and use a little bit of glue to adhere them to the outer edges of the frames to conceal the gaps within the template.

With the plastic glued in place, flip over the template and paint the entire sheet of paper red. This is your opportunity to add any popcorn-themed text or logos. I opted to write, "popcorn" directly over the window as well as, "Pops of Affirmations" just so my bestie knows what she's in for.

STEP 2

Cut out the inner square on page 243. Fold each of the tabs down and glue it along the dotted line on the base template. Fold the base around the square and finish the base off by gluing the tab on the side of the base template. Glue the bottom of the base, but simply fold the top and secure it inside the box. (Your bestie needs a way to open this craft after all.)

STEP 3

Cut out both of the legs as well as the wheels on page 241. Paint the legs to match the rest of the base and color the wheels. Fold the legs and secure them to two adjacent corners on the bottom of the base, leaving part of the legs extended past the base. Glue the wheels extending the same amount as well.

Cut out the handle template on page 243, color it to match the base, fold it along the fold lines and attach it to the front of the popcorn maker just below the window on the opposite side of the wheels. Make sure you glue each of the tabs to the base template so the handle sticks out.

STEP 4

Now, it's time to fill your popcorn cart with little notes of affirmation. Cut small squares of yellow construction paper and write your notes. Crumple the notes to look like popcorn. Place these notes within the popcorn maker, close the top and you're ready to deliver this delightful surprise to your bestie.

For Your BFFs or Your Frenemies

I'm Always Watching You (Eye Ring)

So, you've already tried your hand at making the Friendship Bracelets (page 167) and crafted the adorable Paper Dolls (page 158), but now you're yearning for something more distinctive. After all, your best friend deserves something truly special. But what could it be?

Well, here's a quirky idea—why not wear their eye? Yes, you read that correctly. Not literally of course, but a personalized and intimate piece of jewelry that symbolizes their essence. It's a bit unusual, perhaps even a tad creepy, but also undeniably intriguing. This eye-catching accessory adds a touch of edge, mystery and maybe even a hint of danger to your outfit, all while paying homage to your bestie. If you're thinking, "Friendship bracelets? Been there, done that," but still want to cherish that sentiment, this craft is here to take things up a notch.

MATERIALS

Shrink plastic or #6 plastic

High-resolution photo of your bestie's eye

TOOLS

Rounded wooden dowel

Heat gun

Superglue

Color printer or excellent painting skills

UV resin or gel nail polish top coat

STEP 1

We are going to start with shrink plastic. For the uninitiated, flip back to Shrink Plastic to Grow Love (page 32) for a quick refresher.

With a rounded dowel that matches the size of your finger (for example, I'm using a dowel with a diameter of 22 millimeters), cut out the plastic in a shape similar to the one depicted below as well as a simple circle.

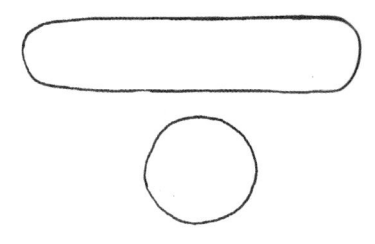

Feel free to adjust the band's thickness, keeping in mind that it will shrink during the process.

Place your dowel next to the first shape of plastic you're going to shrink. Start heating the plastic with your heat gun. The ring will twist and wiggle as it shrinks, but use the dowel to guide it into a curve, eventually wrapping the entire ring around the dowel.

STEP 2

Once the ring has shrunk to fit snugly onto the dowel, carefully remove it and put it to the side. Now heat the circular piece separately, leaving it flat. Glue the flat piece to the center of the curved piece with superglue. Since shrink plastic can vary slightly in size, measure the circle from one side to the other to determine its diameter; we'll need this measurement later.

With your friend's help, take an *eye-catching* picture. And by that, I mean take a high-resolution photo of their eye, capturing the entire iris and pupil. You might need to gently open the eye for the photo, ensuring you capture the iris' intricate details. Avoid harsh highlights on the iris for the best results.

STEP 3

Once you have a suitable photo, print it out, or if your artistic skills are up there, you can try your hand at painting their eye as well. Just be sure that the eye measures the same as the shrink plastic circle you created. Printing it to the correct size may take some trial and error to get the scale just right. Cut out the iris and pupil from the printed photo and use superglue to affix it to the circle. Apply a thick coat of UV resin. UV resin is similar to a gel nail polish top coat, so use what you have available and apply it generously over the eye. Due to its thickness, the UV resin (or top coat) will form a dome shape on top of the photograph, creating a rounded shape that mimics the natural curvature of the eye.

Enjoy your one-of-a-kind friendship ring—a piece of personalized jewelry that lets everyone know that your friendship is truly a *sight* to behold!

TIPS

- ♥ To really celebrate your bestie, consider creating two rings: one with your own eye and one with your bestie's eye. That way, you'll know you and your bestie are always looking out for each other (literally).

- ♥ If this craft seems a little too complicated, and you'd rather not make your own ring from the ground up, you can forgo the ring-making process and purchase a "blank" ring and continue on from there.

You're a Work of Art

♥💔♥💔♥💔♥💔♥💔♥💔♥💔♥💔♥💔♥💔♥💔♥💔

Of course, when the idea of a gift comes to mind, you may consider a card as a staple for birthdays or holidays. It's easy enough to write a heartfelt message within the confines of a card. But a card does not have to simply be a place to house your feelings. Instead, the design of the card itself can easily say more than 100 words. With a little tinkering with a piece of paper, we can say all we'll ever need to say. For this craft, I am comparing my bestie to a glorious piece of artwork, because I know more than anyone that they should be cherished as such.

MATERIALS

Heavyweight paper

Photo of your bestie

Gold paper trim (optional)

TOOLS

Pen or pencil

Scissors or craft knife (I use X-Acto)

Camera or smartphone

Printer

White glue

Coloring utensils

STEP 1

To make the base of your card, fold a piece of 8 x 11-inch (22 x 28-cm) heavyweight paper cleanly in half.

To create your homemade art gallery, start with a picture you absolutely love of your bestie or a special picture featuring both of you. If you have any Polaroids, set them aside because they work great for this craft, but you can also print out a picture that measures 2¼ x 1¾ inches (6 x 4.5 cm) if you choose. Trace this picture on the front cover. Use the tracing as a guide to cut through the paper, revealing the inside of the card through the cutout.

STEP 2

Next, for the backdrop, find a white background and take a photo of yourself with your back to the camera, slightly glancing to the right or left. You can also search the internet for pictures of people at a similar angle admiring artwork. Once you have a few of these photos, cut out the background, leaving only you. Ensure that each person measures approximately 4 x 1 inches (10 x 2.5 cm). Arrange and then glue all these images around the cutout of the card. If you want, you can also add a horizon line below the cutout to indicate that these people are in fact standing on the floor rather than floating in midair.

Now, let's design a frame. You can keep it simple using coloring materials, or if you're feeling a bit extra like me, use gold trim to create an elegant border around the cutout, resembling an antique frame.

(continued)

STEP 3

With the cover now finished, complete with the frame around the cutout and all of the onlookers, open up the inside of the card and place the photograph of your bestie inside, aligning it with the cutout on the outside. Glue it down. Directly below the photo, add a small rectangle, which will act as the artwork's title. Inside this rectangle is your chance to describe your bestie in one word. Here are some examples of words you can use as the title:

- ♥ Masterpiece
- ♥ Perfection
- ♥ Grace
- ♥ The Best
- ♥ My Best Friend
- ♥ LOML ("love of my life" for any boomers reading)

You can give this to your bestie as is, but if you want to fill up the inside just a tad more, feel free to use more photographs of the two of you, and assemble them to either side of the original photo. Add a note if you are feeling so inclined, and you are ready to gift!

When this craft is complete, it should look like your friend's picture is in a popular art gallery with onlookers adoring their beauty. It's a perfect gift for any occasion but especially if your bestie is feeling down and needs some help building their confidence. Sometimes our duty as a friend is to let them know how amazing they really are, even when they don't feel it themselves!

Friendship Bracelets

Ah, friendship bracelets. They're like the middle-school badge of honor for besties. But why buy one when you can make one yourself? Make one for your best friend, for yourself or even make a couple for each other! And the best part about making them from scratch is you'll know that the bracelets are as unique as your friendship.

MATERIALS
Printer paper

Ribbon or string

TOOLS
Scissors

Water-based glue (I use Mod Podge)

Water

Skewer

Coloring utensils

Nail polish or paint

STEP 1
There are two main bead shapes to keep in mind when brainstorming your friendship bracelet: Tubular and rounded.

To make the tubular-shaped beads, cut out several long strips of printer paper measuring 8½ x ½ inches (22 x 1.3 cm). Dunk a paper strip in a 1:1 ratio of water-based glue to water concoction. Wrap the entire strip around your skewer. Wait until the paper is dry, and shimmy it off of the skewer while preserving the tubular shape. Repeat until you've used up all your paper strips.

To make circular beads, cut out several 8½-inch (22-cm) strips of paper that start off ½ inch (1.3 cm) thick, but get thinner and thinner until you reach a point at the other end. Soak your bead in the glue/water concoction and, starting with the thicker end, wrap it around your skewer. Carefully roll the rest of the paper strip around itself until the paper begins to form a bulbous shape. Once it's dry, carefully take it off the skewer. Continue with the rest of your strips.

STEP 2
To color your newly crafted beads, you have two options: You can either color the paper strips with watercolors, markers, colored pencils or whatever you've got on hand, or wait until the beads are totally dry and paint them with acrylic paint, nail polish or even leftover wall paint. Pull the ribbon through the beads, and once you are happy with your creation, tie it off. You have just created your very own friendship bracelet.

For Your BFFs or Your Frenemies

Faux Photobooth Pictures

♥💔♥💔♥💔♥💔♥💔♥💔♥💔♥💔♥💔♥💔♥💔♥💔♥💔

Nothing screams '90s teen movie like cramming into a photobooth with your bestie. But let's face it, spending $10 for a strip of photos feels like daylight robbery, especially when you've already snapped a hundred selfies that day. Fear not, frugal friends, because we're about to DIY our way into photobooth nostalgia—without the outrageous price tag.

MATERIALS
Photo paper

Printer paper

TOOLS
Image software

Color printer

Scissors

Ruler

Glue

Markers

Scanner

STEP 1
First off, embark on a photo-taking spree with your BFF. Channel your inner model and strike those photobooth-worthy poses—the quirkier, the better. Make sure the shots are from head to shoulder, and don't forget the mandatory flash for that authentic photobooth feel. Once you've captured the essence of your friendship in digital form, crank up the exposure and contrast just a smidge to get that 30-year-old camera look.

Next, upload and print around four to six of those beauties, each measuring 1¼ x 1½ inches (3 x 4 cm). You may have to cut or crop the pictures so they fit within that measurement. Print them on your color printer using the photo paper for best results.

STEP 2
Cut a 6½ x 2-inch (17 x 5-cm) strip of printer paper. Organize your printed photos on this strip, leaving a bit of margin at the top and bottom, and glue the images down. Now, get creative and design your own header for the strip.

Here are a few ideas to get you started:

After you're done assembling and designing the images, scan them and print them out on photo paper. Make sure you print at least two so you can give one to your bestie! Cut them into the same strips as before, and find the perfect place to keep them. Whether it's in your wallet or on your wall, these DIY strips are a reminder of good times with your favorite person. And if you want to get even more extra with this craft, pair this gift with the Faux Photobooth (page 170).

Faux Photobooth

If you're looking for a way to make your Faux Photobooth Pictures (page 168) come even more to life, then maybe consider pairing them with an actual photobooth. Okay chill, I don't mean an actual real photobooth. I couldn't even imagine how much one of those things would cost even though now I'm kinda tempted to see if I could buy one. I mean, what a cool party trick? Okay, I'm getting off track. Let me show you how to make a little photobooth out of paper that will perfectly house your real or faux photobooth pics.

MATERIALS

Heavyweight paper

Photos (optional)

Cardboard (optional, see tip on page 172)

Tissue paper

TOOLS

Ruler

Scissors

Pencil

Coloring utensils

Hot-glue gun and hot-glue sticks

Gold marker (optional)

Design it however you want it to look, but here are some of my illustrations to help you get your creative gears turning:

STEP 1

Cut out a 9 x 12-inch (23 x 30-cm) piece of heavyweight paper. Now, cut a rectangle out of this paper, leaving 1 inch (2.5 cm) on the left side of the paper, 2½ inches (6.5 cm) on the right, and 3½ inches (9 cm) on the top. So, that's an 8½ x 5½-inch (22 x 14-cm) rectangle that extends all the way down to the bottom of the paper. Leave the extra rectangle aside for now. Color the rectangle whatever color you want (I opted for pinstripes) and set it aside.

Cut out a 4 x 1½-inch (10 x 4-cm) rectangle out of your remaining scrap paper for the coin slot.

Glue this rectangle to the right border next to your rectangular cutout.

STEP 2

Now it's time for your sign. You can really get as crazy as you would like with this signage. To create those faux Hollywood lights, add little dollops of hot glue surrounding the sign, wait until they dry and go in with a gold marker to make them pop. If you're struggling on a signage design, do not fret; here are some photobooth signs I created that you can either copy or draw from to create your own version. It can really be as big or small as you would like, depending on your preference—mine extends past the top of the photobooth to give it more dimension.

(continued)

When you like the look of your sign, glue it directly onto your heavyweight paper at the center top of the page.

STEP 3

Once everything is glued down to the rectangle, flip it over. Cut out a 10 x 10–inch (25 x 25–cm) piece of tissue paper, and hot glue it to the top of the opening, covering the exposed rectangle. Cut off any excess that extends past the paper. I also decided to cut mine down the middle so it would open like curtains, but that is totally up to you.

Cut out another 9 x 12–inch (23 x 30–cm) piece of heavyweight paper. You can keep this paper white or paint it any color that matches the aesthetic of your photobooth. I chose to paint mine black to match mine. Place glue along the outer margins of the paper, avoiding the center area. Fasten this paper painted side down to the back of the photobooth and let the glue dry. Once everything is connected, write a note to your bestie within the cutout rectangle. Write about how grateful you are to have them in your life or how much they inspire you. Once you have finished writing your note, jam your photobooth pictures in between the two sheets of paper up through the rectangle, and cover them with the sheet of tissue paper. Give this to your bestie, reminding them that every memory you have with them is precious and worth commemorating!

TIP: If you want your photobooth to be a little more substantial than any old card, add a layer of cardboard behind your second sheet of paper. It will make the entire craft feel more heavyweight and expensive.

Lil' Heart Book

For this craft, I am inspired by all of the heart-shaped goodies that people in relationships get to give and receive, and honestly, I'm a little jealous. Why can't we also give these heartfelt cheesy gifts to the ones we love platonically? So this craft's purpose is to combat this and show some extra love to a bestie who may need it. (But c'mon, when is it a bad time to give your bestie a homemade gift made with love?)

MATERIALS

Printer paper

Printed pictures of you and your bestie (optional)

Cardboard

Ribbon

TOOLS

Scissors

Drawing supplies

Pen or marker

Paint

Paintbrushes

Decorative supplies

Glue

STEP 1

Cut an 11 x 2-inch (28 x 5-cm) piece of printer paper. Go ahead, pretend you're back in kindergarten! Fold it in half, and then fold the extended section to the center crease. Do the hokey-pokey and fold it again on the reverse side. Now, fold the entire thing in half (yes, one more time). On the creased side, draw half a heart that is large enough to fit the entire folded section, making sure to leave a small portion of the half heart extended to touch both ends of this folded section.

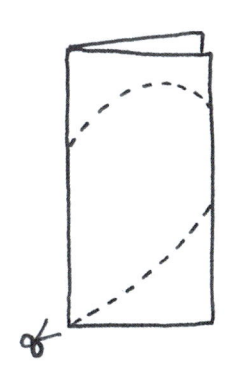

(continued)

For Your BFFs or Your Frenemies - 173

Once the half heart is drawn, take your scissors and cut out the heart. Remember not to completely separate either side from the fold. Unravel your masterpiece and behold—the paper chain of hearts!

Inside each of these hearts, write either affirmations about your bestie, draw pictures or include teeny tiny pictures with the two of you. If you do decide to include pictures, make sure you cut them down to match the shape and size of your hearts.

STEP 2
Now let's create the hardcover for these hearts to make it like a mini book. Trace one of the hearts onto two pieces of cardboard and cut them out. Paint these little pieces of cardboard or decorate them however you like! I painted them red and added pearl beading to the outside edges because it's cute, duh, and to cover up the ugly cardboard cross section.

STEP 3
Glue thin 3½-inch (9-cm)-long ribbons on each side of the cardboard hearts. Glue the last heart on the left and right end of the paper heart chain to each cardboard cover, creating a sort of hardcover end to the chain of hearts. Fold the chain of hearts back into itself and tie the ribbons to the opposite cardboard cover to keep it together. Now your heart chain is the keeper of cherished memories!

When the ribbon is unraveled, pictures of all of you and your bestie's favorite memories come spilling out! Perfect to cheer them up when they're going through a hard time or for Galentine's Day!

You're My Rock

Want the easiest way ever to make your bestie's day? Seriously, no more excuses about not being crafty enough. Showing your BFF some love has never been simpler, and let's face it, we're all about easy wins. If your bestie is always there for you, then take five minutes out of your day and let them know. You never know—this could be the difference between a bad day and making their day ROCK.

MATERIALS
1 rock

TOOLS
Acrylic markers

TIP: And if you want to give this project to an enemy, simply change the wording around a little bit. "You're as dumb as a rock" will do just fine.

STEP 1
Grab a rock, preferably a river rock to make it a nice, smooth canvas. With your acrylic markers, boldly proclaim, "You're My Rock." It's punny, it's cute and it's way cheaper than a Hallmark® card. Go wild decorating the rest of the rock with whatever your artsy heart desires, be it swirls, polka dots, hearts, you name it.

Hand this little gem over to your bestie and watch as their day instantly gets a little better. It's the small things, right? Because sometimes all we really want is for someone to let us know that we are loved. Not to mention that if they're the type who treasures gifts, this rock's going to turn into a cherished keepsake. So, there you have it: a rock-solid way to show some love.

Friend-Chips

Some friends are extra-special. They're the ones who stick with you through thick and thin, share unforgettable memories and, most crucially, endure your absolutely HORRENDOUS puns. This is no different, as we will be making a pun so painful that you can't even help but laugh. So let's dive into this gift for a truly special friend-chip.

MATERIALS
Printer paper

Clear plastic bag

Red glitter (optional)

TOOLS
Ruler

Scissors

Markers and colored pencils

Glue stick or double-sided tape

STEP 1
First things first—let's make a bunch of chips. Cut out 20 or more 3 x 3 x 2½-inch (7.5 x 7.5 x 6.5-cm) triangles from the printer paper. Don't be too concerned with straight lines and perfect edges. To capture that iconic chip color, blend orange and yellow markers, and then use your colored pencil to add that powder finish, just like the real thing. Once colored, give each chip a gentle scrunch. We're aiming for texture and imperfections here—no perfect triangles allowed! Once your chips are colored and crinkled, write a small affirmation to your bestie using the colored pencils we used earlier—just press down a tad harder so it is visible. These affirmations can be full-out letters or a simple "I <3 u." Set these aside.

STEP 2

Next up, the bag. Cut out a 10 x 5½-inch (25 x 14-cm) piece of printer paper. Divide it horizontally into three equal sections. In the middle section, unleash your inner artist to create the chip packaging design. Here are a few drawings for inspiration, but if you want to create your own drawing just be sure to include "Friend-Chips" somewhere in your design.

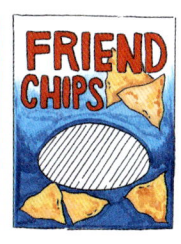

Notice the gray area with crosshatching in my drawings? Leave that part out of your drawing and instead cut out this section. Flip the paper over to the side without your drawing and adhere your plastic film to this cutout area. You can repurpose various materials for this—a clear plastic bag, paper protectors or even cling wrap. As long as it's clear and flexible, it's perfect. Remember, recycling is cool! (I sound like a children's infomercial; how did I get to this point?)

TIP: If you want to add some extra realism, cut a chevron pattern on the edges of the chip bag with some patterned scissors or by patiently snipping it in with regular scissors.

With the paper still flipped over, lay it out horizontally and mark the center of your paper. Bring both the left and right end together at this center point and glue the ends together. Feel free to overlap the sides in order to adhere them properly—we do not want them to stick to the inside paper. To create a proper pocket to house the chips, add glue or tape to the bottom of the inside of the tube and hold it together until the glue dries.

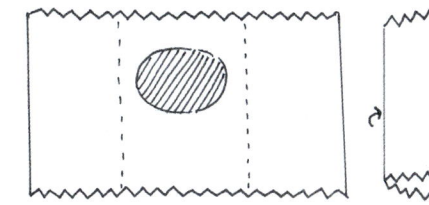

STEP 3

Now you can go ahead and place all of your chips inside the bag. If you want to be extra annoying, which I always recommend being, add a whole lotta red glitter directly inside the bag. Once all of the chips (and glitter) are inside your bag, tape or glue the top of your bag to enclose it all.

Go ahead and give it to your friend. If they decide to open up the bag, their hands will be covered in a cheeky "chip dust" that will undoubtedly haunt them for months to come, reminding them of your super-special friendship along the way.

For Your BFFs or Your Frenemies

Friends Are like Stars

♥ 💔 ♥ 💔 ♥ 💔 ♥ 💔 ♥ 💔 ♥ 💔 ♥ 💔 ♥ 💔 ♥ 💔 ♥ 💔 ♥ 💔

As we navigate through the different stages of life, our friends often become an integral part of our journey. But, let's face it: Growing up means sometimes we can't keep up with everyone like we used to. It's a bit sad, sure, but totally normal. What makes these friendships truly special, though, is knowing that they're like your personal emergency service—always there when you really need them, no questions asked.

To show these stellar friends how much light they bring into your life, here's a craft that captures just that, using the quote, "Friends are like stars. Just because you don't see them doesn't mean they aren't there!" as our inspiration.

MATERIALS

Toilet paper roll

Heavyweight paper

Glitter

Star confetti (optional)

Black string

TOOLS

Ruler

Scissors

Hot-glue gun and hot-glue sticks

Paint

Paintbrushes

Coloring utensils (I chose markers)

STEP 1

Cut your toilet paper roll creating two main pieces, one measuring 1¾ inches (4.5 cm) and the other 2 inches (5 cm). Discard any extra or save it for another craft. We're transforming this humble roll into a cosmic container. For the how-to on how to cut and turn your pieces into a container with a lid, check out the Craft Basics on page 8. Come back once you have created your little TP container.

178 - 100 Ways to Say I Love (or Hate) You

Once you have your container, paint a moon on each of the enclosed sides. You can get as artsy as you like with these moons, but here are a few designs to inspire you:

If drawing feels a little too much like rocket science, just print out a design you love, but make sure it fits the diameter of your toilet paper roll. Also, feel free to add a different phase of the moon on either end of the toilet paper rolls for a more unique look!

Now we don't want to let on that this was once a toilet paper roll, so paint every bit of visible cardboard, including the inside, in dark blue or black to mimic the night sky. Open your container, add a little hot glue and go wild with glitter inside (think gold, silver or black). You can also add tiny white dots inside to mimic faraway stars. Let your container dry while we work on the next step.

STEP 2

Star time! If you're lucky enough to have star confetti, your job here is easy. The rest of us will have to channel our inner Van Gogh and draw simple stars on heavyweight paper. Cut them out and color them in shades of gold, yellow, silver or white. Aim for about six to ten stars, each ¾ inch (2 cm) in size.

Now get out your black string, cut half or fewer pieces of string as you do stars—each measuring 8 inches (20 cm). So, if you have six stars, cut three pieces. Glue one end of one string to the side of the toilet paper roll at the top, just about where it meets the lid. Then glue the other end of the string to the bottom of the container. Space each of the strings evenly around the perimeter of the toilet paper rolls as you repeat this step with all the string pieces.

Once the top and bottom of your container are each connected to either side of the string, sandwich your stars together with glue with one of the strings in between. Do this in different parts of each piece of string so it feels more organic to the stars in the sky.

STEP 3

Close the toilet paper roll container, and on a separate sheet of paper (or simply directly on the exterior of the toilet paper roll container) write, "Friends are like stars. Just because you don't see them doesn't mean they aren't there!" or if you would rather gift this to a frenemy, write, "You aren't the brightest star in the sky!" Cut out this note and glue it to the outside of your container. Now your little piece of the cosmos is ready to gift. When the container is opened, the stars will hang like the night sky, reminding your bestie of the enduring sparkle of your friendship.

For Your BFFs or Your Frenemies

Color Our Friendship

♥ 💔 ♥ 💔 ♥ 💔 ♥ 💔 ♥ 💔 ♥ 💔 ♥ 💔 ♥ 💔 ♥ 💔 ♥ 💔 ♥ 💔 ♥ 💔 ♥

This is a cute gift for besties who love to take pictures together. It's a very sweet way to commemorate your favorite moments that is a little more interactive than just posting pics on social media. And let's be real—as someone who has always loved coloring books, the idea of a customized one created by my best friend seems undoubtably personal and special. And hey, we can even color them all in together.

MATERIALS
Printer paper

Photos

Crayons or colored pencils

TOOLS
Ruler

Scissors

Tape

Window or lightbox

Black marker

Stapler

To get a better idea on how to mark the most prominent details, take a look at how I created my tracings:

STEP 1
Cut three or more pieces of printer paper to 7 x 10½ inches (18 x 27 cm). Lay the pieces down horizontally and fold them down the middle. Keep in mind that each piece of paper equals four pages (including the front and back cover).

Print pictures of you and your bestie that fit within one side of the fold. Plan the order of your photos for the book. If you've been besties for years, arrange the pictures chronologically to see how you both have evolved over time for an extra touch of cuteness.

Now it's time to trace your pictures onto the book. Using a lightbox or a window as a backlight, tape your photos under your book pages. Align each picture to one side of the paper, avoiding the center fold line. As the light shines through, trace the most prominent lines of the photo, capturing outlines, backgrounds and clothing details. With a fine-tip marker or pen, sketch facial features like eyes, nose, lips, and jawline. Keep it simple; focus on the darker lines and shapes.

STEP 2
Once you have traced each and every one of your images, bind the book together by layering the pages on top of each other and stapling the center crease. To avoid issues make sure the staples share the same orientation as the crease itself. If you opted to use heavier paper and are having trouble getting the staples in the middle, you can try using a staple gun and bending the staple backs manually.

Now you can close the book and decorate the cover page however you like! Keep in mind it's the first thing your bestie will see, so make it count! I recommend reserving the cover page for your fav picture with you and your bestie(s) with big bold letters saying, "Color Our Friendship!"

Pair this gift with a set of crayons or colored pencils and gift away! This craft is a special and unique take on a typical photobook, as your bestie will really have a chance to ponder each memory when coloring. It's the perfect gift for a lifelong friend (especially if they're artistic)!

Capture Our Memories

My friends and I are constantly snapping COUNTLESS pictures when we're together. It's practically our trademark activity. And although I cherish these moments, let's face it: We take over a hundred photos on our phones, pick the top three, post them and rarely revisit them unless we're scrolling through our social media notifications. While I absolutely love capturing memories with my besties, let's just say, not all of them are appropriate for public display. So, to give justice for the other 97 photos, here's a creative way to commemorate those moments you've shared with your pals. And you know what? This makes for an adorable gift, especially for birthdays or graduations, serving as a time capsule of all the incredible moments you've experienced together.

MATERIALS

Printed-out pictures

Cardboard

2 binder rings

TOOLS

Ruler

Scissors

Hole punch

Marker

Protractor or round object

Hot-glue gun and hot glue sticks

Paint

Paintbrush

STEP 1

Firstly, gather all the pictures you want to include and print them out on photo paper at a size of at least 4 x 2½ inches (10 x 6.5 cm). This way, we'll be able to shape them to match our cover page later. Aim for at least 20 images, but the more the merrier.

Grab your cardboard and cut out two camera shapes measuring 3¼ x 2½ inches (8 x 6.5 cm). Take a look at the illustration of my camera shape for some help:

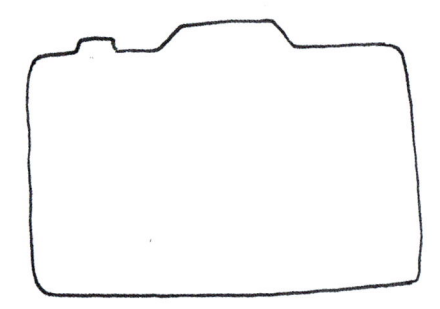

182 - 100 Ways to Say I Love (or Hate) You

STEP 2

Next, use your hole punch to create two holes on the left side of one camera-shaped cardboard. Repeat this process with the second piece of cardboard, ensuring that both the holes and the cardboard pieces are the same size on both pieces.

Before moving on to decoration, let's make sure our pictures will fit within the cardboard pieces. Take your pictures and trace the camera shape directly over each one with a marker. Be sure to mark where the holes need to be punched as well. Then, use the marker lines to cut out the pictures in the same camera shape as the cardboard cover. Don't forget to hole punch the same areas as indicated on the cardboard. Now, your pictures should closely match the shape of the cardboard cutouts.

STEP 3

It's time to decorate the cover to make it look like a real camera. Start with the lens. Use a protractor on a piece of cardboard to trace a 1¾-inch (4.5-cm)-diameter circle. Cut it out and hot glue it to the cardboard cover as the lens of the camera. Paint the entire cardboard piece black or gray, and add repeating circles inside the lens to give it the appearance of a glass lens. For added detail, you can incorporate bits of silver and various shades of gray for the cover, including a brand name and a shutter button.

STEP 4

As for the second piece of cardboard shaped like a camera, I kept it simple by painting it black on both sides. Once your camera cover has dried, sandwich all your pictures between the two cardboard pieces, ensuring that all the holes line up. Secure everything together using the binder rings. And now you've just crafted the most adorable photobook! You can choose to keep it for yourself or give it as a heartfelt gift to your bestie. Or if you're in need of a gift for a not-so-much-of-a-friend, purposely take this opportunity to collect the WORST pictures of them. Keep it a bit sweet and don't go exposing their private photos or anything—but simply go out of your way to choose the less than flattering pictures. This way, gifting it to them will seem like a sweet gesture, but really you both know what your true intentions really are.

For Your BFFs or Your Frenemies

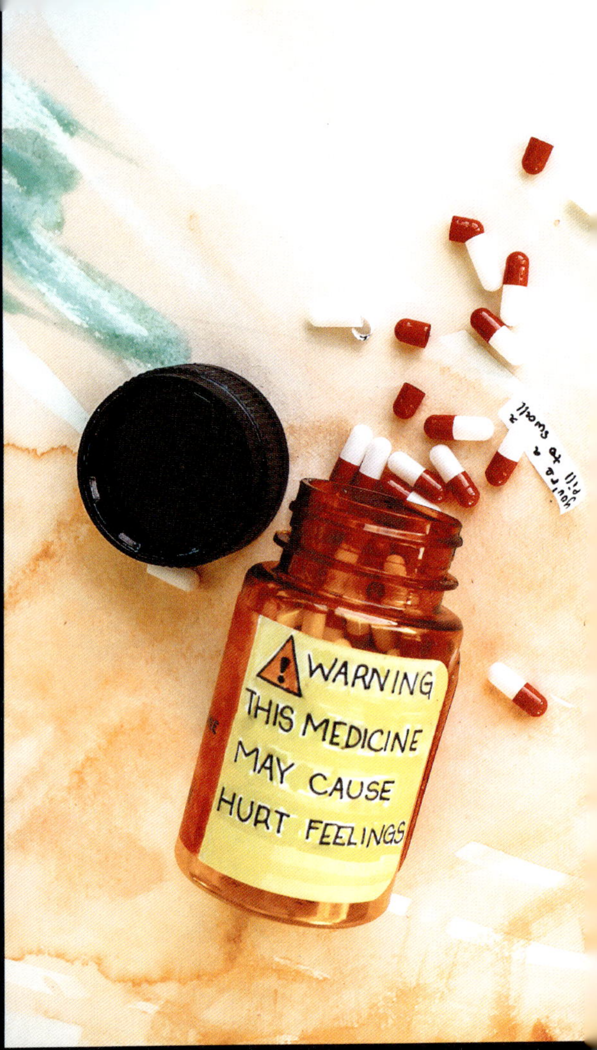
WARNING
THIS MEDICINE
MAY CAUSE
HURT FEELINGS

RIP

I CAN'T STAND YOU!

Never Mind. You Suck.

CRAFTS FOR EXES AND ENEMIES

I get it. You got this book from a former loved one or to make something for someone who is totally not deserving of your love anymore. But you are wrong if you think that crafting is only for the special people in your life. Personally, I have found that crafting some more malicious crafts can be even more cathartic than the lovey dovey ones. Does that make me a psychopath? Either way, trying your hand at some of these "I hate you" crafts may just be the emotional release you have been needing. So, what are you waiting for? Grab your bestie, sob, drink wine, talk shit and craft your little heart away while commiserating over the time you will never get back with this unspeakable person.

You're Such a Tool

♥ 💔 ♥ 💔 ♥ 💔 ♥ 💔 ♥ 💔 ♥ 💔 ♥ 💔 ♥ 💔 ♥ 💔 ♥ 💔

The phrase "You're not the sharpest tool in the shed" brings back a wave of lighthearted insults from my childhood. These kinds of playful jabs are perfect for throwing at someone without causing too much emotional damage (hopefully). I can imagine someone offering this gift to a lazy group project partner or a forgetful partner who missed an anniversary or birthday. It's just enough to call them out on their behavior without leaving any lasting scars.

MATERIALS

Template (page 245)

Skewer

Cardboard

TOOLS

Scissors

Hot-glue gun and hot-glue sticks

Paint

Paintbrushes

Ruler

Superglue

Coloring utensils

Pen

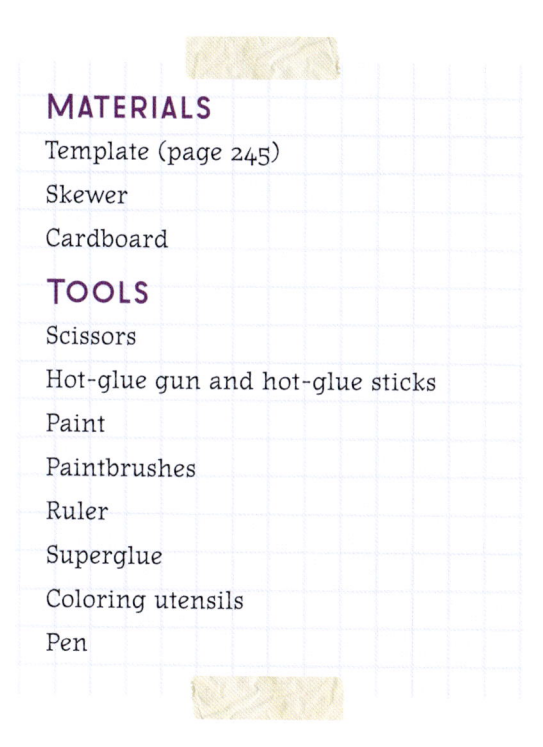

STEP 1

Begin by cutting out the template on page 245. Use the indicated lines and patterns as guides for where to glue and fold. Once you have assembled and glued the template together, paint the entire toolbox, both on the inside and outside, in a bold shade of red. On the top of the triangles attached to the box, you'll notice small "X" shapes; these X lines will be used to attach the handle. Slide a piece of the skewer through both X lines, then cut it down to measure 2¼ inches (6 cm). Secure the skewer in place using a little superglue on both sides, and once it dries, your toolbox should have a functional handle.

STEP 2

Now that your toolbox is complete, it's time to craft some miniature tools to place inside. Instead of making them three-dimensional, we'll keep it simple. To begin making the tools, draw each one to measure approximately 2¼ inches (6 cm) in length so that they will fit perfectly into our toolbox.

You can draw a hammer, a saw, a wrench or any other tool of your choice. Below are some drawings you can use as a reference to draw your tools. Remember to finish each tool in full color, but only do this on one side.

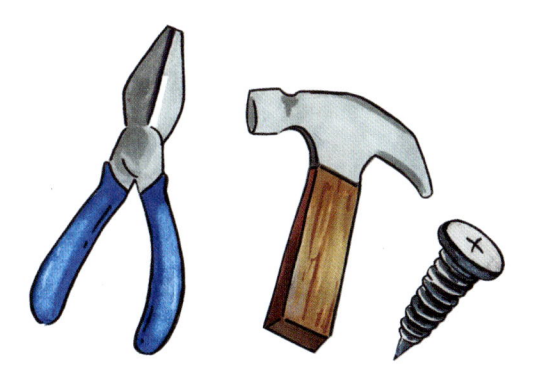

Next, cut out each tool, ensuring there's no extra white paper left on the sides. Now, use each cutout tool as a template to trace the exact shape onto a piece of cardboard. Cut out the cardboard shapes as well and glue each corresponding piece together, leaving the colored side up. On the back of each tool, write a tool-related insult to really "nail" it in there. Here are a few more playful puns to consider:

- You're nuts!
- You're a real wrench in my plans.
- You've got screws loose.
- You're such a hammerhead.
- You're such a tool.
- Screw you!

Assemble the tools drawing side up in your toolbox and either leave it out for your giftee to find or give it to them with the utmost confidence. These are enough to express your frustration at the giftee, but given how adorable the craft is, they really can't get too mad about it!

Never Mind. You Suck.

You're Not a Treat

♥💔♥💔♥💔♥💔♥💔♥💔♥💔♥💔♥💔♥💔♥💔♥💔

As the Halloween season comes around every year, you may take it upon yourself to look around and realize how many people really do seem like they were put on Earth to play a trick on you rather than bring in any sort of sweetness. If you feel like the people around you have personalities more closely resembling ghouls and goblins rather than any sort of princess or fairy, then here is a way to tell them straight to their face while still bringing in some Halloween spirit.

MATERIALS

Heavyweight paper, such as watercolor or multimedia paper

Ribbon

Candy corn

TOOLS

Protractor

Pencil

Scissors

Coloring utensils

Glue

STEP 1

For this craft we are going to recreate Halloween's most iconic candy, the candy corn. To do this start by creating a 5-inch (13-cm)-diameter circle with your protractor on a piece of your heavyweight paper. Create a circle inside this one with a diameter of 3 inches (7.5 cm), and then a third with a diameter of 1 inch (2.5 cm), creating clear boundaries for different sections. Within the parameters of the outer circle, color it yellow. Color the middle circle orange, but leave the center circle white as this will be the tip of our candy corn.

Cut out the largest circle, and then cut the entire paper in half down the middle. To make the cone, twist the paper so that one end of the circle goes underneath the other end, forming a cone. Allow a 1-inch (2.5-cm) border and apply glue within it. Hold down the other side while it dries to secure the cone shape.

STEP 2

Create a 2¼-inch (6-cm)-diameter circle out of your heavyweight paper that has a 1 × 1-inch (2.5 × 2.5-cm) rectangular tab protruding from the circle. This is the lid! Cut out the circle along with the tab, fold this tab and glue it to the inside of the candy corn cone so that it can open and close.

As it is right now, once the craft is picked up from the table, the lid will immediately open. If you fill the cone with candy corn at this point, it will spill out all over your nemesis (which may not be the worst thing). But if you would rather keep the candy corn cone more secure, proceed with the following instructions.

STEP 3

To keep the candy secure, cut out two 5½-inch (14-cm)-long pieces of ribbon. Holding the cone from the bottom, place the first ribbon on the underside of the cone on the opposite side of where the tab was glued down. Glue the other ribbon to the inside of the lid adjacent the other ribbon.

Finish this craft by filling the candy corn cone with actual candy corn and include a small paper note that bluntly states, "You are no sweet treat." Put this in a conference room full of all of your nasty coworkers only for them to devour the candy corn, unknowingly partaking in their own insult (until they find the note and question all of their life choices).

Never Mind. You Suck.

Sad Meal

This craft is fitting for anyone who always has a bad attitude. I'm sure we have all dealt with at least one person who always seems like they have something to complain about. Since they can't seem to enjoy anything, why not create something that they will REALLY hate. Let's do this by taking away the happiness from something that literally has "happy" in the name.

MATERIALS
Template (page 247)
Paper

TOOLS
Scissors
Blue coloring utensils
Hot-glue gun and hot-glue sticks

STEP 1
To begin this craft, start by cutting out the template on page 247. Fold on all of the fold lines, but before we glue, make sure the entire box and handle is painted blue. Once the paint is dry, carefully hot glue the box together. Once everything is folded and glued together, you should be able to open and close your little box and it should stand up on its own, just like a normal takeout box.

To add some pizzazz (or more like sadness) to the box, cut out a little sad face in white and hot glue the frown to the center of the box.

STEP 2
To finish off the gift, write a little note inside the box that says, "Only you could make a happy meal sad," and give it to your enemy. Replace their lunch with the sad meal as a prank, or offer to get them something for lunch, only to come back with this.

Still not fulfilled after this incredibly melancholic meal? If you want to make this a full-scale project, follow the next two projects to add an increasing level of spite to your meal.

Sad Fries

If you just finished your Sad Meal (page 190) and are looking for some more goodies to stuff inside, here is a playful re-creation of everyone's favorite fast-food treat: French fries (or sad fries, since we want to stay on theme).

MATERIALS
Template (page 231)

White and yellow construction paper

TOOLS
Scissors

Blue coloring utensils

Glue

Pen

TIP: Depending on your coloring materials, you may experience some bleed-through. To avoid this, test your coloring utensil and flip over the template to see if it bleeds. If it does, exchange your coloring utensils for something that causes less bleed-through, such as colored pencils.

STEP 1
Begin by cutting out the template on page 231, and fold on the corresponding fold lines (the gray lines). Before you glue, keep one side of the box white, flip it over and color the other side blue.

Once everything is colored, glue your template together, keeping the blue on the outside and the white on the inside.

STEP 2
On a piece of white construction paper, cut out a sad smile, and glue it onto the fry box. Now to add our sad fries. Cut out 20 different rectangles out of the yellow construction paper to act as our fries. On each fry, write an insult. This can either be a lighthearted tease, such as, "I am as happy to see you as I am biting into a soggy fry," or slight roasts, such as, "You're so greasy." Of course, just be sure to bring it back to the fry theme for the biggest impact. Once you're all done, place the sad fries into the happy meal container and either gift it as is or add some sad nuggets to the bunch.

Never Mind. You Suck.

Sad Nuggets

♥💔♥💔♥💔♥💔♥💔♥💔♥💔♥💔♥💔♥💔♥💔♥💔♥

To create your endearingly sad nuggets and complete your delightfully woeful meal, we'll kick things off by making paper clay. Despite the melancholic theme, the process of shaping these little nugs brings me an immense amount of joy for some odd reason.

MATERIALS

Toilet paper or tissues

White glue

Flour

Flexible plastic

Template (page 227)

TOOLS

Bowl

Wooden spoon

Ruler

Scissors

Permanent marker

Brown and tan paint

Paintbrushes

Glue

Coloring utensils

STEP 1

To make the paper clay, in a bowl, mix together 1 part toilet paper, 1 part white glue and 1½ parts flour until they blend into a cohesive mass that you can shape. We're aiming to shape chicken nuggets from this clay, and for an added touch, here are some nuggety shapes you can use as a reference:

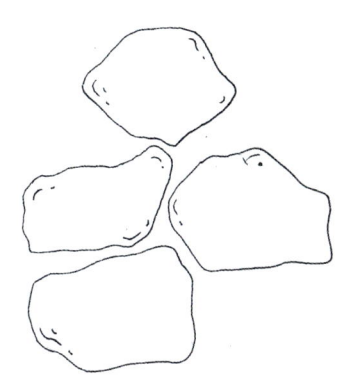

To add insult to injury, we are literally going to be adding an insult within the clay concoction. To do this, cut out a piece of flexible plastic, and write your insult with a permanent marker on it. Then, stuff it in a chicken nugget dough ball as you are shaping it. Feel free to be liberal with whatever plastic you have on hand—use plastic bags, plastic wrap, disposable to-go containers, you name it! Once you've sculpted six chicken nuggets to your satisfaction, place them in the sunlight to dry. Depending on your local climate, this may take a few days or just a few hours.

With your chicken nuggets now dry to the touch, let's move on to painting them to achieve that authentic, crispy fried appearance. Utilize an assortment of brown and tan hues to capture the delightfully crispy look.

STEP 2

Now that you've got six nuggets looking as delectably crisp as can be, it's time to create the box to house them. You can find the template on page 227. Cut it out, fold and glue the template together along all of the indicated lines. Make sure you fold on each of the gray lines and only cut through the black lines. Now that we have a box perfect to contain our sad little nugs, go on to decorate with your preferred coloring utensils. I chose to color my box blue and white, completing the box with the signature sad face we have used for the last collection of gifts.

Now either gift your chicken nuggets with the sad meal and sad fries, or give it as a one-off. When the giftee breaks apart the chicken nugget, the note with the insult will be revealed. While surely the giftee will find the contents of the note annoying, the creativity involved in this elaborate prank will guarantee at least a slight bit of appreciation. And just a little reminder that no matter how much you hate them, make sure your foe knows these are not a pleasant snack.

Never Mind. You Suck.

You're an A-Hole

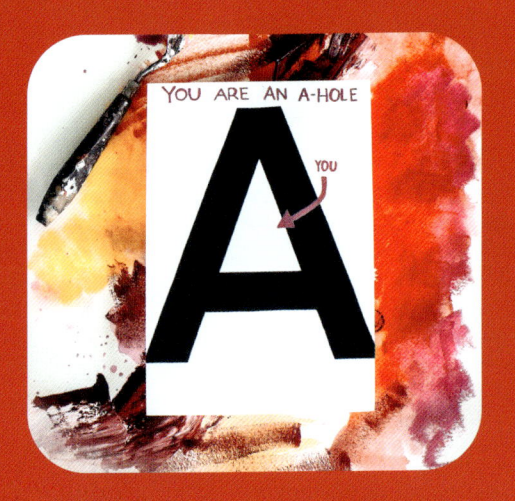

I can totally see this craft being hastily made to leave in the mailbox of an unfavorable relative or slipped into the locker of a bully at school. It's a great way to stick it to someone anonymously, but it's too good of a pun to make them cry about it too much. Sometimes some people just need a small metaphorical slap in the face to fix their behavior, and I would say this craft does that pretty well. And the best part is, it should only take a minute or two to create!

MATERIALS
Paper (any kind)

TOOLS
Black and red pens or markers

STEP 1
In a big bold font taking up the majority of the paper, draw the letter "A" with a black pen. With a red pen, draw an arrow to the hole in the "A" and write, "you." Above the "A," write, "You Are an A-Hole." And that's it! Send it away either anonymously or give it to their face if you have the guts.

Hangman

Ah, hangman, a childhood favorite that somehow went unspoken about how incredibly morbid it is, especially for children. Oh well, at least we can use this morbidity to haunt our exes and enemies. This craft is an efficient way to let your enemies know you're onto them without taking too much time away from your precious day.

MATERIALS
Heavyweight paper

TOOLS
Pen or marker

Ruler

Scissors

Craft knife (I use X-Acto)

STEP 1
Draw the classic hangman shape at the top of a rectangular piece of paper. Now, think about the message you'd like to convey. Some examples could be:

- You are dead to me.
- You are hanging on by a thread.
- You are a dead man walking.

STEP 2
Count the letters in your chosen phrase, and create dashes at the bottom of the page, leaving space for each letter. Write the phrase above these dashes. While you could simply give this as it is, let's add a touch more flair. Use your craft knife to carefully cut the hangman drawing, on the top and sides of the little guy. Just ensure you leave at least a ½-inch (1.3-cm) border at the bottom of the drawing. Press the cutout forward to crease it, causing the hangman to stand up on its own. You can also cut out a picture of their face and transplant it directly onto the man to really target your giftee. Now, you can leave it on a counter for a former "friend" to discover, or use it to playfully tease a sibling who has snuck into your room. Sure it's a little threatening, but thanks to its childhood roots, it won't be mistaken for something more sinister.

Never Mind. You Suck.

A Taste of Their Own Medicine

In a world where some individuals seem to believe they're the ultimate gift to humanity, their overconfidence can often lead to amusing situations. While I can't recommend *actually* gifting this to anyone, we'll leave this craft here . . . just in case you encounter someone who could use a gentle reality check. Now, let's give them a taste of their own medicine (literally)!

MATERIALS

Empty prescription bottle

Printer paper

Empty pill capsules

TOOLS

Ruler

Scissors

Pen

Red and yellow coloring utensils

Glue (any kind)

Black paint

Paintbrushes

STEP 1

To begin, we will need an empty prescription bottle. Remember that time you got pneumonia and got prescribed some antibiotics you could hardly choke down? Grab that bottle because we're gonna need it. Once you have acquired the prescription bottle, completely remove all of the prior prescription stickers. If there is any leftover sticky goo, a little soap and hot water should be all you need for it to go bye-bye.

Now onto creating this medicine specifically for our enemy. Cut out a 5½ x 2-inch (14 x 5-cm) piece of printer paper, and write their new prescription plan. Divide the paper into one side measuring 2 inches (5 cm) and other 3½ inches (9 cm). Color the entire (smaller) left side a scarlet red and the right side yellow. Write your warning label on the yellow section.

You can write:

Warning! This medicine may cause hurt feelings.

On the red side, write your prescription:

RX
DESERVED INSULTS
A taste of your own medicine

Instructions:
Read three pills a day to make you a better person.

Glue the label to the bottle. Remove the cap and paint it black just so the aesthetic of the gift matches our intentions.

STEP 2

Now for the tedious (but totally worth it) part. Get your hands on empty pill capsules. You can typically find either gelatin or plastic capsules online or at your local pharmacy. Open up each container and write a tiny note. Write any sort of insults you feel like this person deserves to know, like "You're a bully," or stay on theme with something like "You're a hard pill to swallow." These are good places to start. Try to think of this as a helpful slap in the face. If you were walking around being a horrible person wouldn't you want someone to let you know? Once you've written at least 20 insults, curl the paper pieces with your finger and stick each into each pill capsule. Place them into your prescription bottle, cap it up and leave it out for your enemy to find. (Just make sure no one actually eats any!)

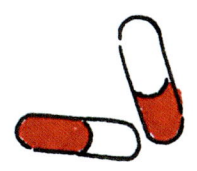

Baby, You Got Baggage

Unfortunately, some people in our lives carry a lot of baggage—from debt to toxic family members or even a criminal record. Whatever this baggage may be, it would be ignorant to assume that those of us who share space with this person are not affected by this baggage, often without them even realizing it. To convey how we're feeling without sparking a heated argument, here's a craft you can whip up to address this challenging situation.

MATERIALS

Small matchbox

Matches

Paper, fabric or Barbie clothes

TOOLS

Acrylic paint

Paintbrushes

Craft knife (I use X-Acto)

Ruler

Superglue

Acrylic markers (or other coloring utensils)

STEP 1

To begin making our tiny suitcase, paint your entire matchbox with acrylic paint. We're aiming for an old American vibe, so I painted mine brown. Cut four matches with the craft knife down to the width of your matchbox. (Make sure the lighting tip is on the side you're cutting off.) Superglue two on both sides, positioning them close to the edges of the box.

Cut four more matches, each measuring the height of your matchbox. Superglue them to go down the height of your box, lining them up the same distance from the edge as the other matches.

To create a handle for your suitcase, cut two pieces from a matchstick, one measuring ½ inch (1.3 cm) and the other two measuring ¼ inch (6 mm). Superglue the edges of two shorter pieces at a 90-degree angle to the center piece, allowing it to set for 1 minute. Once it feels secure, apply a small amount of glue to the ends and affix it to the top of your matchbox in the center.

STEP 2

Now that it looks like a miniature briefcase, take the opportunity to add some "stickers" with your acrylic markers. This is a perfect time to reference any memories where your recipient brought their emotional baggage into your shared experiences, such as the time you were planning a trip together and their mother came along without your permission, or when they didn't pay their fair share of bills until debt collectors came knocking.

STEP 3

To finish off the gift, cut out bits of paper or fabric in the shape of clothes and stuff them inside the matchbox. Even better, if you have leftover Barbie clothes hanging around, use those instead! On one of these pieces of clothing, write the words, "You have so much baggage." Gift the suitcase to your foe. While I cannot guarantee this won't lead to an argument, at least this way is way more adorable than a simple nag.

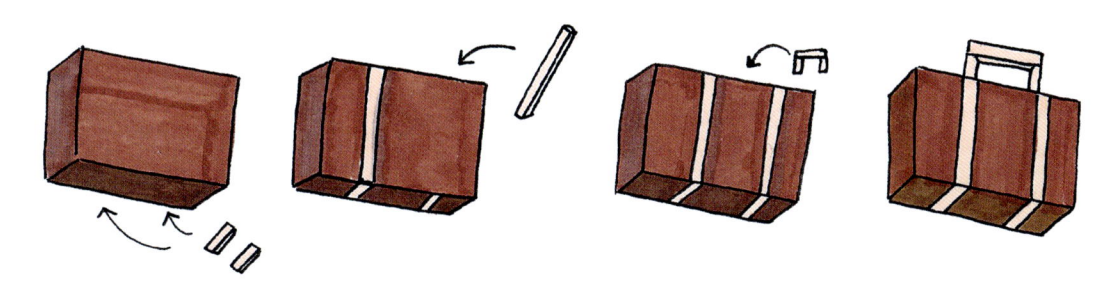

Never Mind. You Suck.

You're Dead to Me . . . Literally

♥💔♥💔♥💔♥💔♥💔♥💔♥💔♥💔♥💔♥💔♥💔♥

So you've just been completely and utterly betrayed by someone you thought you could trust. Oh, hon, I get it. The pain is an absolutely indescribable emotion, and it has you confused about the past, present and future. And in one fell swoop, they took all of it away from you . . . Sometimes in specific cases like this, all you can think of is "You're dead to me."

If we're feeling like this right now, instead of resorting to something that may get you a free night's stay on the jail cell floor or with a lifelong restraining order, let's get out a little bit of this anger with a hot-glue gun rather than an actual gun.

MATERIALS

Small matchbox

Cardboard

Green construction paper

Personal objects that remind you of this foe

TOOLS

Paint

Paintbrushes

Ruler

Scissors

Hot-glue gun and hot-glue sticks

White glue or water-based glue (I use Mod Podge)

Tissue or toilet paper

White gel pen or acrylic marker (optional)

STEP 1

Let's begin with our little cemetery plot. Remove the matches from your matchbox. Save them for a global blackout, an apocalypse or whatever normal people use matches for. Paint the outside of the matchbox green to resemble grass. Color the inside brown to resemble dirt. Set this aside.

Cut out a piece of cardboard that measures the width of your matchbox and at least double its height. Shape your cardboard to resemble a gravestone. Feel free to use some creative liberty with this. Take a look at my illustrations (below) for some inspiration.

With your hot-glue gun on low heat, write "RIP" on the cardboard. Wait until the glue is dry and brush the entire cardboard piece with white glue. Use either some pieces of tissue or toilet paper and place them over the entire gravestone to give it some texture. Paint over the entire piece of cardboard with silver or gray paint, and use a small amount of white paint on a dry brush to accentuate the hot glue letters as well as any imperfections due to the toilet paper. This should give your gravestone a worn-in, old cemetery look to it.

(continued)

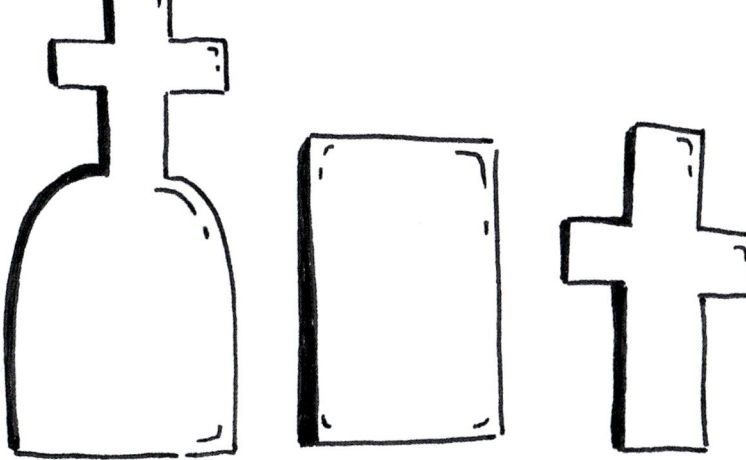

If you would like to personalize this craft to your betrayer, use a white gel pen to write either the name of your betrayer or the relationship that you had with this person. Attach the headstone to the top portion of your matchbox with hot glue. It may have a little trouble standing upright so be sure to hold it in place until all of the glue dries and the headstone stays upright by itself.

STEP 2

Now to make the grass. Cut out square pieces of green construction paper that match the width of your box. Fold the square in half and cut multiple slits into the squares, but leave at least ½ inch (1.3 cm) uncut. Once you add enough slits, the edges should look like fringe, or better yet, like grass. Take the folded edge of the square and glue it directly to the top of the matchbox. I did this with 20 squares, but keep layering the fringe pieces very closely together to ultimately get an appearance similar to a small patch of grass.

STEP 3

Now your matchbox should look transformed into a miniature cemetery plot. Grab any small knickknacks that remind you of your betrayer as well as pictures of you two together or simply of the betrayer. Stuff them inside the matchbox and invite your friends over and have a proper funeral to mourn the person you thought they were. Hover around the tiny cemetery plot and give speeches about the betrayal or even happy memories that you have to mourn. Just remember that the betrayal is not your fault, or any indication of your own self-worth. The betrayal only shows who THEY are; it does not reflect your ability to be loved or treated well by the people in your life. I mean, they must simply be crazy because who would ever hurt such an artsy and loving person who has excellent taste in craft books?

Bloody Knife

For legal reasons, I must address that I do not believe in violence, which is relevant because in this project, we will be making a knife. Okay, hold your horses. I know it looks pretty convincing in the photo, but it's just cardboard, I promise.

So like, maybe don't go around chasing people with it because you may get the cops called on you, but I will say that anonymously leaving it in your *ex's* mailbox isn't technically illegal, is it?

MATERIALS
Cardboard

Smooth heavyweight paper, such as bristol paper

TOOLS
Pen or pencil

Craft knife (I use X-Acto)

Hot-glue gun and hot-glue sticks

Glue stick

Red, black and white paint

Paintbrushes

Water-based glue (I use Mod Podge)

Silver chrome marker

STEP 1
While the diagram for this craft is provided on the next page, you don't really need it if you have a knife set at home. I am legitimately just tracing my kitchen knife onto the cardboard, but of course, you can also reference my little illustration.

> **CAUTION**: If your family is not accustomed to very bizarre antics in the name of crafts (such as mine are), they may be very concerned by you grabbing the kitchen knife and bringing it to your room. Just saying.

(continued)

Never Mind. You Suck.

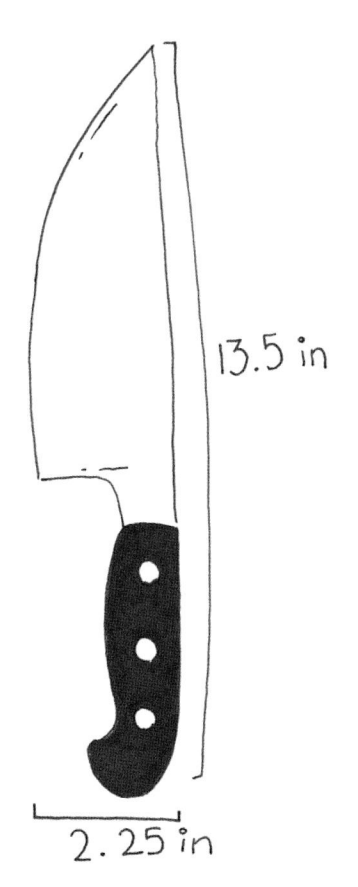

Okay, with that being said, let's start by tracing your kitchen knife onto a piece of cardboard. Make sure you mark where the handle ends and when the blade starts. Now cut out your knife. If this is the first craft you're trying out in this book, then you may be surprised to find out that cardboard is not so easy to cut. Refer to Cutting Cardboard (page 8) for details on how to cut cardboard like a professional crafter.

Now that the entire base of your knife is cut out, draw a line marking when the handle begins and the blade ends. Use the cardboard knife as a tracing tool to cut out two more handle pieces. We want the handle to be thicker than the blade to give it a more realistic look.

STEP 2

Once you have three cardboard pieces, hot glue the two extra handle pieces to either side of your original knife, lining them up together at the bottom of the base. You may notice that the sides of the cardboard look very unclean. If you're simply going for a quick scare and don't want to fret about the details, then you can skip this step, but I highly recommend coating the base of the knife with paper to cover up the texture of the sides. To do this, measure the height of your knife at the handle. Cut out a long strip of heavyweight paper matching the height measurement. Dollop hot glue along the edges of the knife, and slowly wrap the paper strip along the sides of the knife. Just be sure that you stop at the knife blade—you will see why in a moment.

To make the blade appear sharp, trace your knife on a sheet of smooth heavyweight paper such as bristol paper. Stop tracing once you get to the handle section and extend the protruding section of the blade out another ½ inch (1.3 cm) past the tracing. Cut out two of these blades.

Using a glue stick, glue the pieces of paper onto the cardboard blade on both sides. You will notice your paper extends past the cardboard; add just a touch of glue to the inside of either sheet of paper and connect them to form the appearance of a sharp blade. This little step is crucial to mark the difference between chasing someone around with a piece of cardboard versus chasing someone around with a knife. One is definitely a tad more threatening. If there is still any cardboard exposed on the side, or on the back of the blade for example, feel free to cut out another strip of paper to cover any imperfections.

STEP 3

Now that that's done, let's move on to the handle. I painted my handle black to resemble my actual kitchen knives, and I added three white dots in the middle because, for some reason, knives have that. If you're a knife expert, please tell me why.

Once the handle is dry, let's move on to making this legitimately realistic. Coat the blade in water-based glue and color the entirety of the blade with a silver chrome marker. Once it is dry, I swear you can put it in the knife drawer and no one will be the wiser.

STEP 4

To add a note for your ex or enemy, mix red paint and water. Lather this concoction together with a paintbrush and lash the paintbrush so the little droplets sit on the knife. In the creepiest font you can muster (or even using your finger for that oh, so, "I've just gotten stabbed and I need to write a message before I die" look), write, "I am cutting you OFF."

And I think this eloquently finishes off this craft, if I do say so myself. You know, it's threatening without being dangerous, to the point and very clear on its intention. Truly, the perfect gift to give someone who has betrayed you and a good warning for everyone else.

Pack o' Smokes

Alright, let's not point fingers at smokers here—this is a judgment-free zone, after all. But, come on, we all know smoking's bad for you, right? You know what else is a health hazard? Toxic people. So, naturally, what better gift than one that literally increases your risk of cancer.

So whether you're planning to actually hand this over to your personal human pollutant or just crafting for some much-needed art therapy (which, by the way, I wholeheartedly endorse), this is your go-to project.

MATERIALS
Template (page 249)

Printer paper

TOOLS
Scissors

Glue (any kind)

Ruler

Coloring utensils

Pen

Double-sided tape (optional)

STEP 1
Cut out the template on page 249. I could give you a long spiel about cutting along some horizontal line, but let's not kid ourselves—that can get as confusing as explaining why you still hang out with said toxic person. Just stick to the template, folding along the gray lines and cutting along the black, and you'll be fine. Glue the template together on the connecting tabs, and voilà: You've got yourself a faux cigarette container.

Now, for the fun part—decorating. I went for the classic cigarette pack look because authenticity is key in passive-aggressive crafts. But really, as long as it screams "cigarette box," go wild with your creativity. Cut out a 1½ x 2-inch (4 x 5-cm) piece of printer paper. Color the top ⅗ inch (1.5 cm) a lovely shade of brownish orange—you know, to mimic those appealing cigarette filters.

On the non-colored side, it's time to unleash your inner poet of pettiness. Write whatever snarky comment fits the bill. Extra points if you tie it to the whole smoking theme—it keeps it classy. Some suggestions:

- You make me feel like I'm dying.
- You make it hard to breathe around you.
- Your presence pollutes the air.
- I'm quitting you.

STEP 2
Roll up this masterpiece, with your note craftily hidden inside. If it keeps unrolling, tear off a teeny tiny bit of double-sided tape and attach it to the end of your roll, roll it up again and it will stick. Be careful though because adding too much double-sided tape risks ripping the paper when the notes are unraveled. Now all you need to do is load up about 16 to 20 of these cigarettes into your box and there you have it.

A pack of cigarettes brimming with burn-worthy insults! What more could you want? Forgiveness? Peace? Solitude? Ugh, as if. We're all about that petty revenge life.

I Can't Stand You

This craft is a playful take on the popular phrase "I can't stand you." Since whoever you're gifting this to is clearly either very annoying or a huge pain in the ass, let's make our message abundantly clear with this craft.

MATERIALS

6 toothpicks

2 bottle caps

Paper towel

Cotton ball

TOOLS

Hot-glue gun and hot-glue sticks

Wire cutters

Ruler

Pliers

Paint

Paintbrushes

Superglue

Markers

Gel ink pen

STEP 1

Hot glue 4 of the toothpicks to the bottom of 1 bottle cap as chair legs. Space them out evenly so the cap stands firmly.

Use wire cutters to make two incisions into the other bottle cap, no more than ½ inch (1.3 cm) apart. Use pliers to flatten out this small piece, separating it from the rest of the rim. Apply hot glue to this straightened piece and attach it to the rim of the first bottle cap, forming the chair's back. Hold it steady until it's completely dry.

Glue 2 toothpicks to the sides of the seat to serve as tiny armrests, and cut off any excess that extends past the first bottle cap.

STEP 2

It's painting time. Feel free to give it whatever aesthetic you want. I opted for a black and white polka dot chair, but if you like the bottle cap look, you can even leave it as is.

STEP 3

We can probably assume that your giftee isn't the brightest star in the sky, so let's make a little pillow to drive the message home. Cut out a 1 x 1½-inch (2.5 x 4-cm) piece of paper towel. Add a small amount of superglue to the sides of the rectangle and fold it in half, adhering the edges together. When the glue is dry, stuff the "pillowcase" with a bit of cotton until it is filled. Glue the open top together so all of the fluff stays confined inside the pillow. This is your chance to color your pillowcase any color you choose, using a marker. Once it is colored, use a gel ink pen to write, "I can't stand you" in the smallest font you can muster.

I have to say that while some elements of this craft are a little trickier than one would expect, the end result is just the right amount of, "Aww, a tiny chair, how cute and innocent," while still being totally snarky. My favorite combo!

You're So Sour

♥💔♥💔♥💔♥💔♥💔♥💔♥💔♥💔♥💔♥💔♥💔♥

If there's someone in your life who's constantly oozing sour vibes, it might be time for a little creative intervention. This craft is perfect for subtly (or not so subtly) letting those sourpusses know that their attitude could use a little sugar. We're taking a cue from the classic lip-puckering candies, because, trust me, breaking the news with candy is way better than without—a universal law for all things that are hard to swallow.

MATERIALS

Printer paper

Construction paper

TOOLS

Ruler

Scissors

Glue or double-sided tape

Coloring utensils

Pen or marker

STEP 1

First up, we're crafting the bag to stash our candied messages. Cut out a 9 x 9-inch (23 x 23-cm) piece of printer paper. Bring two sides together, add a bit of glue on one of the edges, fold over the other edge to overlap where the glue is and press it down until they are adhered. Now, add some glue along the inside bottom and pinch it together.

STEP 2

Now, about those candies. I was inspired by a few different sour candy package designs. I ended up drawing a yellow chevron pattern and the a sour candy logo on the front of my candy bag. In the lower left corner, I mimicked a black splash design, but instead of incorporating any official sour candy branding, I wrote, "You're so sour" in bold blue and green letters.

STEP 3

Time to switch gears to the candy notes. Cut several 2½ x 2-inch (6.5 x 5-cm) pieces of construction paper. Use green, yellow, red, blue and pink. Fold them just like you did with the larger bag, glue the ends and cinch the bottoms.

Now on a small piece of paper, write why this person gives you a sour taste. As always, extra points if you stay on our sour candy theme. Slide your notes into these faux candies. Once filled, seal the ends with glue. Stuff all these into the bag and seal the larger bag with glue or double-sided tape.

For an extra flair, snip a chevron pattern along the top and bottom of your bag and candies with patterned scissors. There you have it—a craft that's as creative as it is cheeky. The final result? A vibrant collection of paper "candies" bursting with your not-so-sweet messages. It's the perfect blend of crafty fun and playful revenge. Go ahead and gift it, and watch as they unwrap each colorful piece, revealing a message that's anything but sugary.

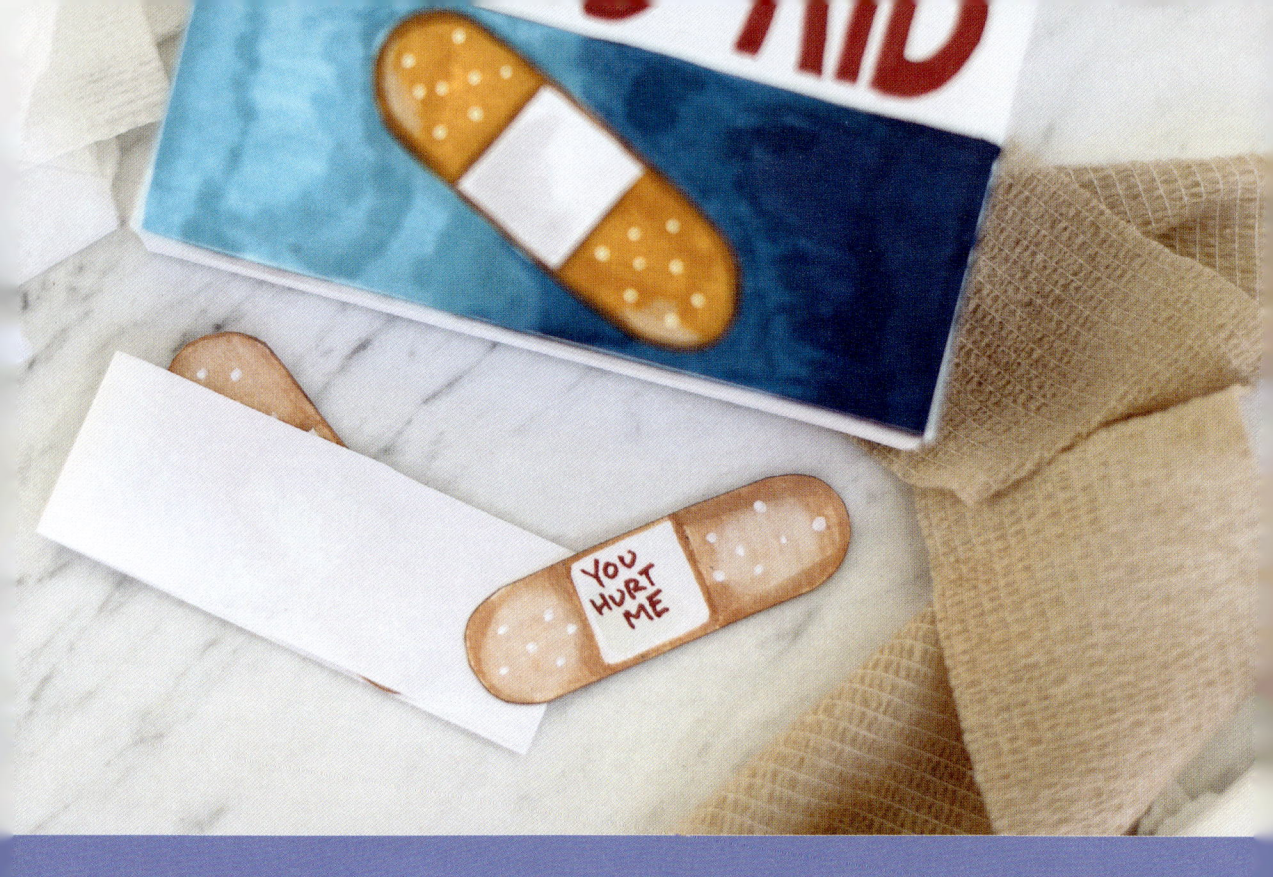

Bandage for My Boo-Boo

Remember those childhood days when you'd get into trouble, look up at your parents with those big innocent eyes and ask, "Are you mad?" And then they'd hit you with the "I'm not mad, I'm disappointed." Talk about a gut punch. The word "disappointed" alone felt like a claw tearing through my insides. It's undeniably one of the most soul-crushing feelings still to this day.

This horrible feeling? Oh, of course, we are going to weaponize it. Has someone really, really betrayed you? Then why bother spending your precious energy trying to get them back when you can hit them where it hurts. Their guilty conscience. Less work for you, and yet the most pain for them. The ultimate revenge, reserved only for the few who really, really deserve it. To perfectly weaponize this guilt, we are going to create a craft that is simple, effective and to the point. Literally, just letting our giftee know that they hurt us. Sometimes that is the best course of action.

MATERIALS

Heavyweight paper

Printer paper or tracing paper

Template (page 219)

TOOLS

Ruler

Pencil

Coloring utensils

Scissors

Glue stick

Pen

STEP 1

Let's prove our point by creating the ultimate symbol of a boo-boo: a box of bandages, of course! Sketch a rectangle on your heavyweight paper measuring 2¼ x ½ inches (6 x 1.3 cm). Now, round out the two ends until you have a bandage shape. Once that is done, sketch out a square that measures ¾ x ¾ inch (2 x 2 cm) in the middle of your bandage. Keep this square white and color the rest of the shape a pale-peachy color—the most generic shade of a bandage. For added detail, you can put little white dots on the outskirts of the bandage to mimic the air holes. But the real kicker, the soul-crushing statement of death, is to write, "You hurt me" in a red font within the white square, imitating blood coming from a wound. Once you are satisfied with the way your bandage looks, cut it out.

STEP 2

It's time to create the packaging. Cut two 1⅛ x 3–inch (3 x 7.5-cm) rectangles from your printer paper. These will be the outer cover of your bandage. With a glue stick, glue the outer side edges of one rectangle, place your bandage inside, and then sandwich it together with the second rectangle. Feel free to add any sort of designs or branding to really convey the vibe. Complete it with a little piece folded at the top for easy opening.

If you still don't feel totally satisfied with a simple little bandage, create a whole box of them just spewing with all the intricacies of how this person hurt you. To make the box, just grab the template on page 219, cut, glue and draw some doctor-worthy bandage branding on the box and either gift it or leave it with the person who hurt you for them to rummage through and (hopefully) feel a little bit of well-deserved guilt.

This craft, while simple, carries a weighty message. It isn't only about petty revenge like some of the other crafts. Instead, it exposes a bit of vulnerability that represents the betrayal. This craft, out of all the other "I hate you" crafts, may be the most effective in the entire book for the best chances of receiving a true heartfelt apology and potential reconciliation. So, do not proceed with this powerful craft if you are not prepared for what may follow.

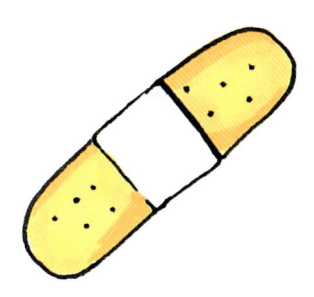

Douchebag Day

♥💔♥💔♥💔♥💔♥💔♥💔♥💔♥💔♥💔♥💔♥💔♥💔

In high school when my friends got their very first boyfriends, and then inevitably got their first broken hearts, we came up with a very mature and adult "solution" to combat the intense feelings that accompany a break. We turned their birthday into a holiday called Douchebag Day.

I know what you're thinking right now: This is the most ingenious way to heal a broken heart ever! And I would simply have to agree with you. What makes it even better is that, even ten years later when we don't even remember our former partners' middle names, we still celebrate every year together like it is a national holiday. So, if you're looking for a craft to celebrate being free from this person's reach, let's make a little Douchebag Day cake to bring to the most anticipated holiday party of the year.

MATERIALS

Toilet paper roll

Heavyweight paper

Red slime or clear glue and red food coloring

TOOLS

Ruler

Scissors

Hot-glue gun and hot-glue sticks

Craft knife (I use X-Acto)

Pen or pencil

White paint

Paintbrushes

Red gel pen or acrylic marker

STEP 1

Cut out a 3-inch (7.5-cm) piece out of a toilet paper roll. Cut a line down the center. Curl either side next to the slit. Add a line of hot glue to connect these two curled pieces together. Directly on the opposite side of the slit, pinch the toilet paper roll to a point creating a heart-shaped tube. Very carefully, using craft knife, cut the tube in half leaving you with two heart-shaped tubes. Slightly widen one of the glued curl pieces so it is just slightly larger than the other one, allowing you to slide the smaller tube into the other. I typically cut off the excess cardboard that has rolled inside the tube, allowing the other piece to slide in with ease.

Trace one heart-shaped opening for each toilet paper heart on a piece of heavyweight paper. Cut out the hearts, add hot glue to the rim of the toilet paper rolls that match each tracing and stick the hearts to the end of the tubes. Now when you slip the smaller tube into the other, it creates an adorable heart-shaped container. (I know what you're thinking: Hearts for Douchebag Day? Just trust me with this.)

Paint both of the container pieces white and allow the paint to dry. Use a bit of hot glue and "ice" the cake by adding a little hot glue to the border of the top of the bigger heart and at the edge of the bottom of the bigger heart. Once the hot glue dries, paint it white to match the rest of the cake.

STEP 2

Open the cake and fill the smaller tube with either red slime, or if you do not have slime on hand, add clear glue and red food coloring and dump this concoction all up in there. Close up the container again, and with a red gel pen (or acrylic marker) write, "Happy Douchebag Day" on the top of the cake.

Pair this cake with a sharp knife, and amidst the celebration of Douchebag Day, cut the cake to reveal a horror of a blood-red substance. It's a perfect way to spin the birthday of the douchebag into something much more malicious.

TIP: If you do decide to take this Douchebag Day and incorporate it into your life with your very own besties, make sure to bring this book with you to all the future celebrations so you can all craft up some hate to send to the former lover in question!

You're a Sour Grape

♡💔♡💔♡💔♡💔♡💔♡💔♡💔♡💔♡💔♡💔♡💔♡💔

You know what? Some people are just sour grapes. A little underripe perhaps, they never got the chance to sweeten up. If there is someone in your life who is a little too sour for taste, who you just have to *wine* about, here is the perfect craft to get all that bitterness off your chest.

MATERIALS

Template (page 249)

Printer paper

TOOLS

Scissors

Hot-glue gun and hot-glue sticks

Coloring utensils

Pen

STEP 1

Cut out the template on page 249. You will notice this template is a little tricky because it isn't a simple "glue here, fold here" template, specifically around the "wings" of the juice box. Just make sure you fold the gray lines in the same direction and fold the pink lines in the opposite direction.

Once everything is folded, hot glue the side of the box together as well as the bottom of the juice box and the top—excluding the wings. For the wings, make sure they are folded to resemble a triangle on either side, add a dollop of glue to the underside of the triangles and fold them down to adhere to the side of the juice box.

Now that our juice box has taken shape, let's design our box to get the message across. I am rethinking a classic grape juice box to serve as the initial message for our giftee, titling it "You're a Sour Grape," with a drawing of a grape serving as the primary subject matter. Feel free to design your juice box in many different ways. In fact, here are some more designs you can take for inspiration:

Now you may be wondering what the little hole is at the top of our box. This is the perfect place for us to fit in a little straw—but not just any straw. This is where you can really "wine" about said sour grape.

On a small piece of paper measuring 1¾ x 3½ inches (4.5 x 9 cm), write all of your complaints. Of course, I love when these crafts share an overarching theme, so I encourage you to connect your insults back to grapes somehow. Here are some (admittedly cheesy) examples:

- You're a sour grape.
- You look like a shriveled-up raisin.
- You're a grape disappointment.
- You're more like a shriveled-up grape than a fine wine.
- You're the reason why some wines come with a headache.
- You smell very ripe.

Once your straw is filled with all of your insults, hold it vertically, roll it up and fit it into the hole at the top of your juice box. Bend down the top of the straw and you're done!

Templates

♥ 💔 ♥ 💔 ♥ 💔 ♥ 💔 ♥ 💔 ♥ 💔 ♥ 💔

Black Lines: Cut
Gray Lines: Fold
Pink Lines: Fold in Opposite Direction

LOOPY FOR YOU
(PAGE 48)

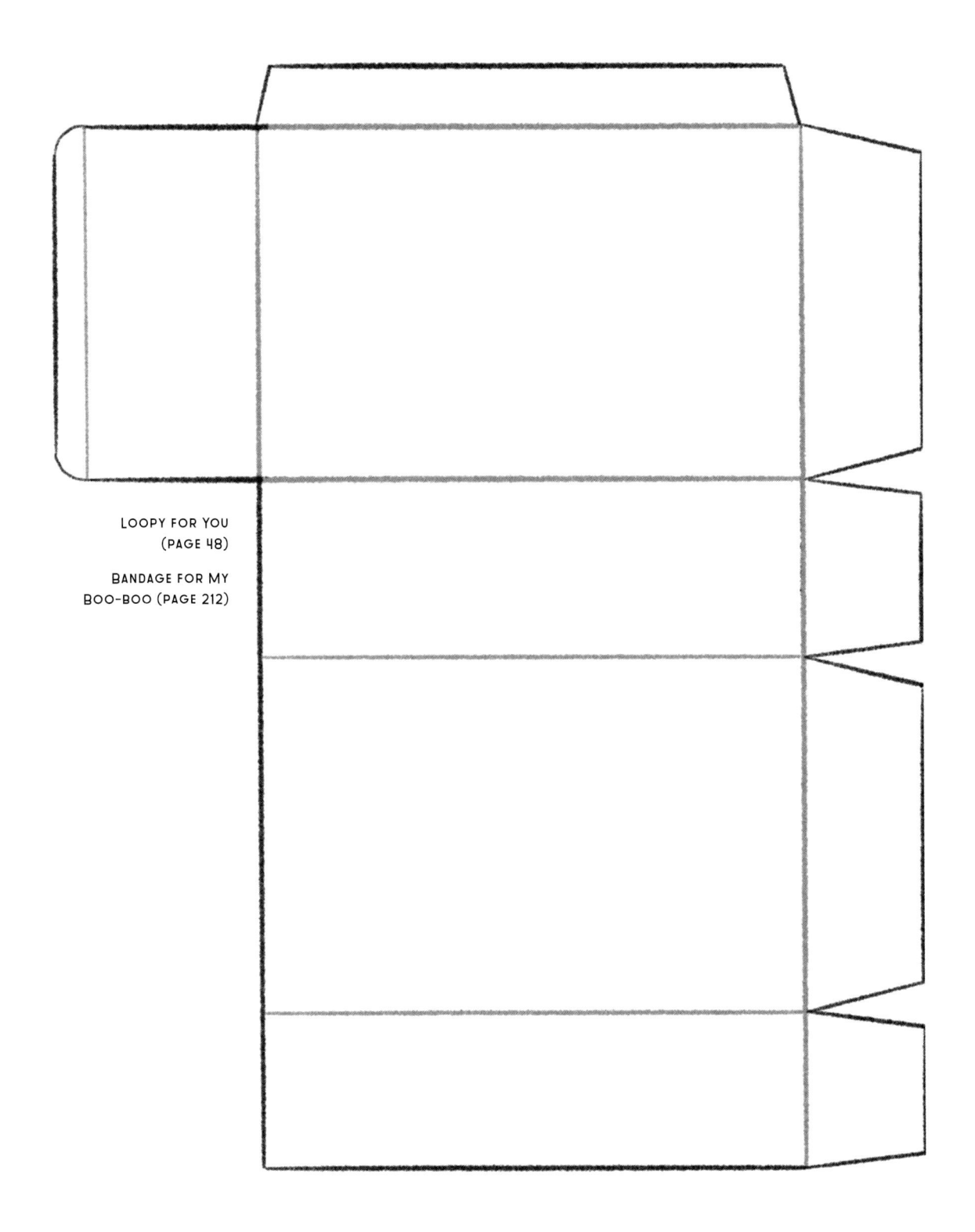

BANDAGE FOR MY
BOO-BOO (PAGE 212)

WILL YOU WEAR YOUR
BOWTIE? (PAGE 118)

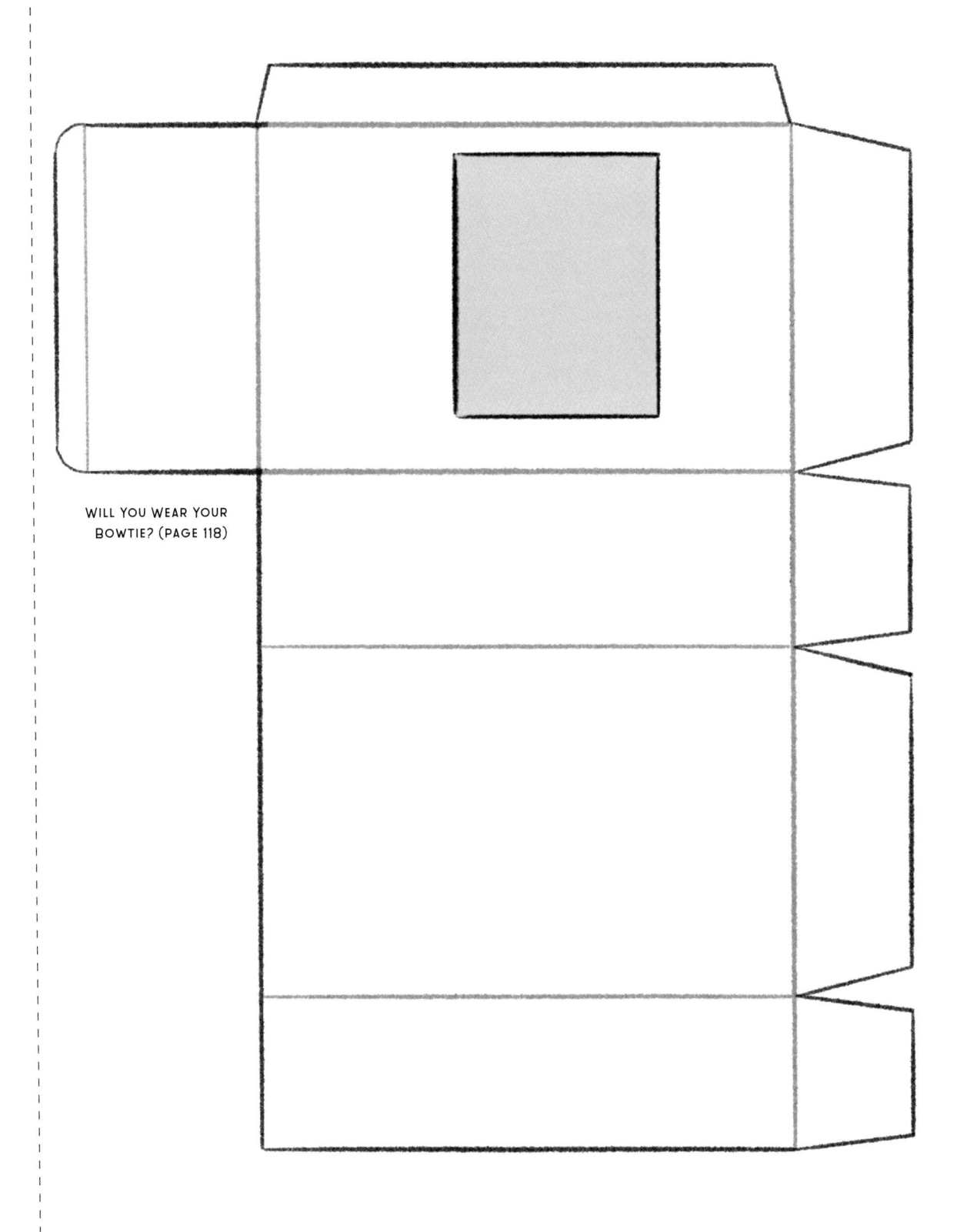

Templates - 221

MACHINE CLAW GAME
(PAGE 54)

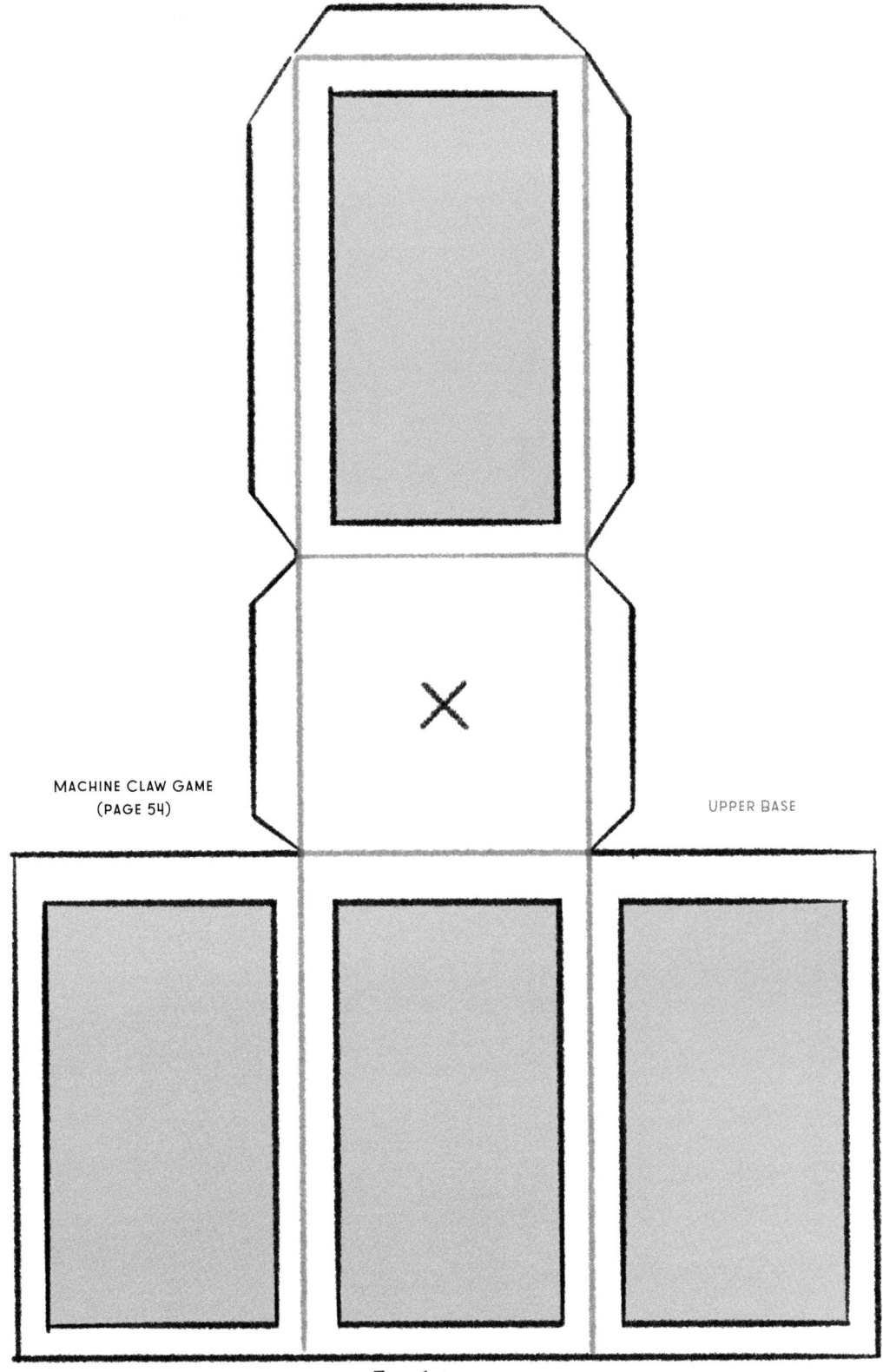

UPPER BASE

Templates - **223**

MACHINE CLAW GAME
(PAGE 54)

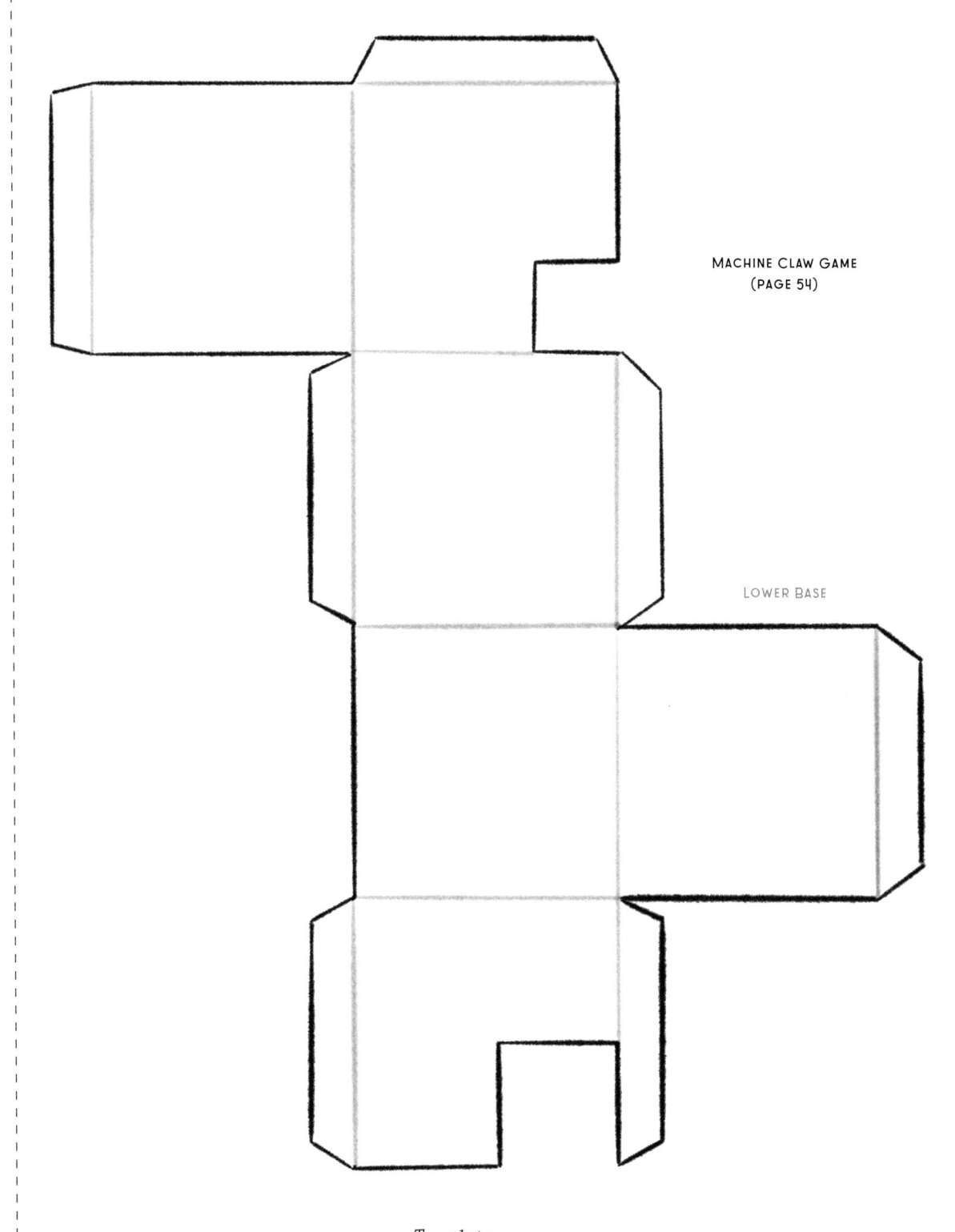

LOWER BASE

Templates - **225**

MACHINE CLAW GAME
(PAGE 54)

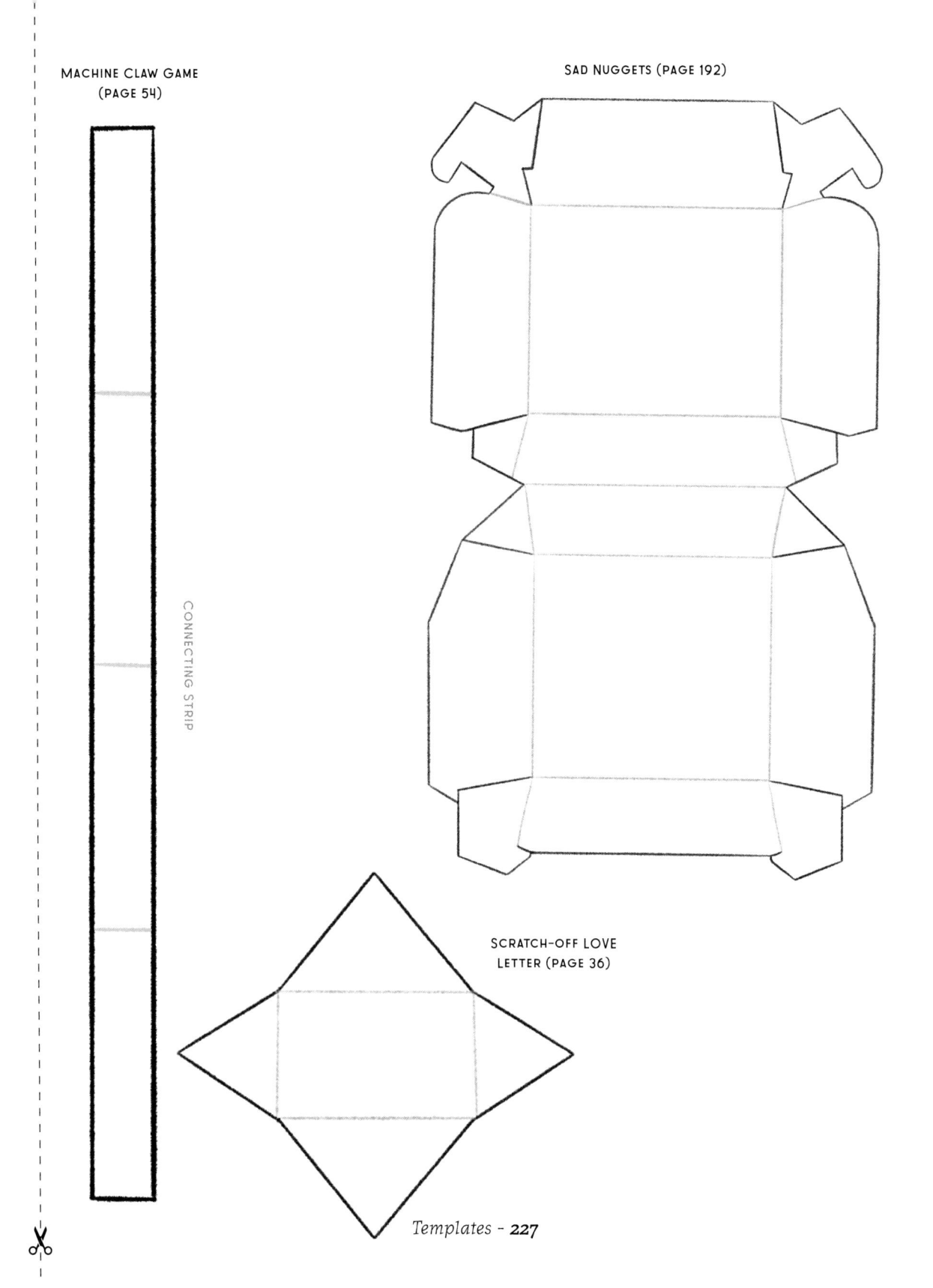

SAD NUGGETS (PAGE 192)

CONNECTING STRIP

SCRATCH-OFF LOVE
LETTER (PAGE 36)

Templates - **227**

Main Piece (My Favorite Sweet Treat [page 64])

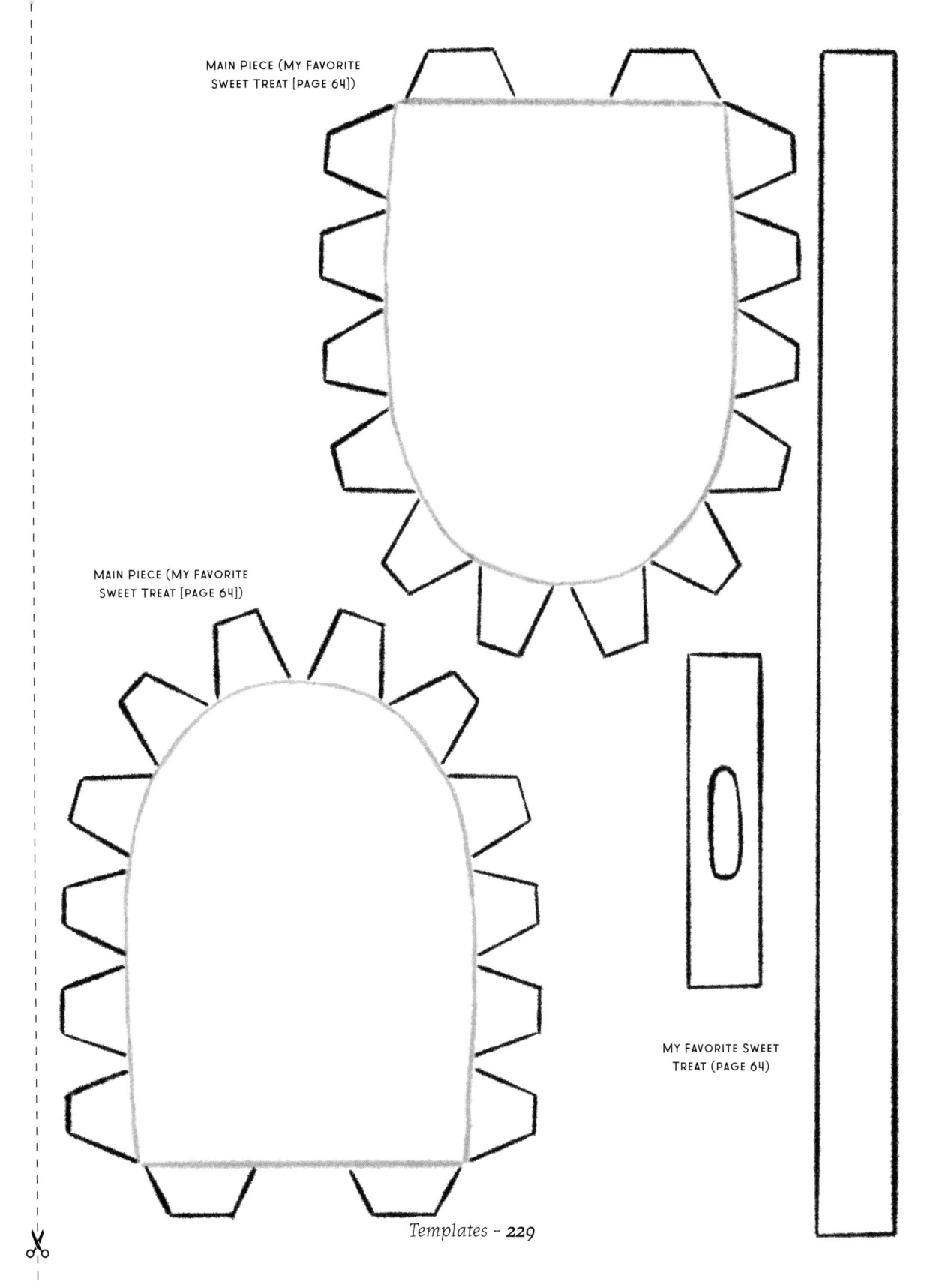

Main Piece (My Favorite Sweet Treat [page 64])

My Favorite Sweet Treat (page 64)

Templates - 229

SAD FRIES
(PAGE 191)

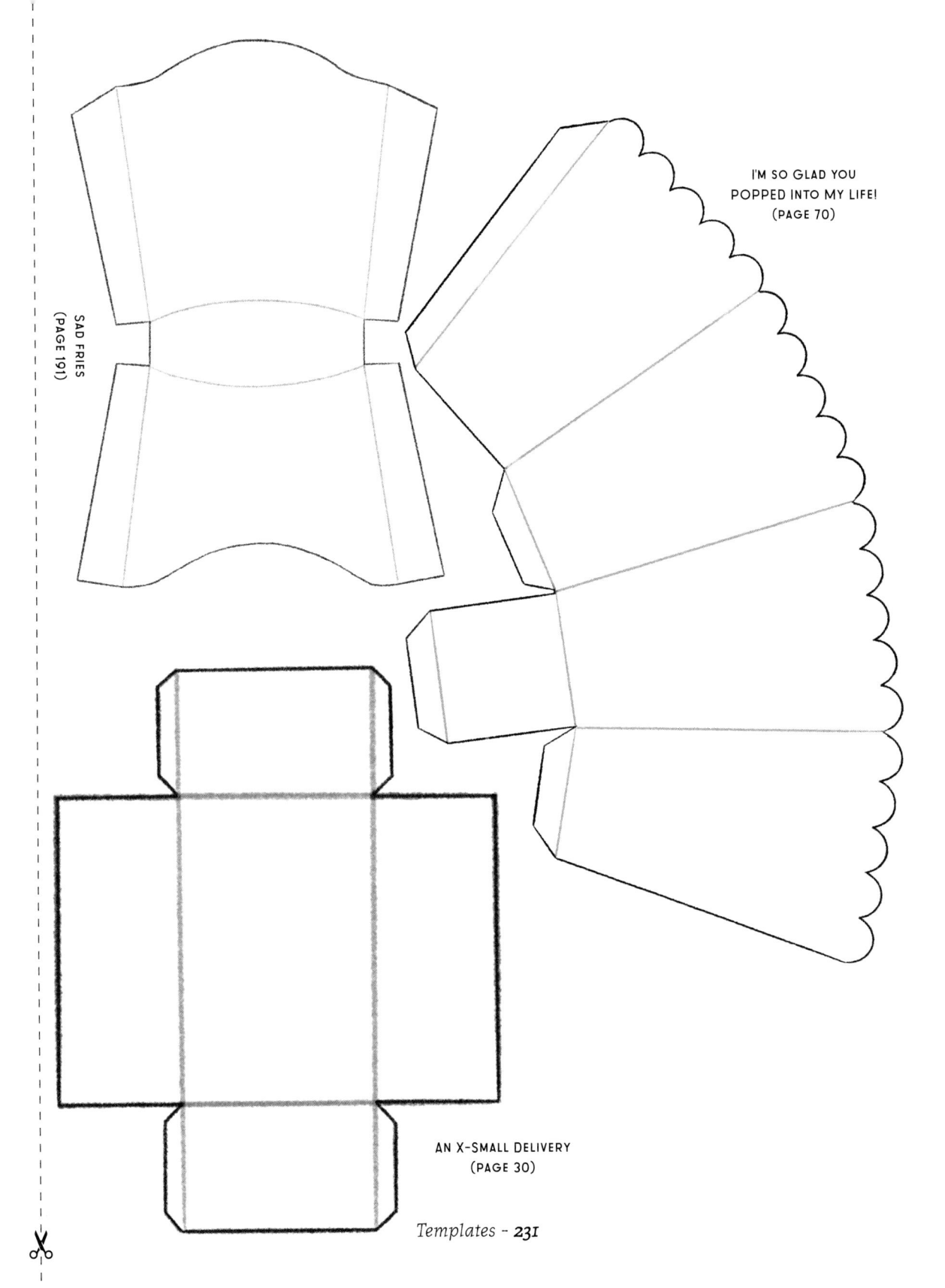

I'M SO GLAD YOU
POPPED INTO MY LIFE!
(PAGE 70)

AN X-SMALL DELIVERY
(PAGE 30)

Templates - 231

FRONT TAB

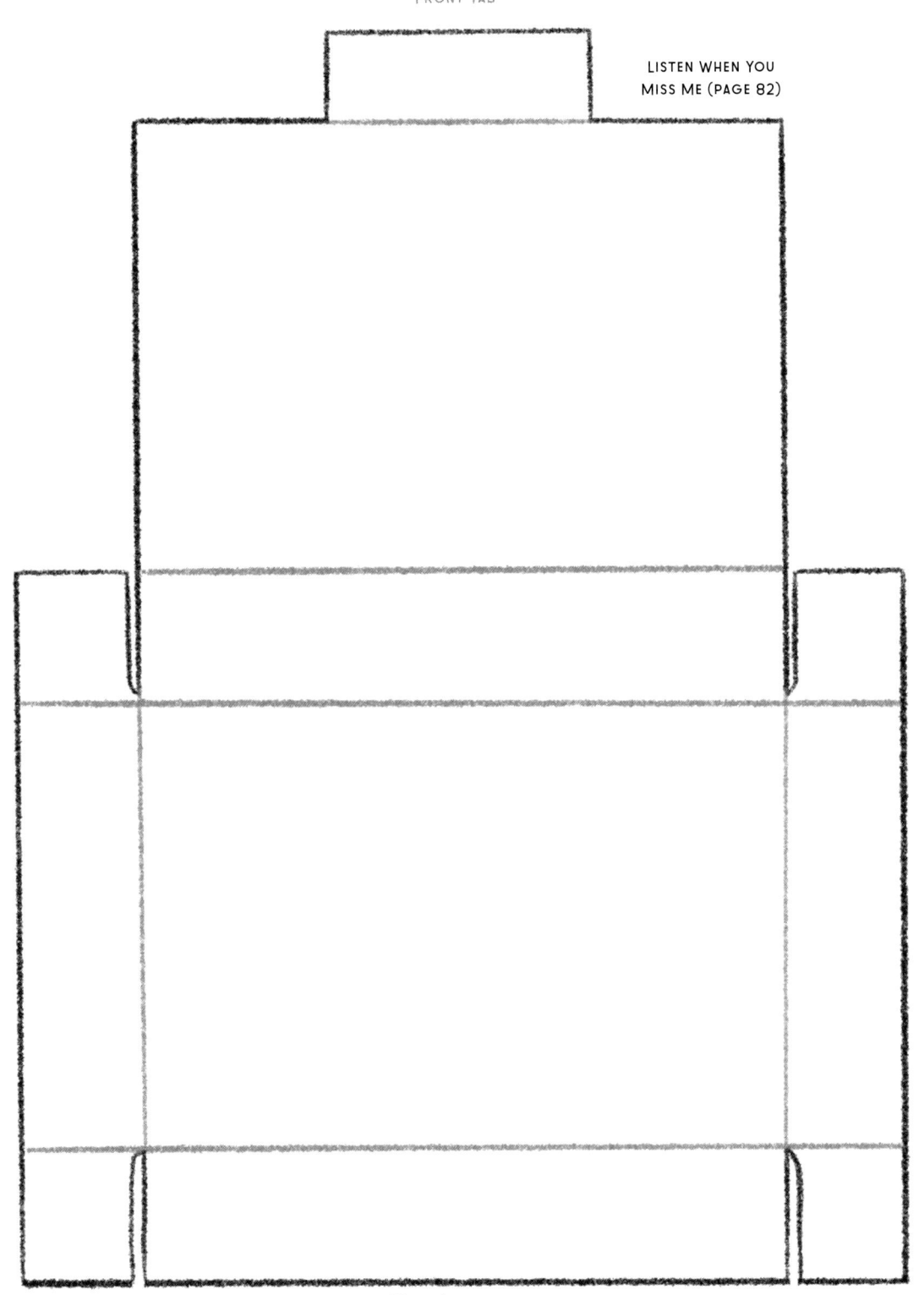

LISTEN WHEN YOU
MISS ME (PAGE 82)

Templates – **233**

YOU ARE MY FAVORITE SONG (PAGE 96)

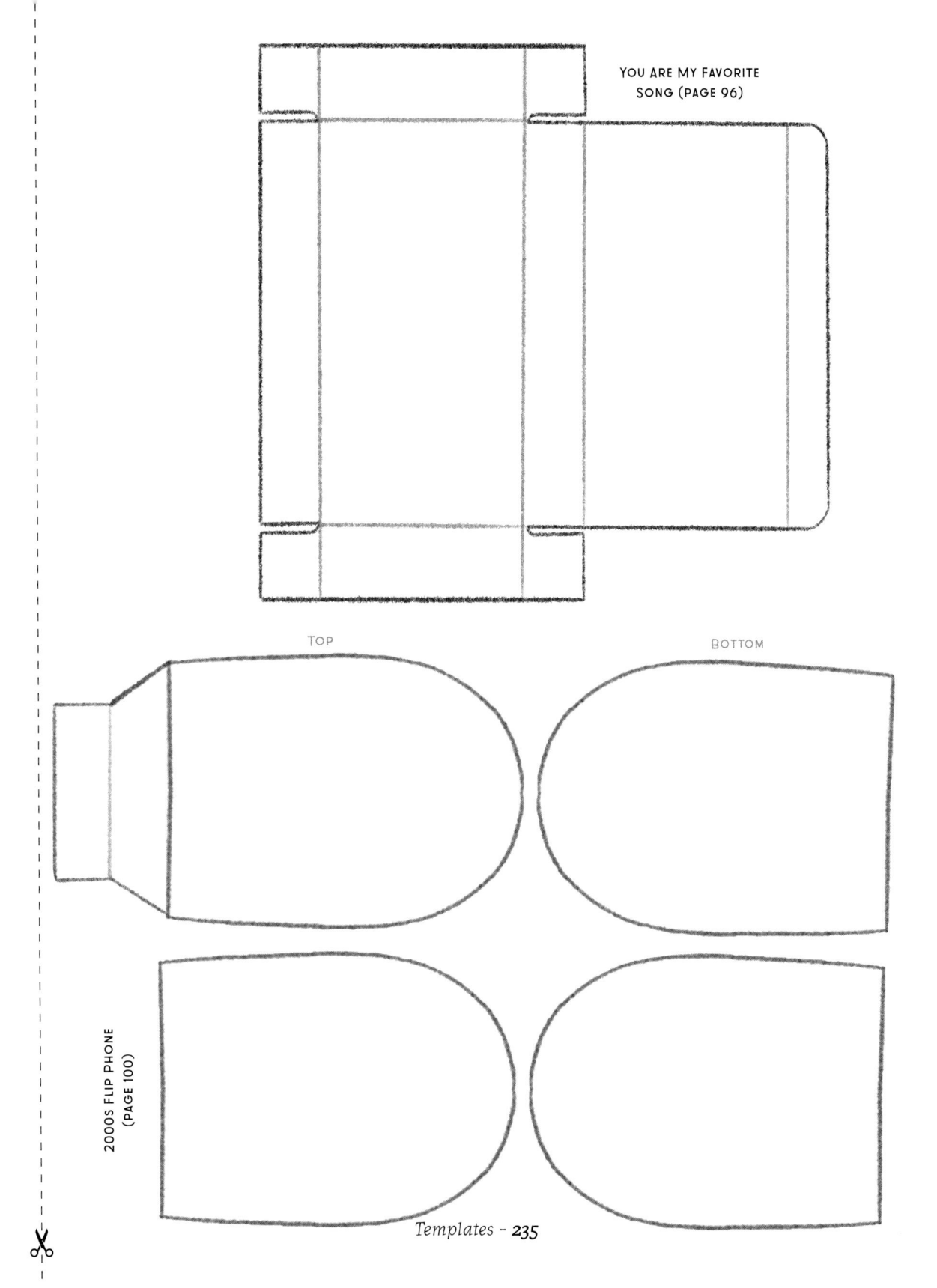

2000S FLIP PHONE (PAGE 100)

TOP

BOTTOM

Templates - **235**

MY MOTHER'S PURSE
(PAGE 138)

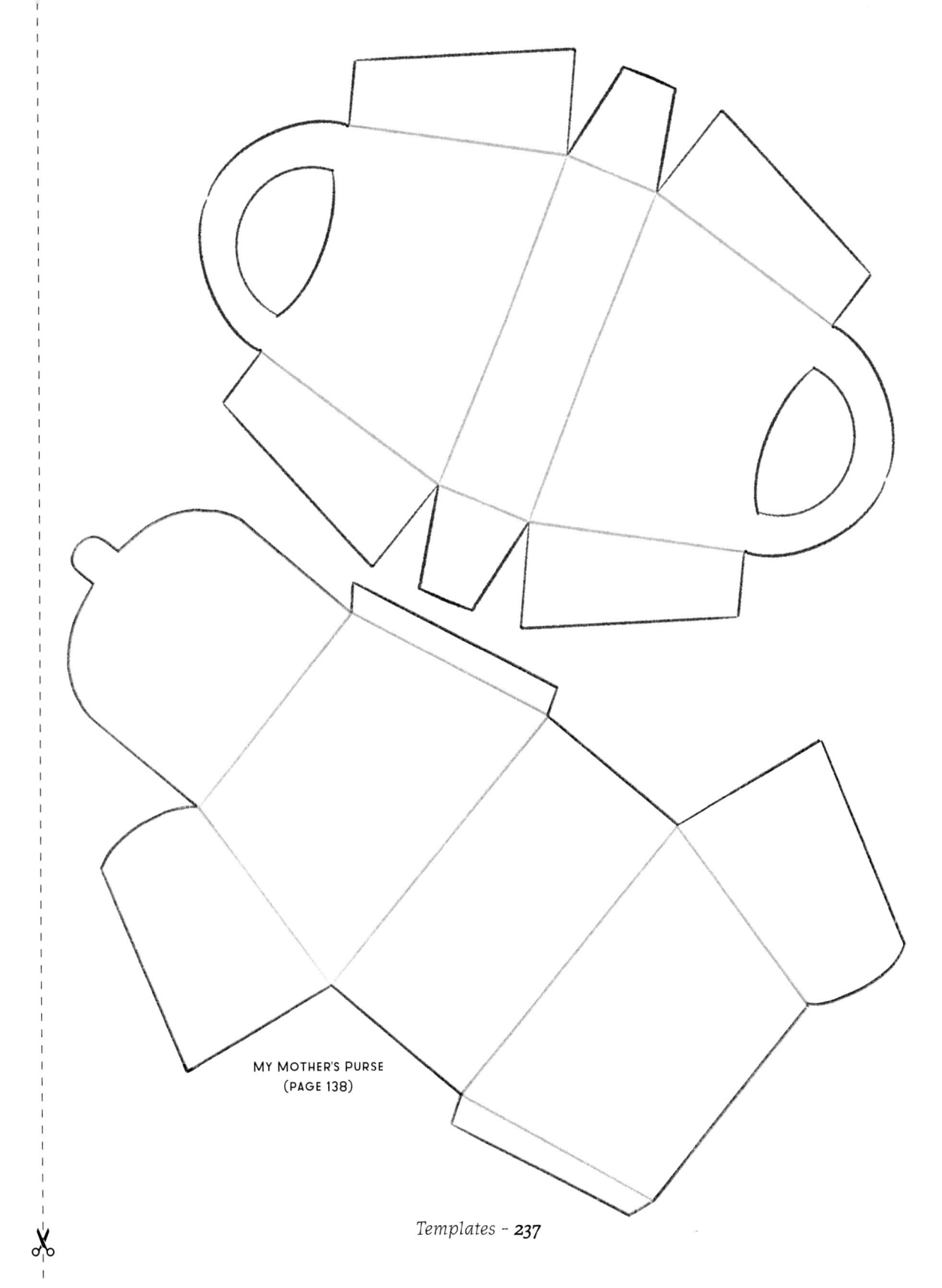

Templates – 237

SURPRISE PARTY IN A
BOX (PAGE 150)

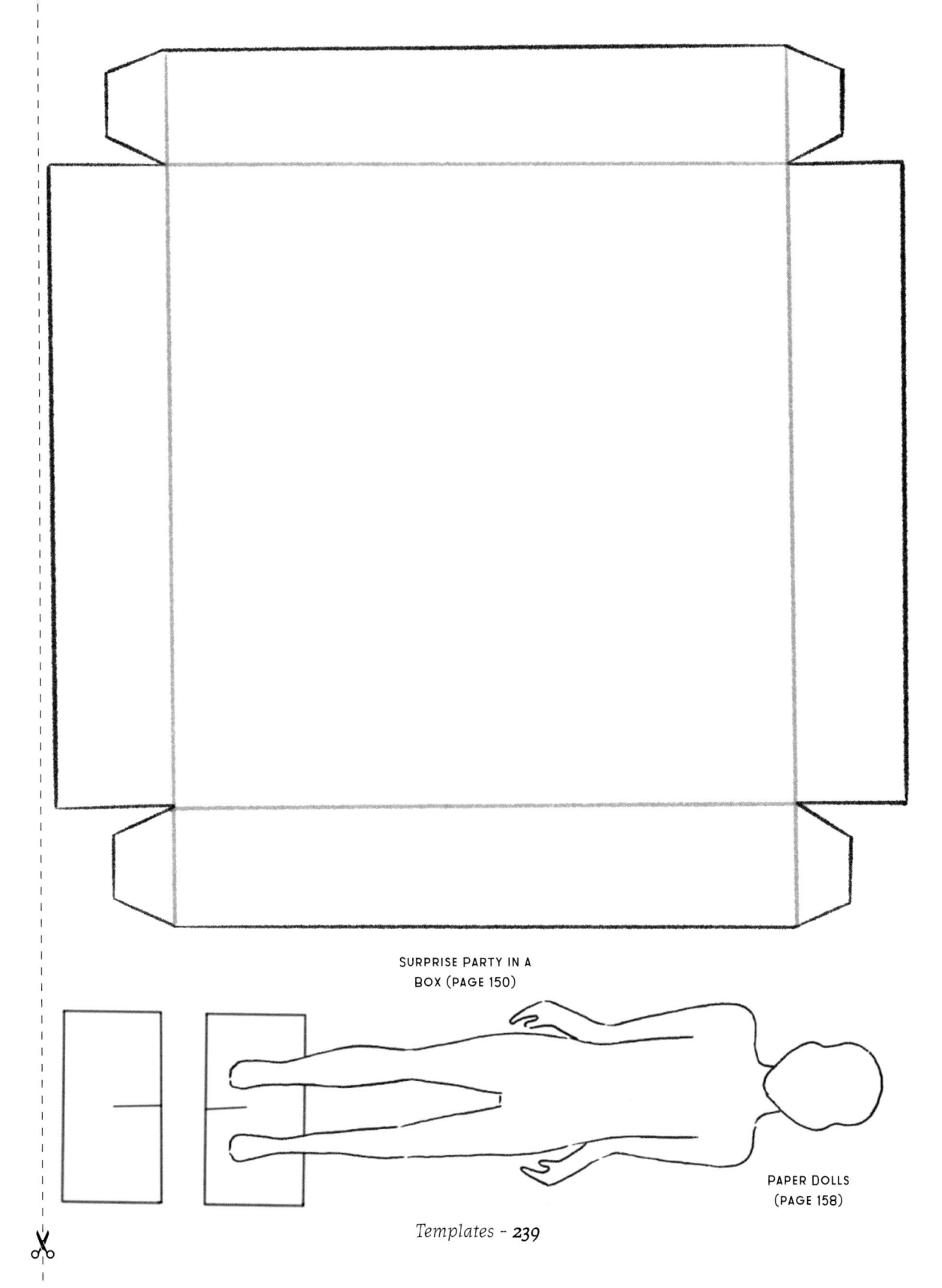

PAPER DOLLS
(PAGE 158)

Templates – 239

PAPER DOLLS
(PAGE 158)

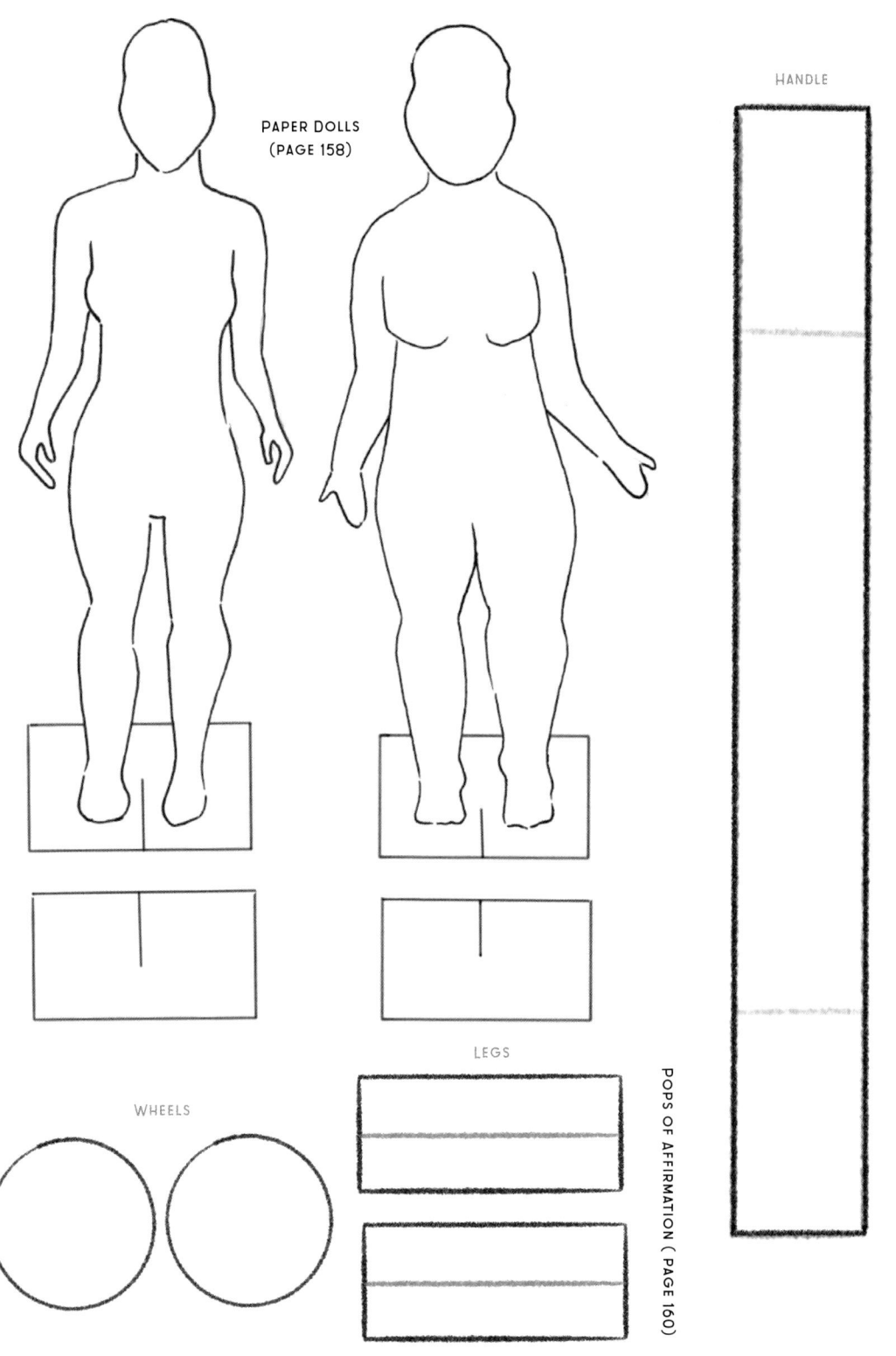

HANDLE

LISTEN WHEN YOU MISS ME (PAGE 82)

WHEELS

LEGS

POPS OF AFFIRMATION (PAGE 160)

Templates - **241**

POPS OF AFFIRMATION (PAGE 160)

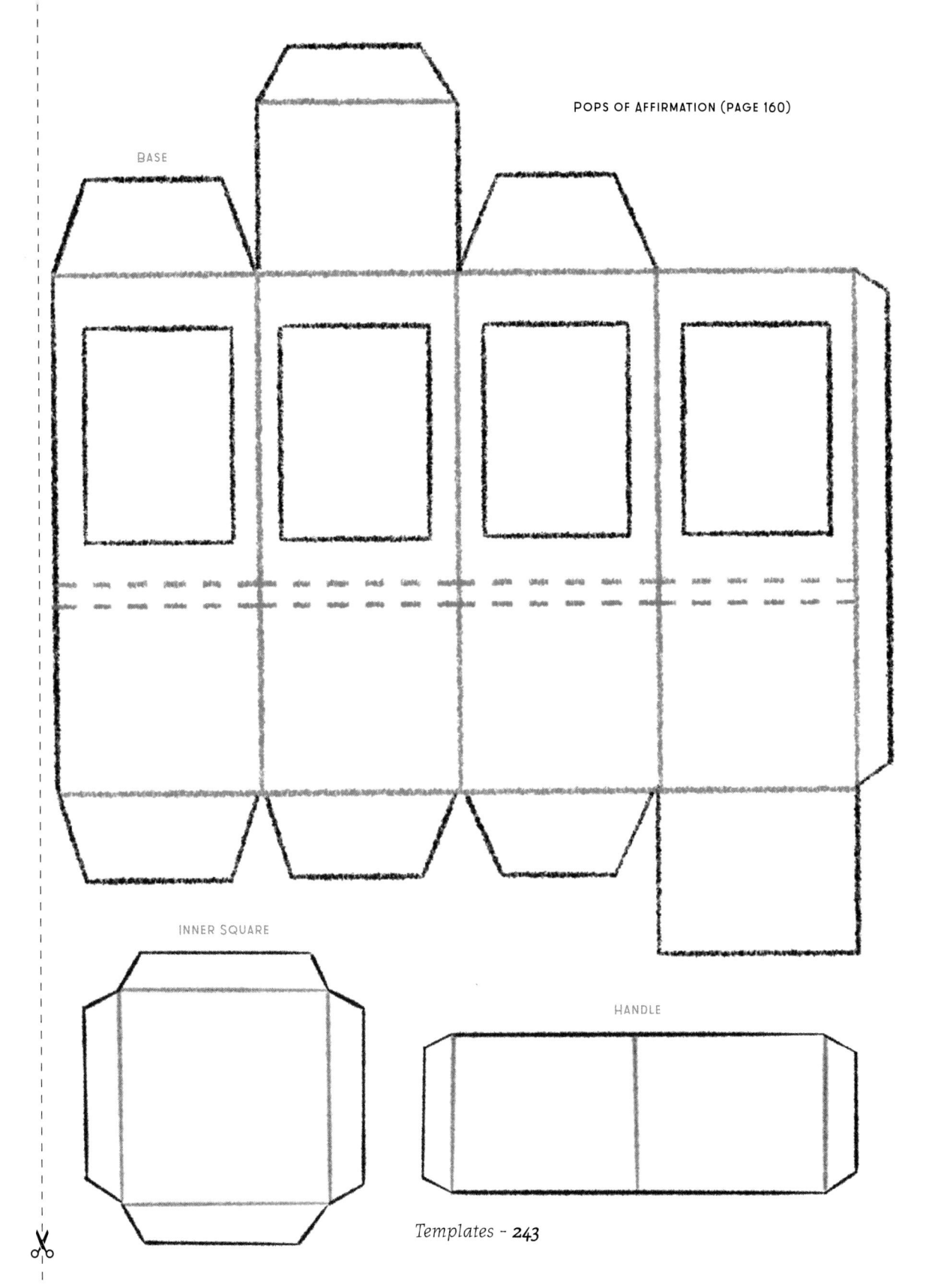

BASE

INNER SQUARE

HANDLE

Templates - 243

MY MOTHER'S PURSE
(PAGE 138)

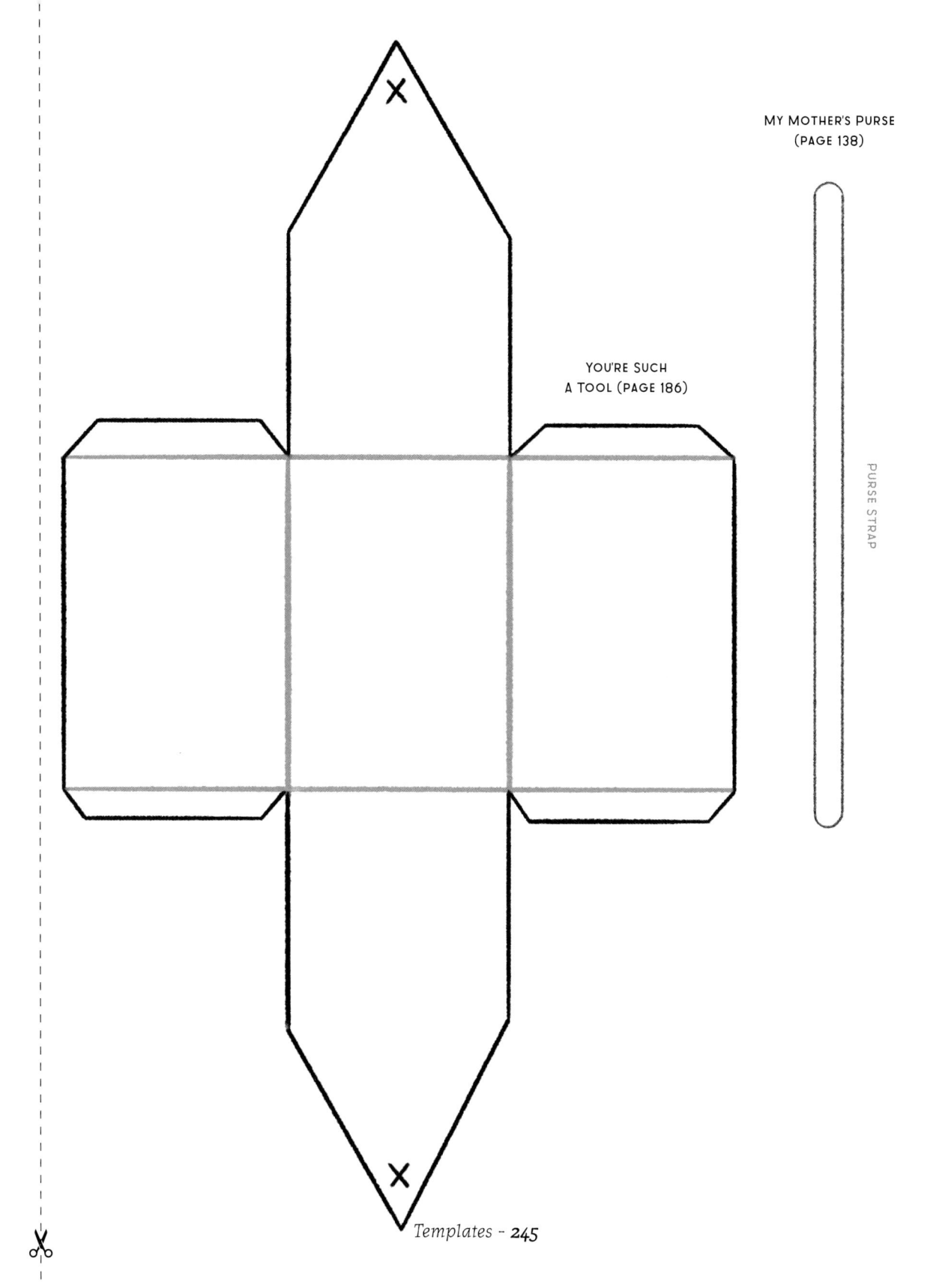

YOU'RE SUCH
A TOOL (PAGE 186)

PURSE STRAP

Templates - **245**

STRIPS (2000S FLIP
PHONE [PAGE 100])

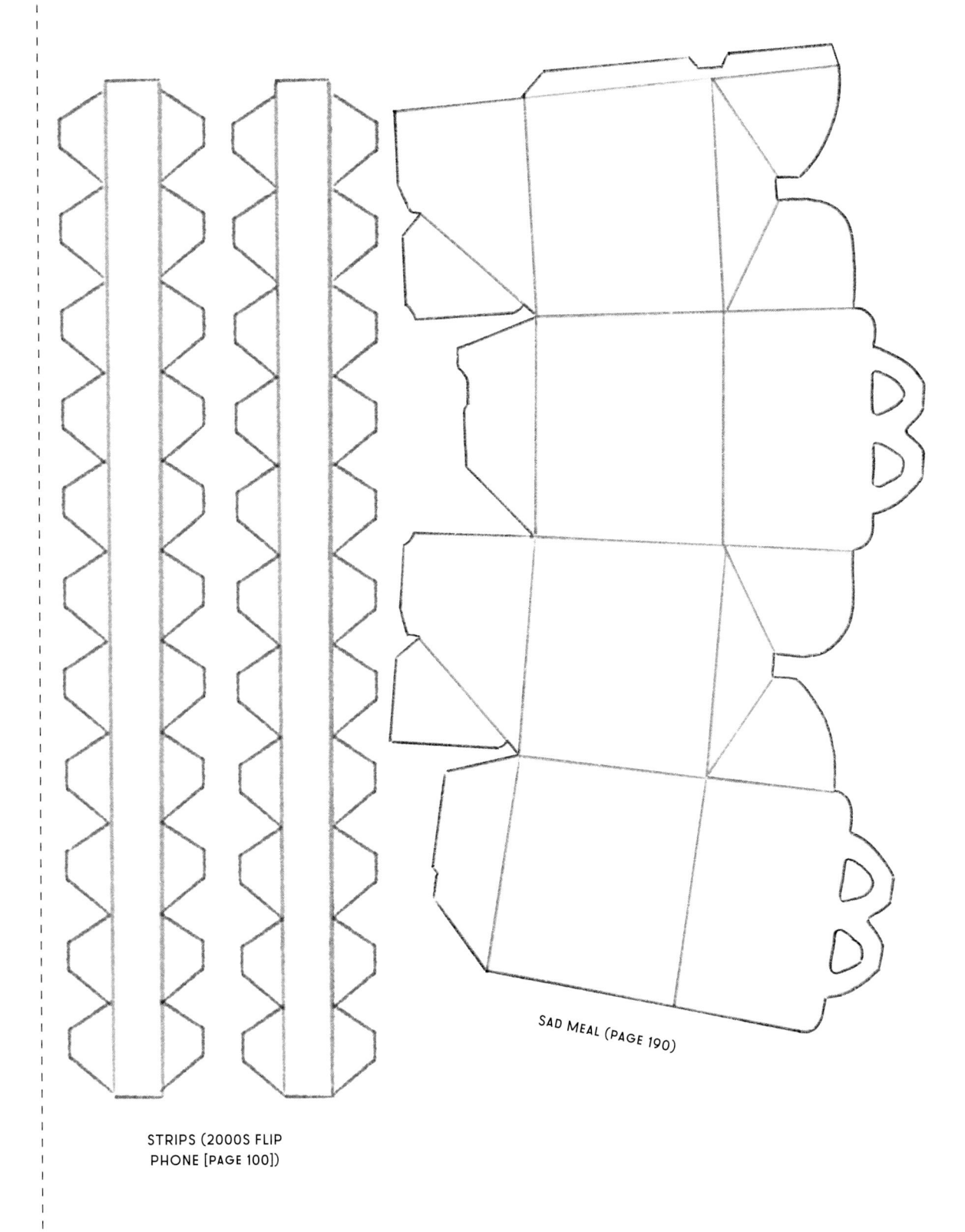

SAD MEAL (PAGE 190)

Templates – 247

PACK O' SMOKES
(PAGE 206)

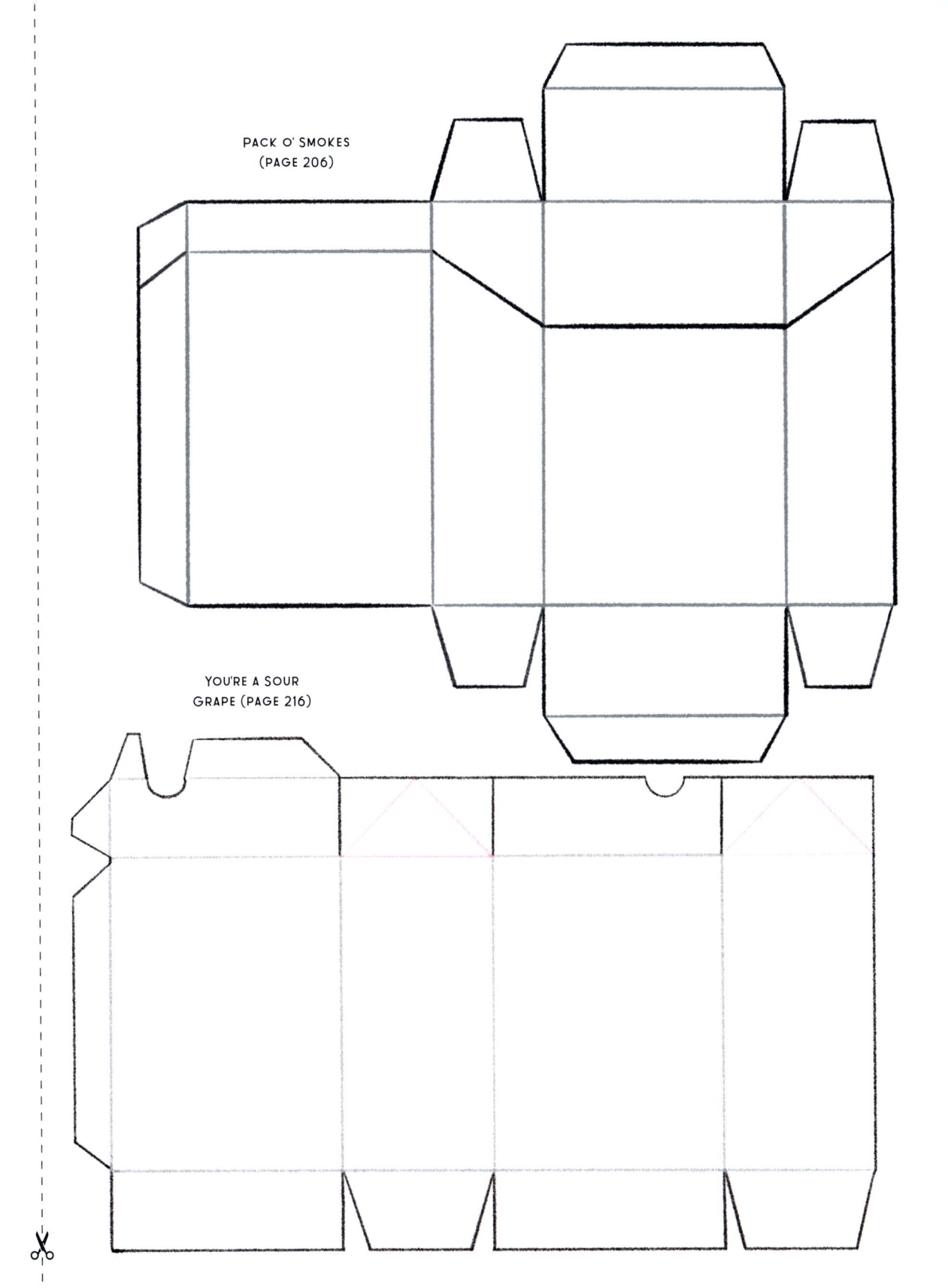

YOU'RE A SOUR
GRAPE (PAGE 216)

Acknowledgments

Being the little social media influencer that I am, I had connected with Page Street Publishing to promote some of their other amazing art books on my social media pages. While reading these books, I realized that these authors were not too different from me. Minnie Small, who wrote *The 30-Day Sketchbook Project*, owns her own popular art channel on YouTube. Sosha Davis, who wrote *Galaxy Watercolor*, posts her original watercolor paintings on her popular Instagram account. With that in mind, I realized if I wanted to write a book, I could, and I already had the connection to do it.

After reading them, I set the books down on my family's living room coffee table and my mom stopped me dead in my tracks. "These are the most beautiful books I have ever seen!" she said. My mom, being a self-diagnosed design snob, made me realize just how special the collection of books from Page Street Publishing was and made me think about a book I wrote potentially garnering the same reaction. I sent a message to them the next day asking them if they would consider granting me the opportunity to write (what eventually became) this book.

With that being said, I have to thank Charlotte Lyman, for reaching out to me on behalf of Page Street Publishing for me to promote their books, giving me the direct connection to make this thing happen.

I would like to thank my editor Marissa Giambelluca, for believing in me and encouraging me throughout this whole process.

This book's photographer Katelyn Prisco also needs a big round of applause for her incredible talent as well as being able to translate the ideas in my head into real-life photographs.

A quick nod to some of my most influential teachers, such as my college professor Ryan Buyssens, whose assignments made me realize that I enjoy my writing voice in its offbeat and conversationalist manner, which again, cracked open the door for me to pursue this opportunity in the first place. And special thanks to my high school art teacher Dr. Jackie Henson-Dacey, who adamantly encouraged me to pursue art in college and eventually in the real world. Without her confidence in me, I may have cracked under the pressure many years ago.

And lastly of course, thank you to my family, friends and partner for having an unwavering amount of faith in me, even when my dreams extended past what their eyes could see. They never, not even for a moment, doubted that I could write a book—instead they just couldn't wait to get their hands on it.

About the Author

Devyn realized she was an artist at the age of 15, when she transferred out of her freshman-year choir class into the art class where all the switches in her brain suddenly flipped. After discovering her lost love of art from her childhood, Devyn went head-first into art, dedicating all of her time to improving her skill. This also sparked the beginning of Devyn's unwavering stubbornness that she was in fact going to be an artist. There was simply no other path forward for her. Starving artist living in a van or penthouse New York modern artist, it didn't matter. As long as Devyn's hands were stained with some sort of art supply, then in her opinion, her purpose in life was being fulfilled.

Fast-forward a few years . . . Devyn started college at New College of Florida, pursuing a degree in fine art, but then the pandemic hit. With Covid-19 keeping everyone indoors, a new app emerged called TikTok that suddenly everyone was spending all of their time on. This piqued Devyn's interest, as this could be her opportunity to get exposure for her art. So, with that in mind, she posted every single day on the platform for two years. And guess what? It worked. People started following Devyn for her art, so she kept posting!

Four years after her first post, Devyn's social media page is stronger than ever, with 2.9 million followers on TikTok, 400,000 on Instagram and 560,000 on YouTube and growing!

When Devyn is not out there pursuing her dreams, she enjoys spending her time with her mom going thrifting and yard saleing to get the next big beautiful project on her hands, as well as spending time with her friends, enjoying wholesome picnics to dancing the night away. She also spends an adequate amount of time ooing and gooing over her three cats, Spanky, Aurora and Healy.

Index

A
Antique Love Letter, 90–91
Art, You're a Work of, 164–66

B
Baby, You Got Baggage, 198–99
Baby, You're a Firework, 50–51
Baggage, Baby You Got, 198–99
balloons, 34–35
Bandage for My Boo-Boo, 212–13, 219
basics, 8–9
BFFs or frenemies, crafts for, 155–83
    Capture Our Memories, 182–83
    Color Our Friendship, 180–81
    Faux Photobooth, 170–72
    Faux Photobooth Pictures, 168–69
    For the Record, You're My Best Friend, 156–57
    Friend-Chips, 176–77
    Friends Are like Stars, 178–79
    Friendship Bracelets, 167
    I'm Always Watching You (Eye Ring), 162–63
    Lil' Heart Book, 173–74
    Paper Dolls, 158–59, 239–41
    Pops of Affirmation, 160–61, 241–243
    You're a Work of Art, 164–66
    You're My Rock, 175
Bloody Knife, 203–5
Book, Lil' Heart, 173–74
Bookmark, Secret, 112–13
books, 114–15
boombox, 82–83, 233, 241
bottle caps, 208–9
Bow Tie (Pasta)?, Will You Wear Your, 118–20, 221
Bracelets, Friendship, 167
Butterflies, You Give Me, 110–11

C
cake, 214–15
Candy, Piece of, 20
candy corn, 188–89
Capture Our Memories, 182–83
cardboard
    Bloody Knife, 203–5
    Capture Our Memories, 182–83
    cutting, 8–9
    DIY "Operation" Game, 46–47
    Faux Photobooth, 170–72
    ILove Your iMessages, 79–81
    Instant Love (Ramen Noodles), 86–87
    Lil' Heart Book, 173–74
    Listen When You Miss Me, 82–83, 233, 241
    Love: Delivered to Your Door, 60–62
    My Family's Cookbook, 133–35
    Opening Doors, 140–41
    Surprise Party in a Box, 150–51, 239
    You're Dead to Me . . . Literally, 200–202
    You're My Muse, 104–6
    You're Such a Tool, 186–87, 245
    You Rock My World, 66–67
cards
    Conceal to Reveal, 124–25
    Cuddles from Afar, 37
    Fiery Feels, 40–41
    It's Been a Bumpy Road, 152–53
    Lemon Juice Secret Letter, 102–3
    Message in a Bottle, 38–39
    The Never-Ending Card, 44–45
    Opening Doors, 140–41
    Rip-Up Card, 22–23
    The Way to My Heart, 25
    What Makes Up My Heart?, 24
    You Blow My Mind, 34–35
    You're an A-Hole, 194
    You're a Work of Art, 164–66
cemetery plot, 200–202

chair, 208–9
chip can, 68–69
Chips, Friend-, 176–77
chrome marker, 9
Claw Game, Machine, 54–56, 223–227
Cocoon, You Were My, 144–45
Color Our Friendship, 180–81
Conceal to Reveal, 124–25
confessions of love, 99–125
    Conceal to Reveal, 124–25
    Decipher Your Love, 107–9
    I Love Learning about You, 114–15
    Lemon Juice Secret Letter, 102–3
    The Love Equation, 121
    Mirror Writing, 122–23
    Read between the Lines, 116–17
    Secret Bookmark, 112–13
    2000s Flip Phone, 100–101, 235, 247
    Will You Wear Your Bow Tie (Pasta)?, 118–20, 221
    You Give Me Butterflies, 110–11
    You're My Muse, 104–6
Cookbook, My Family's, 133–35
cotton swabs, 110–11
Cozy Cup of Love, A, 58–59
craft basics, 8–9
craft sticks
    Home Is Wherever My Family Is, 128–30
    My Favorite Sweet Treat, 64–65, 229
    You're My Muse, 104–6
Cuddles from Afar, 37
Cutie for My Cutie, A, 14–15

D

Decipher Your Love, 107–9
DIY "Operation" Game, 46–47
Dollar Bill, 148–49
Dolls, Paper, 158–59, 239–41
Doodly Gesture, A, 19
Doors, Opening, 140–41
Douchebag Day, 214–15

E

enemies. See exes and enemies, crafts for
Everlasting Flowers, 136–37
exes and enemies, crafts for, 185–217
    Baby, You Got Baggage, 198–99
    Bandage for My Boo-Boo, 212–13, 219
    Bloody Knife, 203–5
    Douchebag Day, 214–15
    Hangman, 195
    I Can't Stand You, 208–9
    Pack o' Smokes, 206–7, 249
    Sad Fries, 191, 231
    Sad Meal, 190, 247
    Sad Nuggets, 192–93, 227
    A Taste of Their Own Medicine, 196–97
    You're an A-Hole, 194
    You're a Sour Grape, 216–17, 249
    You're Dead to Me . . . Literally, 200–202
    You're Not a Treat, 188–89
    You're So Sour, 210–11
    You're Such a Tool, 186–87, 245
Eye Ring, (I'm Always Watching You), 162–63

F

family, crafts for, 127–53
    Dollar Bill, 148–49
    Everlasting Flowers, 136–37
    Family Flowers, 142–43
    Home Is Wherever My Family Is, 128–30
    It's Been a Bumpy Road, 152–53
    My Family's Cookbook, 133–35
    My Father's Wallet, 146–47
    My Mother's Purse, 138–39, 237, 245
    Opening Doors, 140–41
    Surprise Party in a Box, 150–51, 239
    Thank You for Helping Me Grow, 131–32
    You Were My Cocoon, 144–45
Family Flowers, 142–43
Faux Photobooth, 170–72
Faux Photobooth Pictures, 168–69
Fiery Feels, 40–41
Firework, Baby, You're a, 50–51
Flip Phone, 2000s, 100–101, 235, 247
Flowers, Everlasting, 136–37
Flowers, Family, 142–43
folding, 9
For the Record, You're My Best Friend, 156–57
frenemies. See BFFs or frenemies, crafts for
Friend-Chips, 176–77
Friends Are like Stars, 178–79
Friendship Bracelets, 167
Fries, Sad, 191, 231

G

glues, working with, 9
guitar, 66–67

H

Hangman, 195
Heart Book, Lil,' 173–74
Home Is Wherever My Family Is, 128–30
hot-glue gun, 9

I

I Can't Stand You, 208–9
ice cream, 64–65
I Love Learning about You, 114–15
iLove Your iMessages, 79–81
I'm Always Watching You (Eye Ring), 162–63
I'm So Glad You Popped into My Life!, 70–71, 231
Instagram IRL, 52–53
Instant Love (Ramen Noodles), 86–87
It's Been a Bumpy Road, 152–53

J

juice box, 216–17, 249

K

Kisses, Pocket, 21
Knife, Bloody, 203–5

L

Lemon Juice Secret Letter, 102–3
Lil' Heart Book, 173–74
Listen When You Miss Me, 82–83, 233, 241

Little Stamp of Love, A, 17
Loopy for You, 48–49, 219
love, confessions of. See confessions of love
Love: Delivered to Your Door, 60–62
Love Equation, The, 121
Love Letter, Antique, 90–91
Love Letter, Scratch-Off, 36, 227
Love Letters, Tiny, 12–13

M

Machine Claw Game, 54–56, 223–27
mailbox, 60–62
Map of Our Love, 74–75
Match, We Are a Perfect, 16
Matchbox TV, 76–78
matches / matchboxes
   Baby, You Got Baggage, 198–99
   Fiery Feels, 40–41
   Home Is Wherever My Family Is, 128–30
   Lemon Juice Secret Letter, 102–3
   Matchbox TV, 76–78
   Puzzle to My Heart, 57
   We Are a Perfect Match, 16
   You Make My Heart Bounce, 63
   You're Dead to Me . . . Literally, 200–202
Medicine, A Taste of Their Own, 196–97
Message in a Bottle, 38–39
Mine to Be Mine, 84–85
Mirror Writing, 122–23
money, 148–49

music, 82–83, 233, 241
My Family's Cookbook, 133–35
My Father's Wallet, 146–47
My Favorite Sweet Treat, 64–65, 229
My Mother's Purse, 138–39, 237, 245

N

Never-Ending Card, The, 44–45
Nuggets, Sad, 192–93, 227

O

Old Timey Scroll, 26–27
Opening Doors, 140–41
"Operation" Game, DIY, 46–47

P

Pack o' Smokes, 206–7, 249
Paper Dolls, 158–59, 239–41
Passport to My Heart, 93–95
Photobooth, Faux, 170–72
Photobooth Pictures, Faux, 168–69
photos
   Capture Our Memories, 182–83
   Color Our Friendship, 180–81
   Dollar Bill, 148–49
   A Doodly Gesture, 19
   Faux Photobooth, 170–72
   Faux Photobooth Pictures, 168–69
   For the Record, You're My Best Friend, 156–57
   iLove Your iMessages, 79–81

I'm Always Watching You (Eye Ring), 162–63
Instagram IRL, 52–53
Lil' Heart Book, 173–74
Passport to My Heart, 93–95
You're a Work of Art, 164–66
Piece of Candy, 20
plane ticket, 88–89
Pocket Kisses, 21
popcorn box, 70–71, 231
popcorn cart, 160–61, 241–243
Pops of Affirmation, 160–61, 241–243
potato chip can, 68–69
Purse, My Mother's, 138–39, 237, 245
Puzzle to My Heart, 57

R

ramen noodles, 86–87
Read between the Lines, 116–17
recipes, 133–35
Record, For the, You're My Best Friend, 156–57
record player, 96–97, 235
Rip-Up Card, 22–23
rocks
    You're My Rock, 175
    You Rock (Literally), 18
romantic partner, gifts for current or former, 43–97
    Antique Love Letter, 90–91
    Baby, You're a Firework, 50–51
    A Cozy Cup of Love, 58–59
    DIY "Operation" Game, 46–47
    iLove Your iMessages, 79–81

I'm So Glad You Popped into My Life!, 70–71, 231
Instagram IRL, 52–53
Instant Love (Ramen Noodles), 86–87
Listen When You Miss Me, 82–83, 233, 241
Loopy for You, 48–49, 219
Love: Delivered to Your Door, 60–62
Machine Claw Game, 54–56, 223–27
Map of Our Love, 74–75
Matchbox TV, 76–78
Mine to Be Mine, 84–85
My Favorite Sweet Treat, 64–65, 229
The Never-Ending Card, 44–45
Passport to My Heart, 93–95
Puzzle to My Heart, 57
Ticket to My Heart, 88–89
Tootsie Rolls for My Tootsie, 72–73
You Are a Snack!, 68–69
You Are My Favorite Song, 96–97, 235
You Make My Heart Bounce, 63
You Rock My World, 66–67

S

Sad Fries, 191, 231
Sad Meal, 190, 247
Sad Nuggets, 192–93, 227
Scratch-Off Love Letter, 36, 227
Scroll, Old Timey, 26–27
Secret Bookmark, 112–13
secret messages
    Conceal to Reveal, 124–25

Lemon Juice Secret Letter, 102–3
The Love Equation, 121
Mirror Writing, 122–23
Read between the Lines, 116–17
shrink plastic
    I'm Always Watching You (Eye Ring), 162–63
    Shrink Plastic to Grow Love, 32–33
Shrink Plastic to Grow Love, 32–33
Smokes, Pack o,' 206–7, 249
Sour, You're So, 210–11
Sour Grape, You're a, 216–17, 249
Spotify song code, 82–83, 233, 241
Stamp of Love, A Little, 17
Stars, Friends Are like, 178–79
Stickers of My Affection, 28–29
Surprise Party in a Box, 150–51, 239
Sweet Treat, My Favorite, 64–65, 229

T

Taste of Their Own Medicine, A, 196–97
templates, 218–49
10-minute crafts, 11–41
    Cuddles from Afar, 37
    A Cutie for My Cutie, 14–15
    A Doodly Gesture, 19
    Fiery Feels, 40–41
    A Little Stamp of Love, 17
    Message in a Bottle, 38–39
    Old Timey Scroll, 26–27
    Piece of Candy, 20

Pocket Kisses, 21

Rip-Up Card, 22–23

Scratch-Off Love Letter, 36, 227

Shrink Plastic to Grow Love, 32–33

Stickers of My Affection, 28–29

Tiny Love Letters, 12–13

The Way to My Heart, 25

We Are a Perfect Match, 16

What Makes Up My Heart?, 24

An X-Small Delivery, 30–31, 231

You Blow My Mind, 34–35

You Rock (Literally), 18

Thank You for Helping Me Grow, 131–32

Ticket to My Heart, 88–89

tin mint containers

    Lemon Juice Secret Letter, 102–3

    Mirror Writing, 122–23

Tiny Love Letters, 12–13

toilet paper rolls and containers, 8

    Baby, You're a Firework, 50–51

    Douchebag Day, 214–15

Friends Are like Stars, 178–79

Love: Delivered to Your Door, 60–62

Old Timey Scroll, 26–27

Thank You for Helping Me Grow, 131–32

You Are a Snack!, 68–69

You Give Me Butterflies, 110–11

You Rock My World, 66–67

Tool, You're Such a, 186–87, 245

toothpicks, 208–9

Tootsie Rolls for My Tootsie, 72–73

Treat, You're Not a, 188–89

2000s Flip Phone, 100–101, 235, 247

W

Wallet, My Father's, 146–47

watering can, 131–32

Way to My Heart, The, 25

We Are a Perfect Match, 16

What Makes Up My Heart?, 24

Will You Wear Your Bow Tie (Pasta)?, 118–20, 221

Work of Art, You're a, 164–66

X

X-Small Delivery, An, 30–31, 231

Y

You Are a Snack!, 68–69

You Are My Favorite Song, 96–97, 235

You Blow My Mind, 34–35

You Give Me Butterflies, 110–11

You Make My Heart Bounce, 63

You're an A-Hole, 194

You're a Sour Grape, 216–17, 249

You're a Work of Art, 164–66

You're Dead to Me . . . Literally, 200–202

You're My Muse, 104–6

You're My Rock, 175

You're Not a Treat, 188–89

You're So Sour, 210–11

You're Such a Tool, 186–87, 245

You Rock (Literally), 18

You Rock My World, 66–67

You Were My Cocoon, 144–45